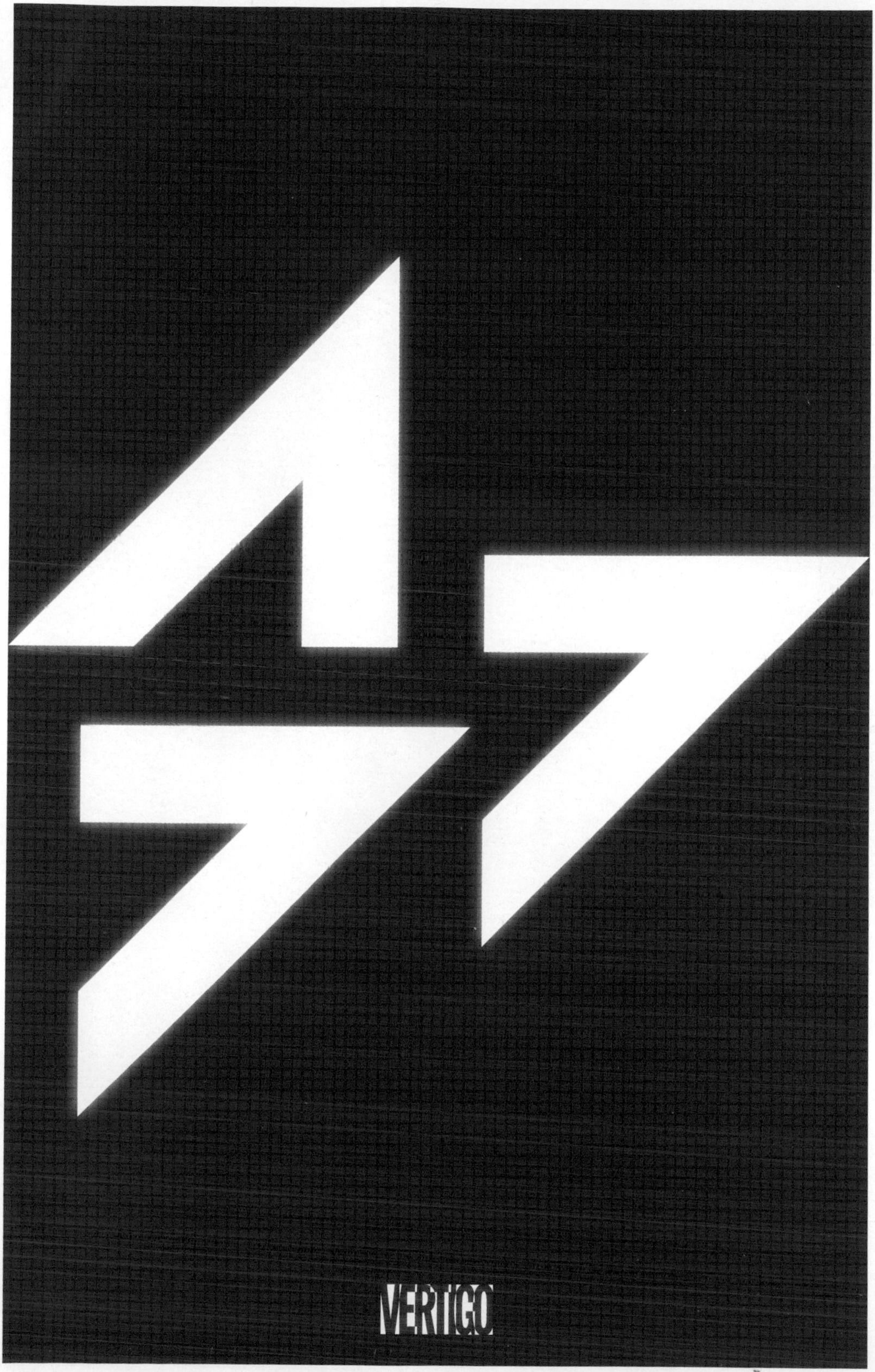
VERTIGO

A.D.D.

ADOLESCENT DEMO DIVISION

Writer: **Douglas Rushkoff** Artist: **Goran Sudžuka**

Inker (page 61-144): **Jose Marzan, Jr.** Colorists: **Tanya** and **Richard Horie**

Letterers: **Steve Wands** and **Jared K. Fletcher**

Jonathan Vankin	Editor
Joe Hughes and Sarah Litt	Assistant Editors
Robbin Brosterman	Design Director – Books
Louis Prandi	Publication Design
Karen Berger	Senior VP – Executive Editor, Vertigo
Bob Harras	VP – Editor-In-Chief
Diane Nelson	President
Dan DiDio and Jim Lee	Co-Publishers
Geoff Johns	Chief Creative Officer
John Rood	Executive VP – Sales, Marketing and Business Development
Amy Genkins	Senior VP – Business and Legal Affairs
Nairi Gardiner	Senior VP – Finance
Jeff Boison	VP – Publishing Operations
Mark Chiarello	VP – Art Direction and Design
John Cunningham	VP – Marketing
Terri Cunningham	VP – Talent Relations and Services
Alison Gill	Senior VP – Manufacturing and Operations
David Hyde	VP – Publicity
Hank Kanalz	Senior VP – Digital
Jay Kogan	VP – Business and Legal Affairs, Publishing
Jack Mahan	VP – Business Affairs, Talent
Nick Napolitano	VP – Manufacturing Administration
Sue Pohja	VP – Book Sales
Courtney Simmons	Senior VP – Publicity
Bob Wayne	Senior VP – Sales

Printed in the USA. DC Comics, a Warner Bros. Entertainment Company. HC ISBN: 978-1-4012-2355-7 SC ISBN 978-1-4012-2356-4

Cover concept and color by Miroslav Mrva.

SUSTAINABLE FORESTRY INITIATIVE
Certified Chain of Custody
60% Certified Fiber Sourcing and 40% Post-Consumer Recycled
www.sfiprogram.org
This label applies to the text stock
SGS-SFI/COC-US10/81072

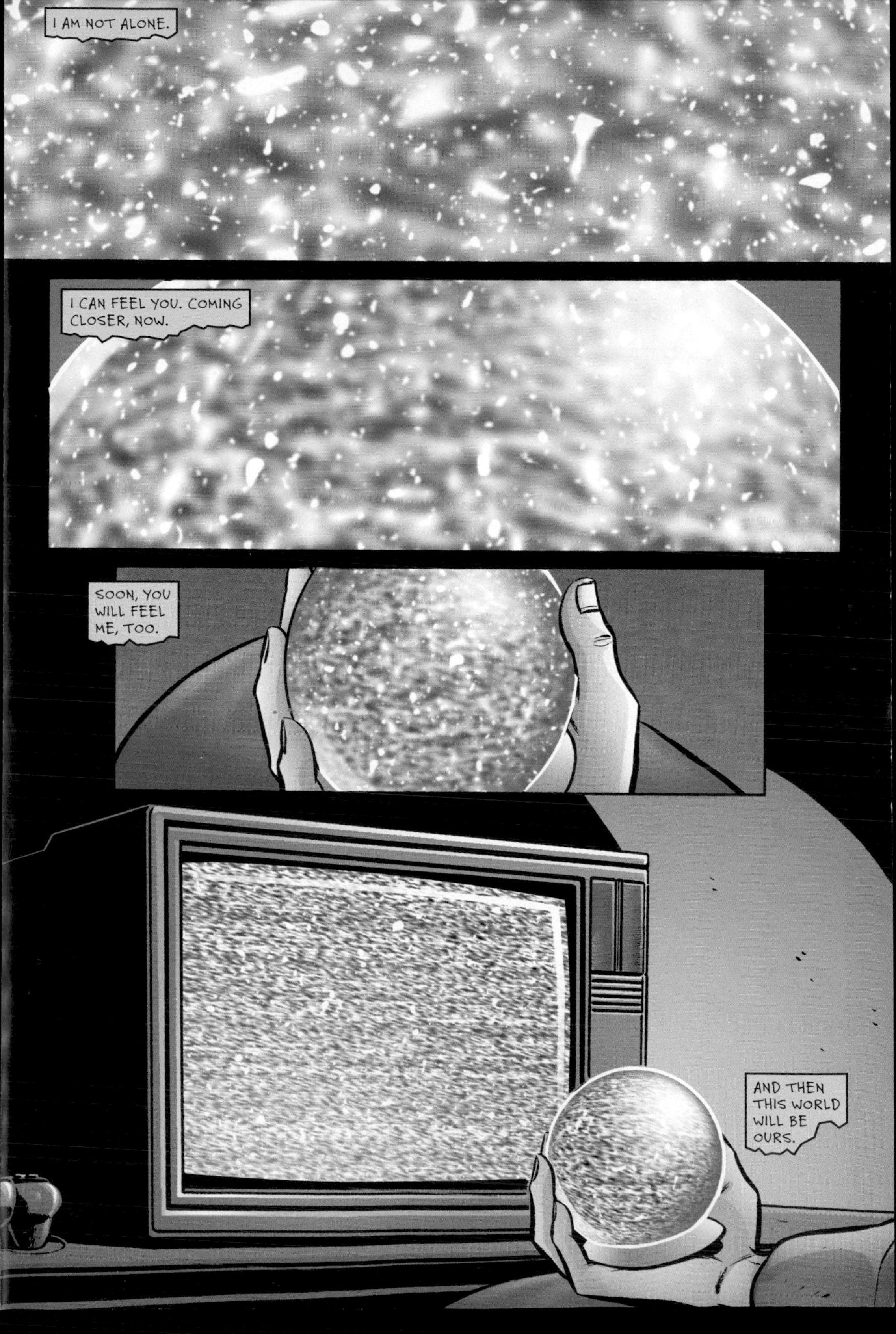
I AM NOT ALONE.
I CAN FEEL YOU. COMING CLOSER, NOW.
SOON, YOU WILL FEEL ME, TOO.
AND THEN THIS WORLD WILL BE OURS.

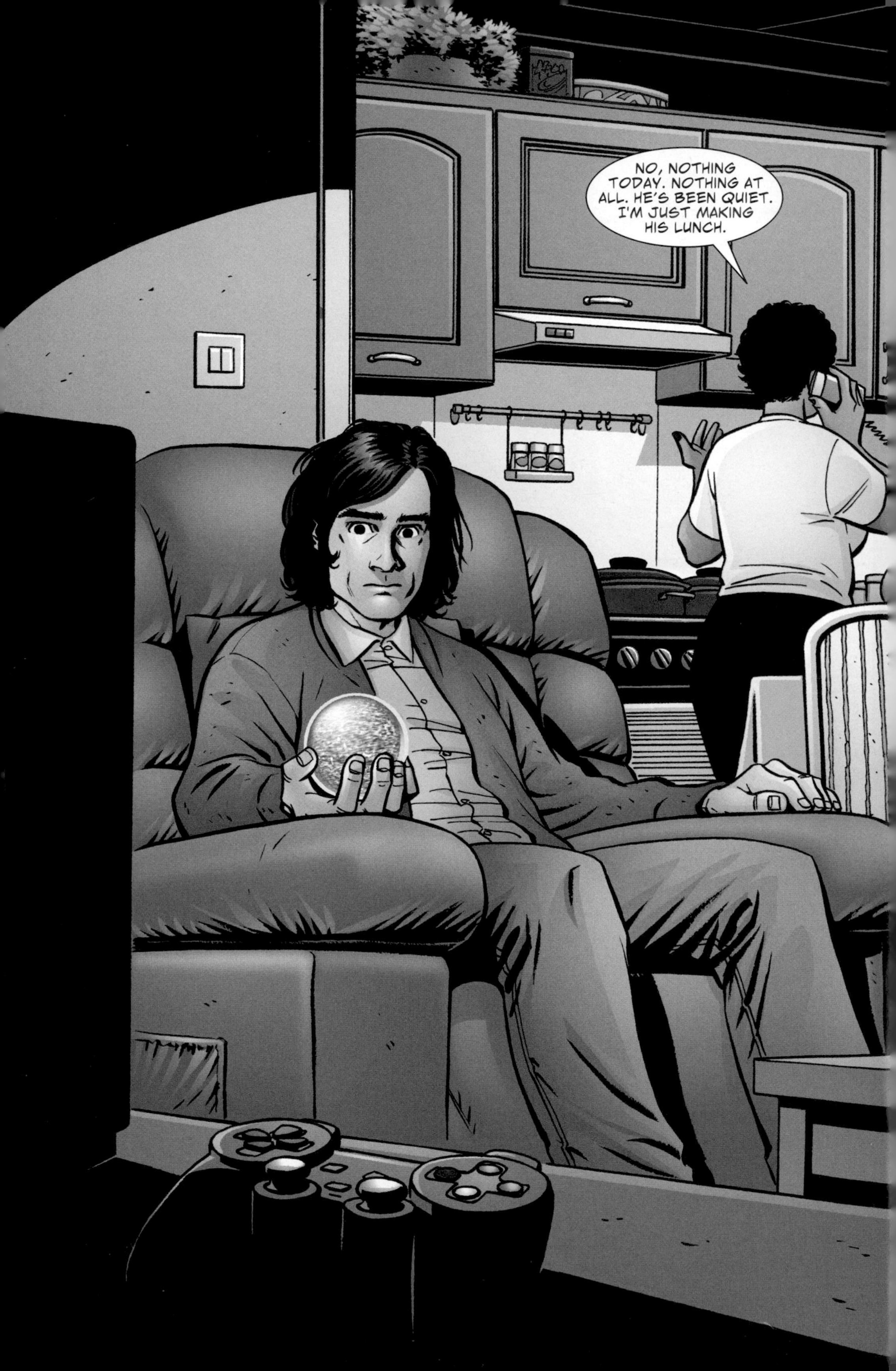
NO, NOTHING TODAY. NOTHING AT ALL. HE'S BEEN QUIET. I'M JUST MAKING HIS LUNCH.

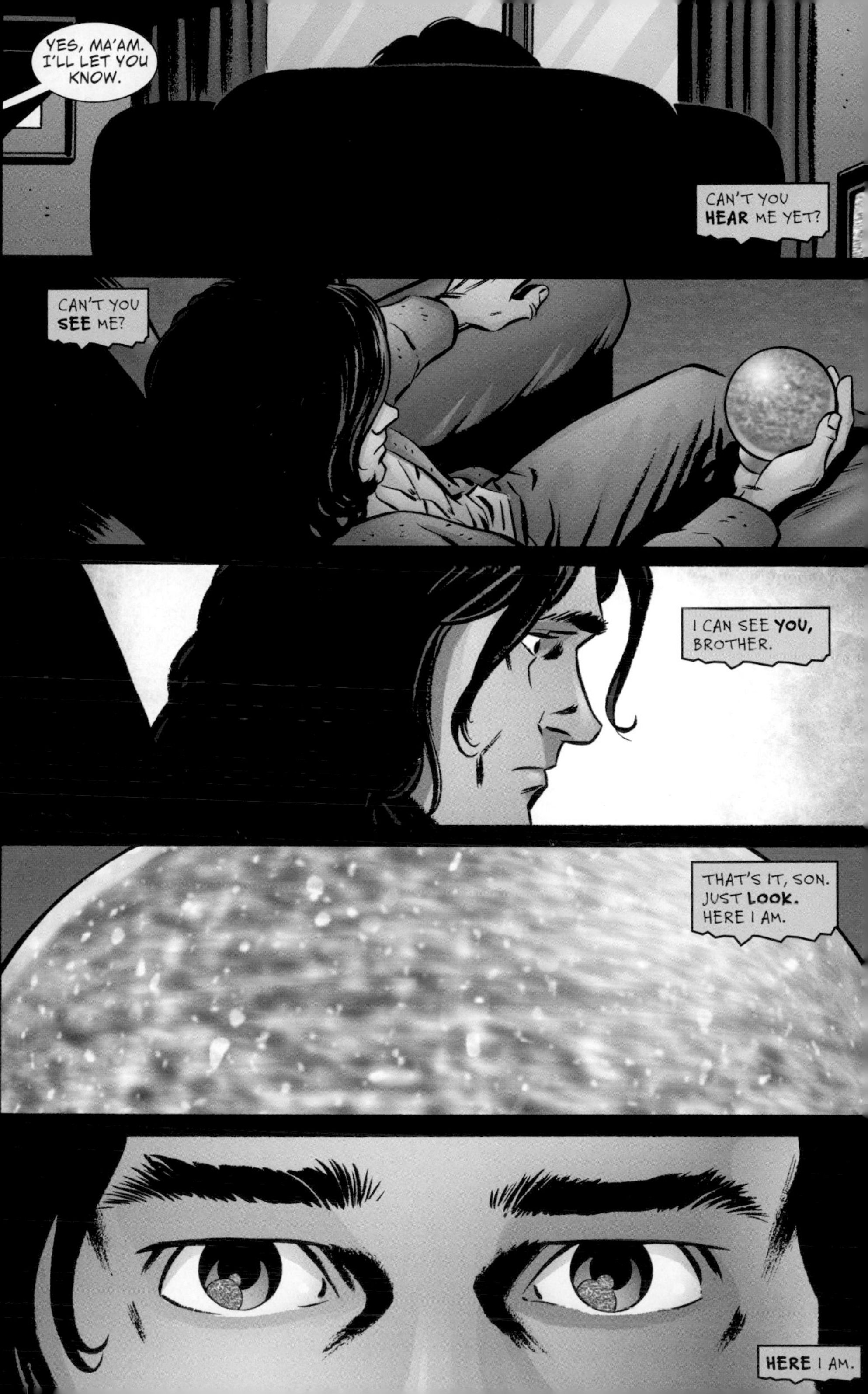
YES, MA'AM. I'LL LET YOU KNOW.
CAN'T YOU HEAR ME YET?
CAN'T YOU SEE ME?
I CAN SEE YOU, BROTHER.
THAT'S IT, SON. JUST LOOK. HERE I AM.
HERE I AM.

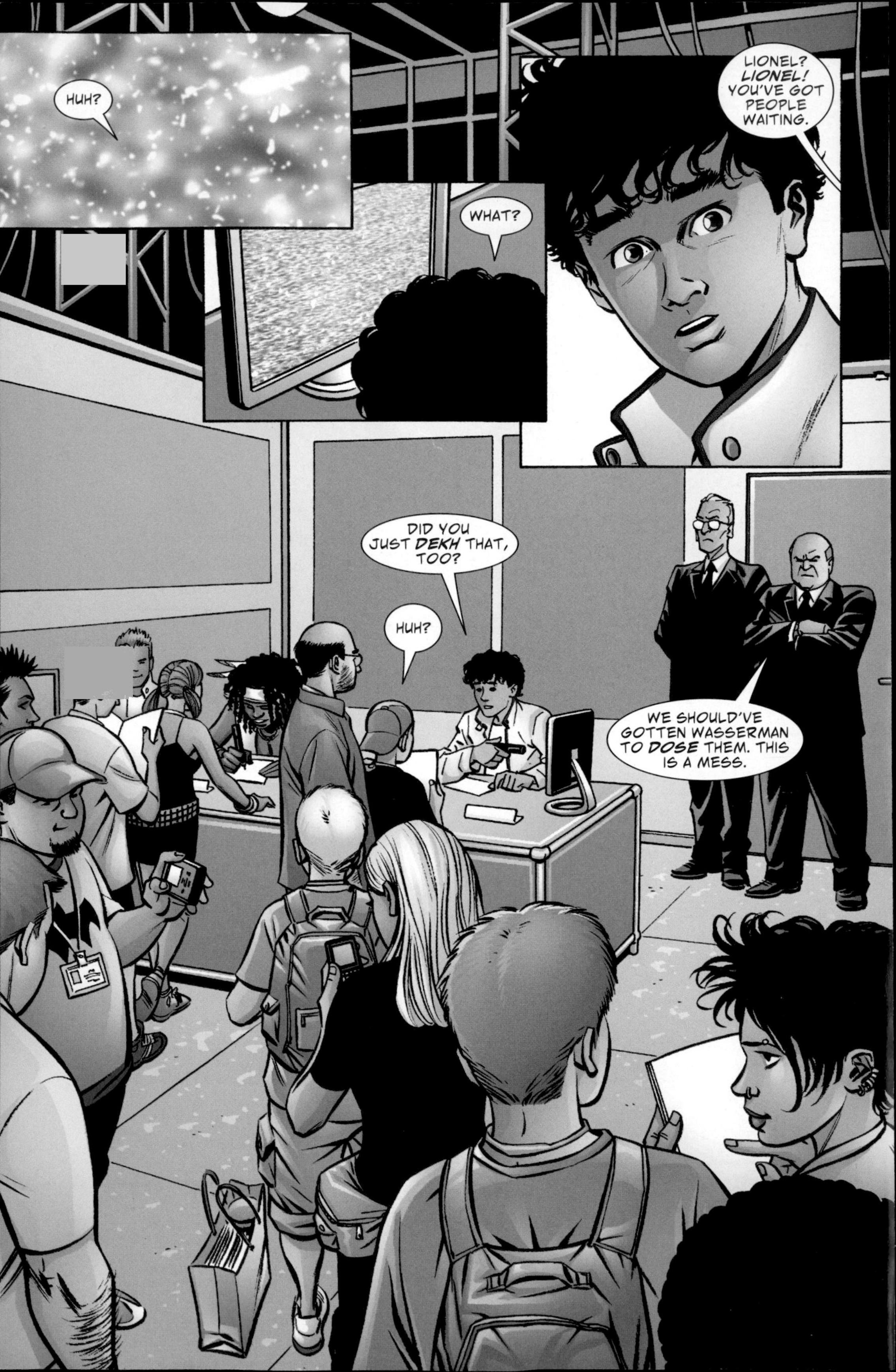

HUH?
LIONEL? LIONEL! YOU'VE GOT PEOPLE WAITING.
WHAT?
DID YOU JUST DEKH THAT, TOO?
HUH?
WE SHOULD'VE GOTTEN WASSERMAN TO DOSE THEM. THIS IS A MESS.

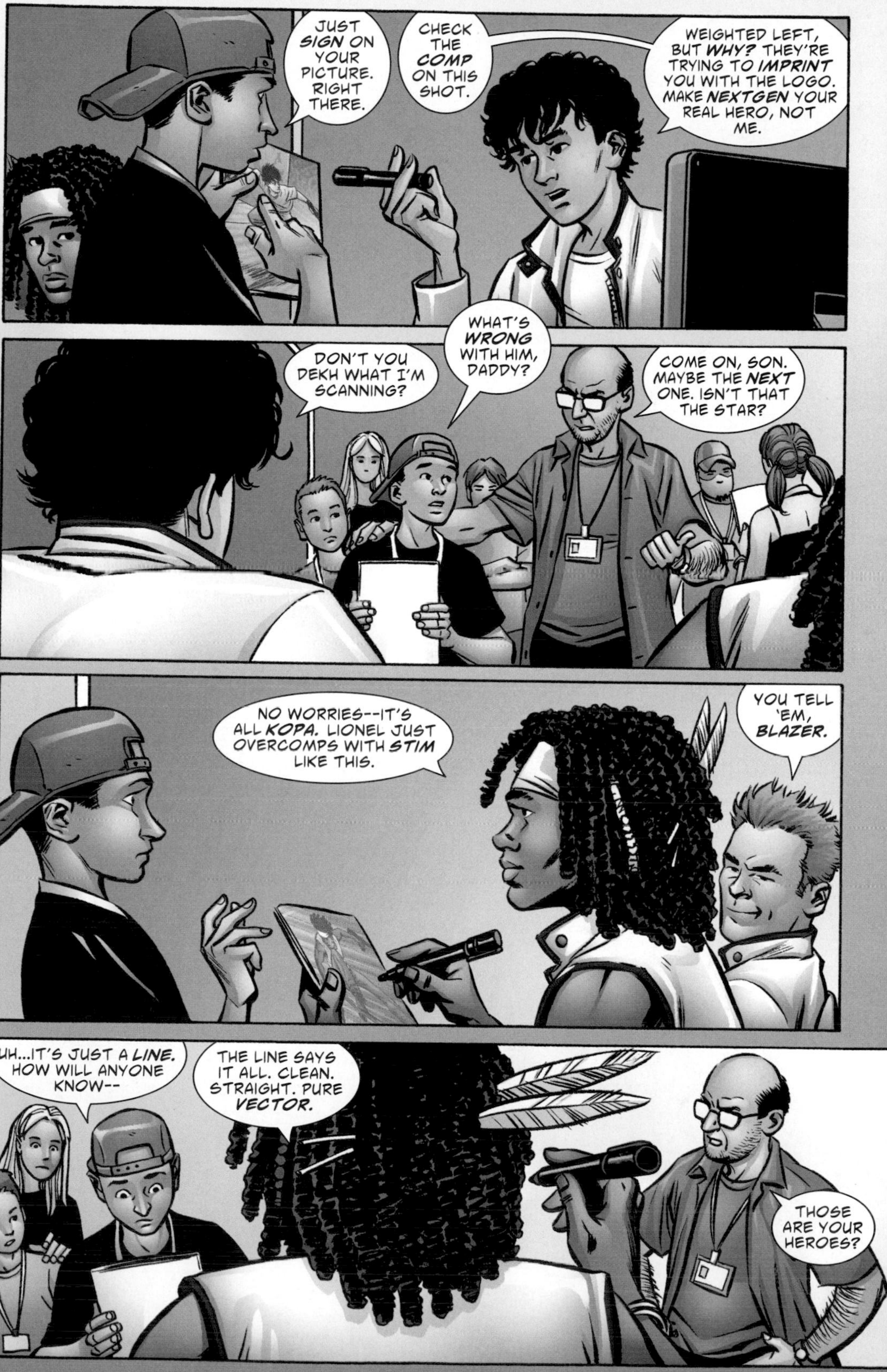
JUST SIGN ON YOUR PICTURE. RIGHT THERE.
CHECK THE COMP ON THIS SHOT.
WEIGHTED LEFT, BUT WHY? THEY'RE TRYING TO IMPRINT YOU WITH THE LOGO. MAKE NEXTGEN YOUR REAL HERO, NOT ME.
DON'T YOU DEKH WHAT I'M SCANNING?
WHAT'S WRONG WITH HIM, DADDY?
COME ON, SON. MAYBE THE NEXT ONE. ISN'T THAT THE STAR?
NO WORRIES--IT'S ALL KOPA. LIONEL JUST OVERCOMPS WITH STIM LIKE THIS.
YOU TELL 'EM, BLAZER.
UH...IT'S JUST A LINE. HOW WILL ANYONE KNOW--
THE LINE SAYS IT ALL. CLEAN. STRAIGHT. PURE VECTOR.
THOSE ARE YOUR HEROES?

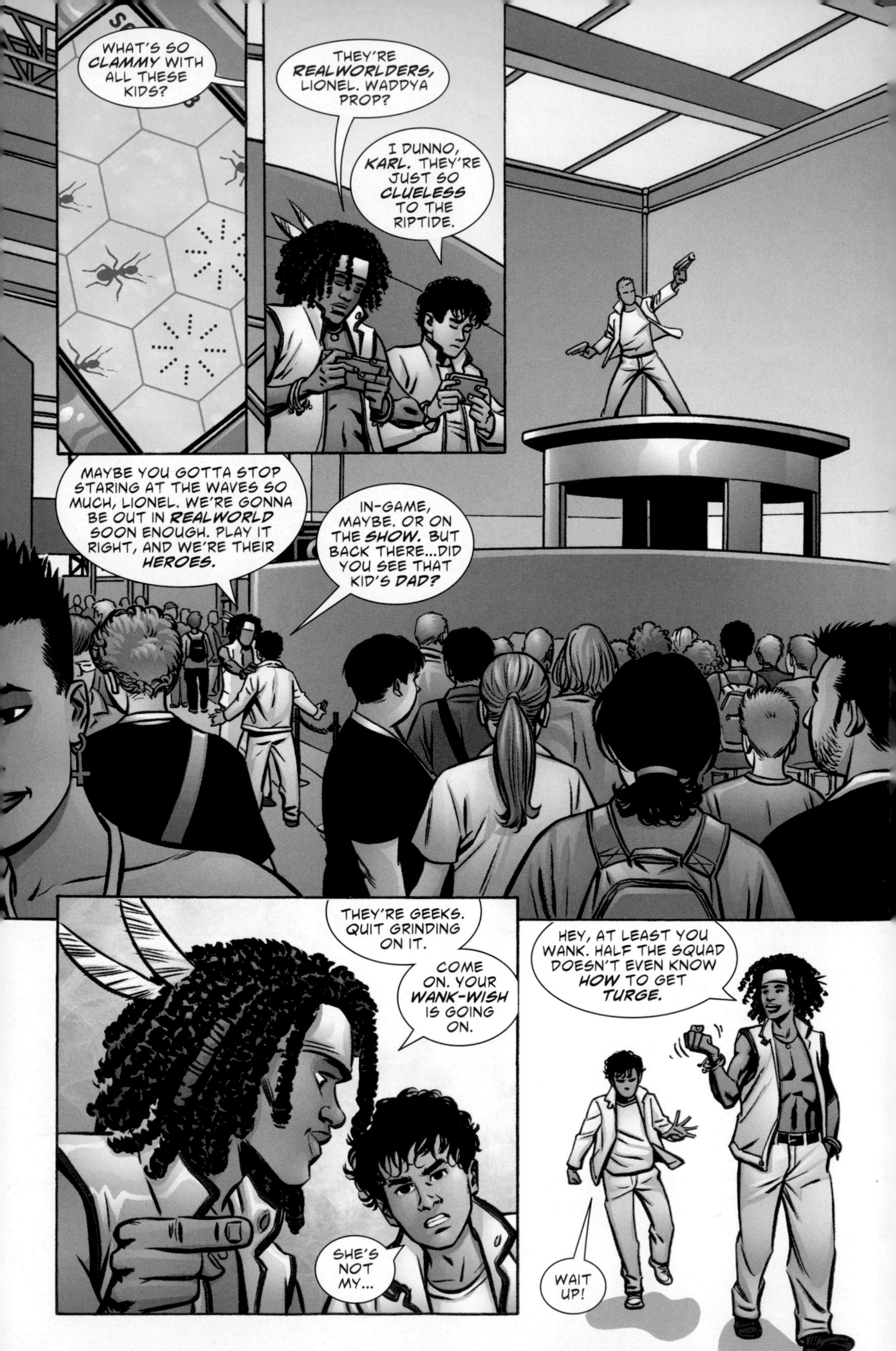
WHAT'S SO CLAMMY WITH ALL THESE KIDS?
THEY'RE REALWORLDERS, LIONEL. WADDYA PROP?
I DUNNO, KARL. THEY'RE JUST SO CLUELESS TO THE RIPTIDE.
MAYBE YOU GOTTA STOP STARING AT THE WAVES SO MUCH, LIONEL. WE'RE GONNA BE OUT IN REALWORLD SOON ENOUGH. PLAY IT RIGHT, AND WE'RE THEIR HEROES.
IN-GAME, MAYBE. OR ON THE SHOW. BUT BACK THERE...DID YOU SEE THAT KID'S DAD?
THEY'RE GEEKS. QUIT GRINDING ON IT.
COME ON. YOUR WANK-WISH IS GOING ON.
SHE'S NOT MY...
HEY, AT LEAST YOU WANK. HALF THE SQUAD DOESN'T EVEN KNOW HOW TO GET TURGE.
WAIT UP!

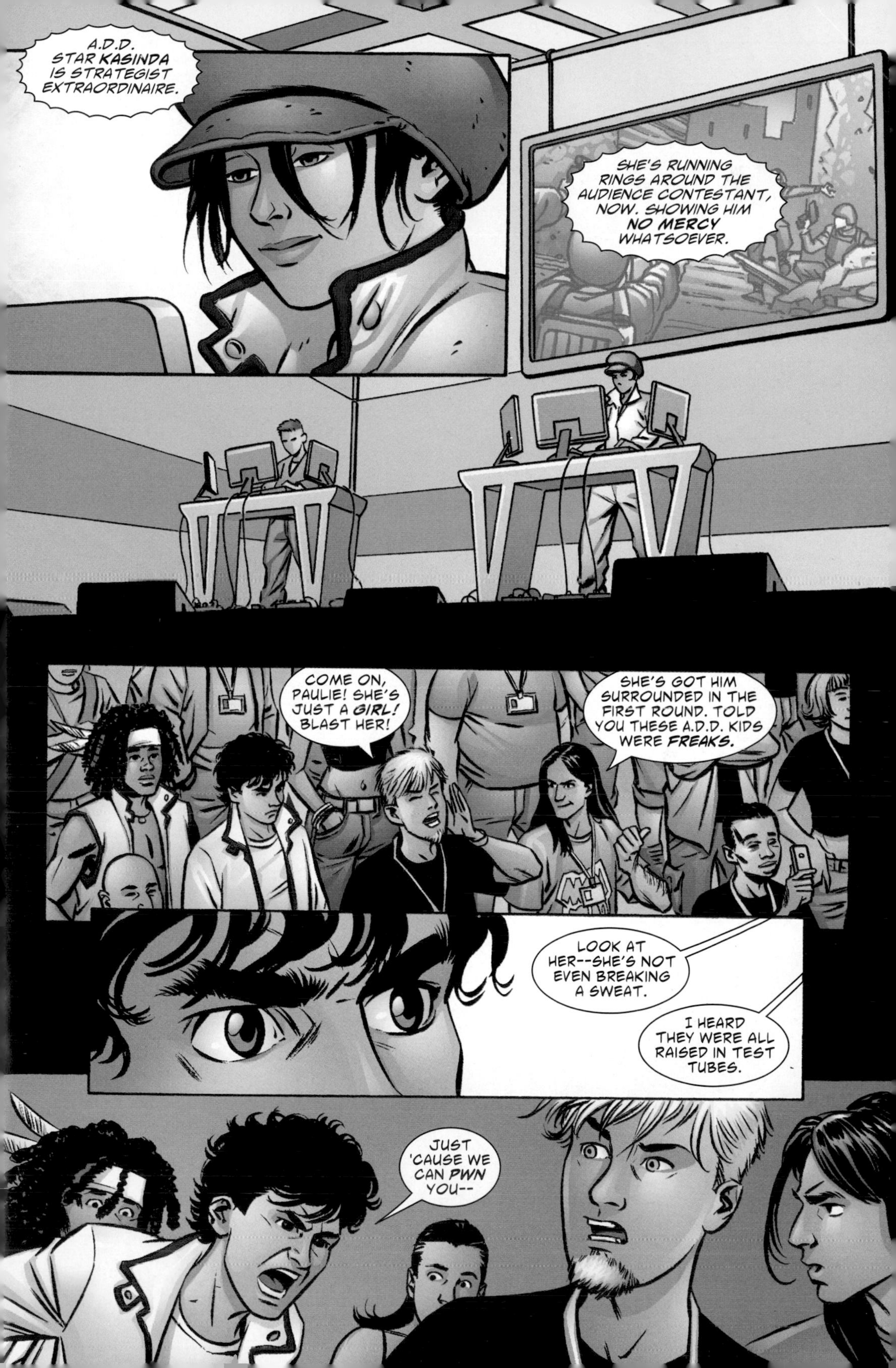
A.D.D. STAR KASINDA IS STRATEGIST EXTRAORDINAIRE.
SHE'S RUNNING RINGS AROUND THE AUDIENCE CONTESTANT, NOW. SHOWING HIM NO MERCY WHATSOEVER.
COME ON, PAULIE! SHE'S JUST A GIRL! BLAST HER!
SHE'S GOT HIM SURROUNDED IN THE FIRST ROUND. TOLD YOU THESE A.D.D. KIDS WERE FREAKS.
LOOK AT HER--SHE'S NOT EVEN BREAKING A SWEAT.
I HEARD THEY WERE ALL RAISED IN TEST TUBES.
JUST 'CAUSE WE CAN PWN YOU--

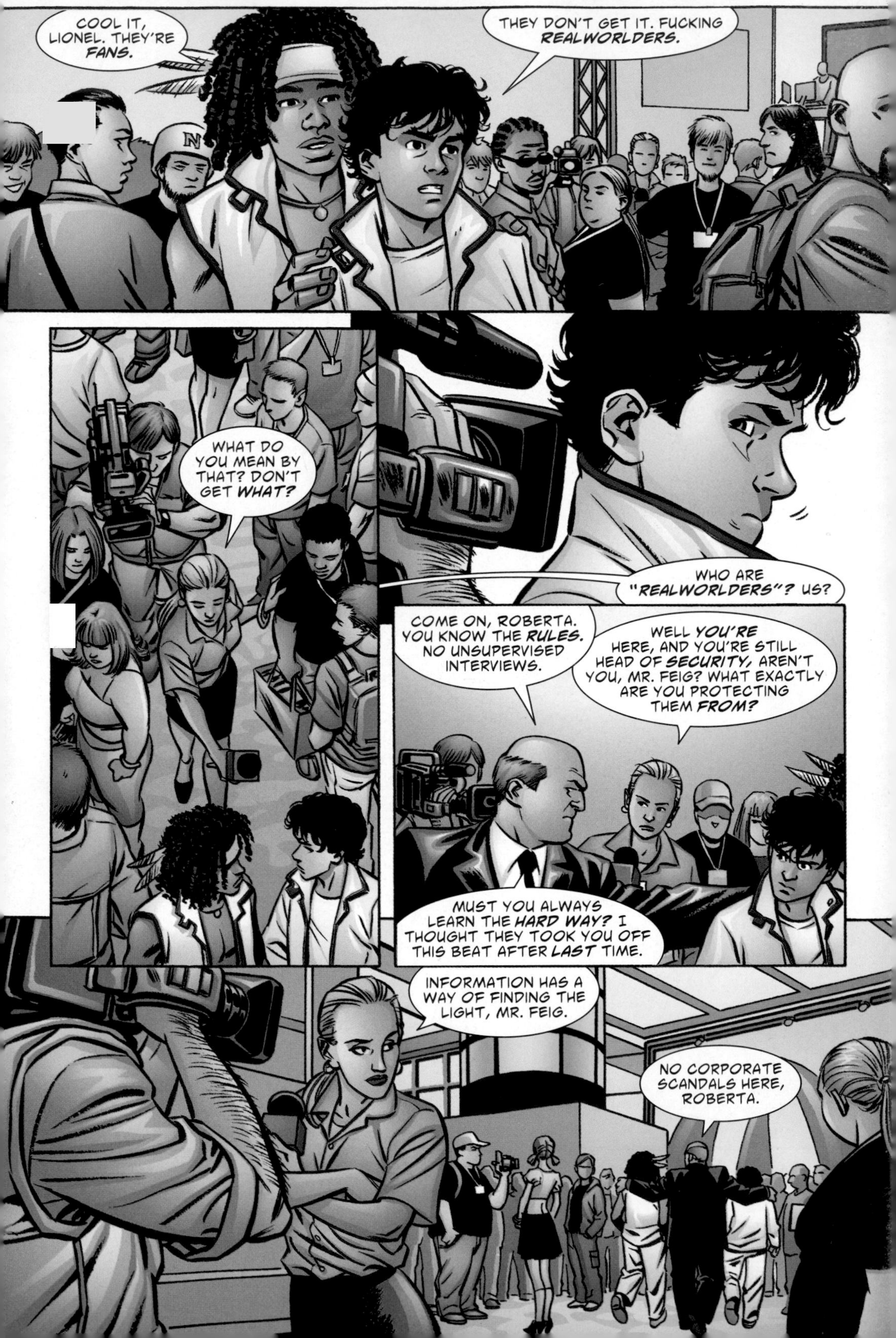

COOL IT, LIONEL. THEY'RE FANS.
THEY DON'T GET IT. FUCKING REALWORLDERS.
WHAT DO YOU MEAN BY THAT? DON'T GET WHAT?
WHO ARE "REALWORLDERS"? US?
COME ON, ROBERTA. YOU KNOW THE RULES. NO UNSUPERVISED INTERVIEWS.
WELL YOU'RE HERE, AND YOU'RE STILL HEAD OF SECURITY, AREN'T YOU, MR. FEIG? WHAT EXACTLY ARE YOU PROTECTING THEM FROM?
MUST YOU ALWAYS LEARN THE HARD WAY? I THOUGHT THEY TOOK YOU OFF THIS BEAT AFTER LAST TIME.
INFORMATION HAS A WAY OF FINDING THE LIGHT, MR. FEIG.
NO CORPORATE SCANDALS HERE, ROBERTA.

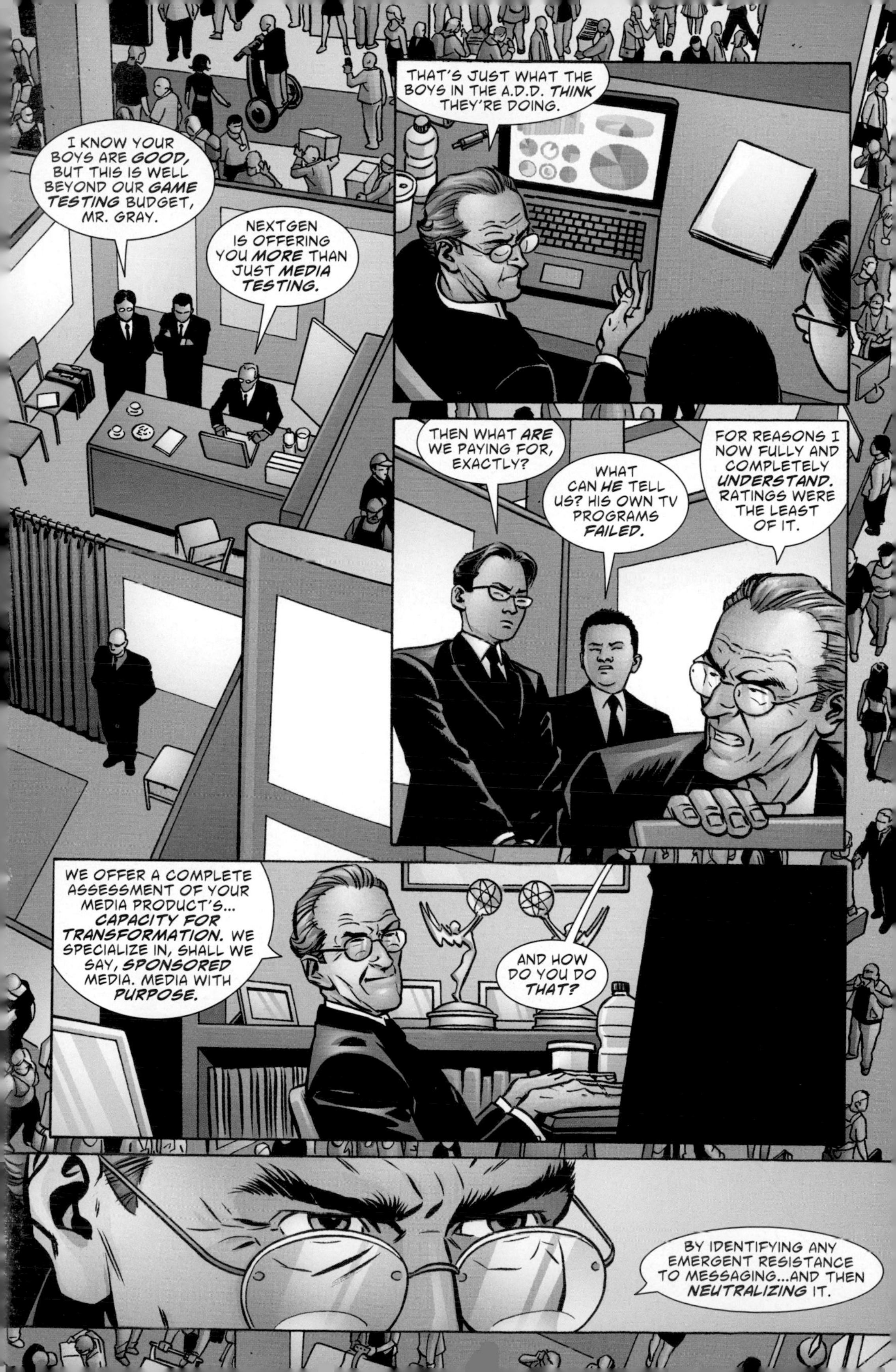
I KNOW YOUR BOYS ARE GOOD, BUT THIS IS WELL BEYOND OUR GAME TESTING BUDGET, MR. GRAY.
NEXTGEN IS OFFERING YOU MORE THAN JUST MEDIA TESTING.
THAT'S JUST WHAT THE BOYS IN THE A.D.D. THINK THEY'RE DOING.
THEN WHAT ARE WE PAYING FOR, EXACTLY?
WHAT CAN HE TELL US? HIS OWN TV PROGRAMS FAILED.
FOR REASONS I NOW FULLY AND COMPLETELY UNDERSTAND. RATINGS WERE THE LEAST OF IT.
WE OFFER A COMPLETE ASSESSMENT OF YOUR MEDIA PRODUCT'S... CAPACITY FOR TRANSFORMATION. WE SPECIALIZE IN, SHALL WE SAY, SPONSORED MEDIA. MEDIA WITH PURPOSE.
AND HOW DO YOU DO THAT?
BY IDENTIFYING ANY EMERGENT RESISTANCE TO MESSAGING...AND THEN NEUTRALIZING IT.

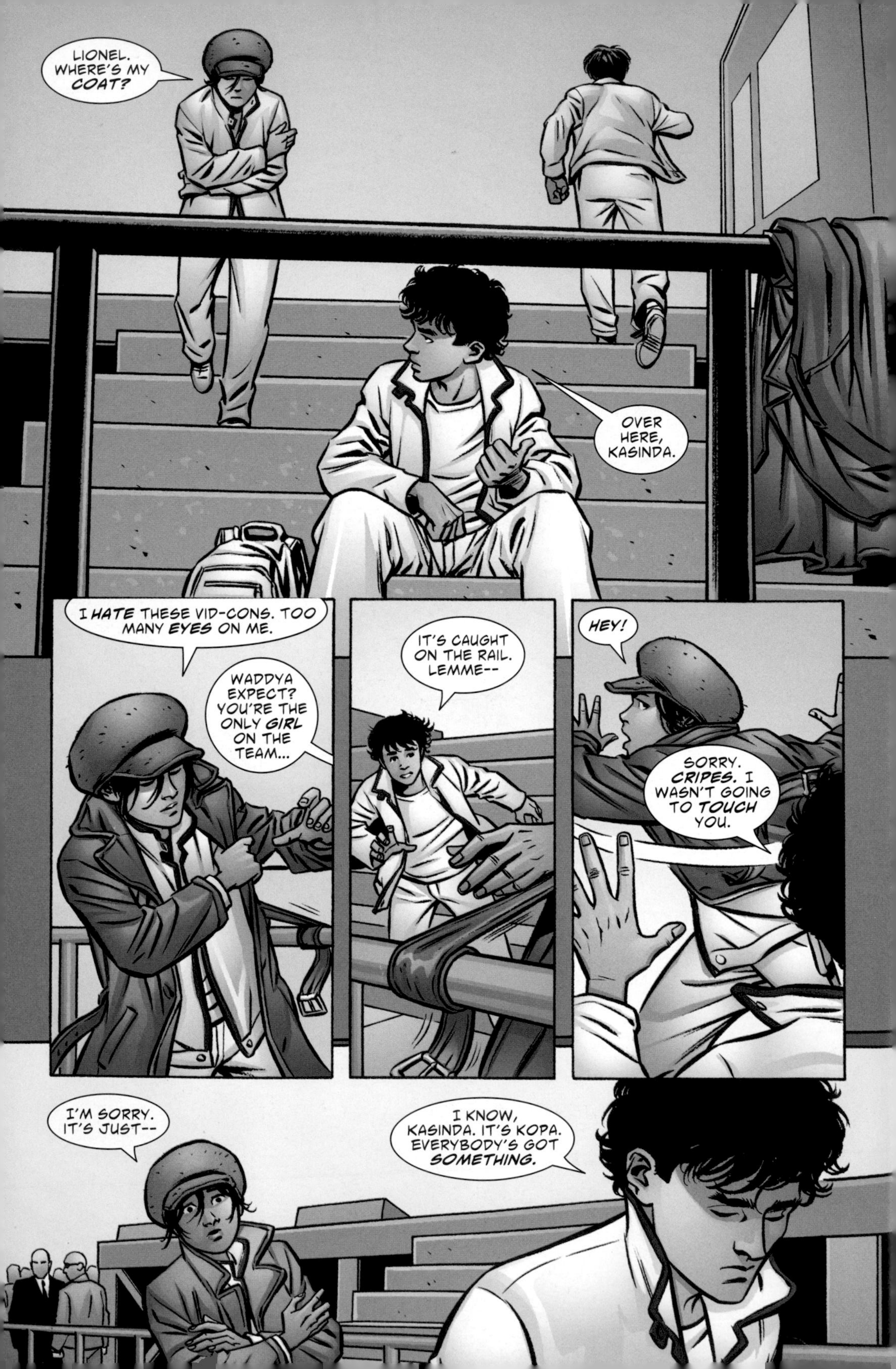
LIONEL. WHERE'S MY COAT?
OVER HERE, KASINDA.
I HATE THESE VID-CONS. TOO MANY EYES ON ME.
WADDYA EXPECT? YOU'RE THE ONLY GIRL ON THE TEAM...
IT'S CAUGHT ON THE RAIL. LEMME--
HEY!
SORRY. CRIPES. I WASN'T GOING TO TOUCH YOU.
I'M SORRY. IT'S JUST--
I KNOW, KASINDA. IT'S KOPA. EVERYBODY'S GOT SOMETHING.

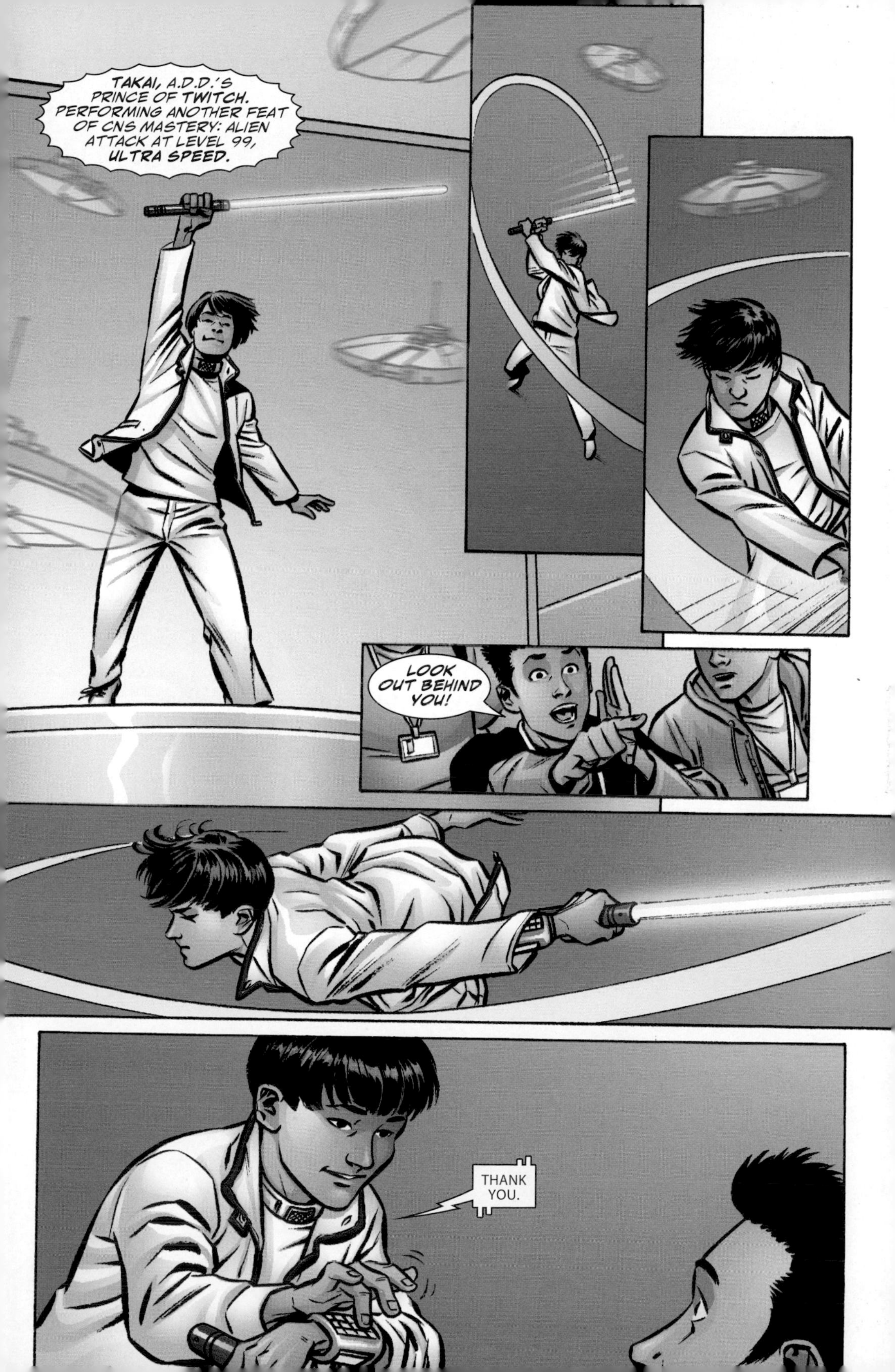
TAKAI, A.D.D.'S PRINCE OF TWITCH. PERFORMING ANOTHER FEAT OF CNS MASTERY: ALIEN ATTACK AT LEVEL 99, ULTRA SPEED.
LOOK OUT BEHIND YOU!
THANK YOU.

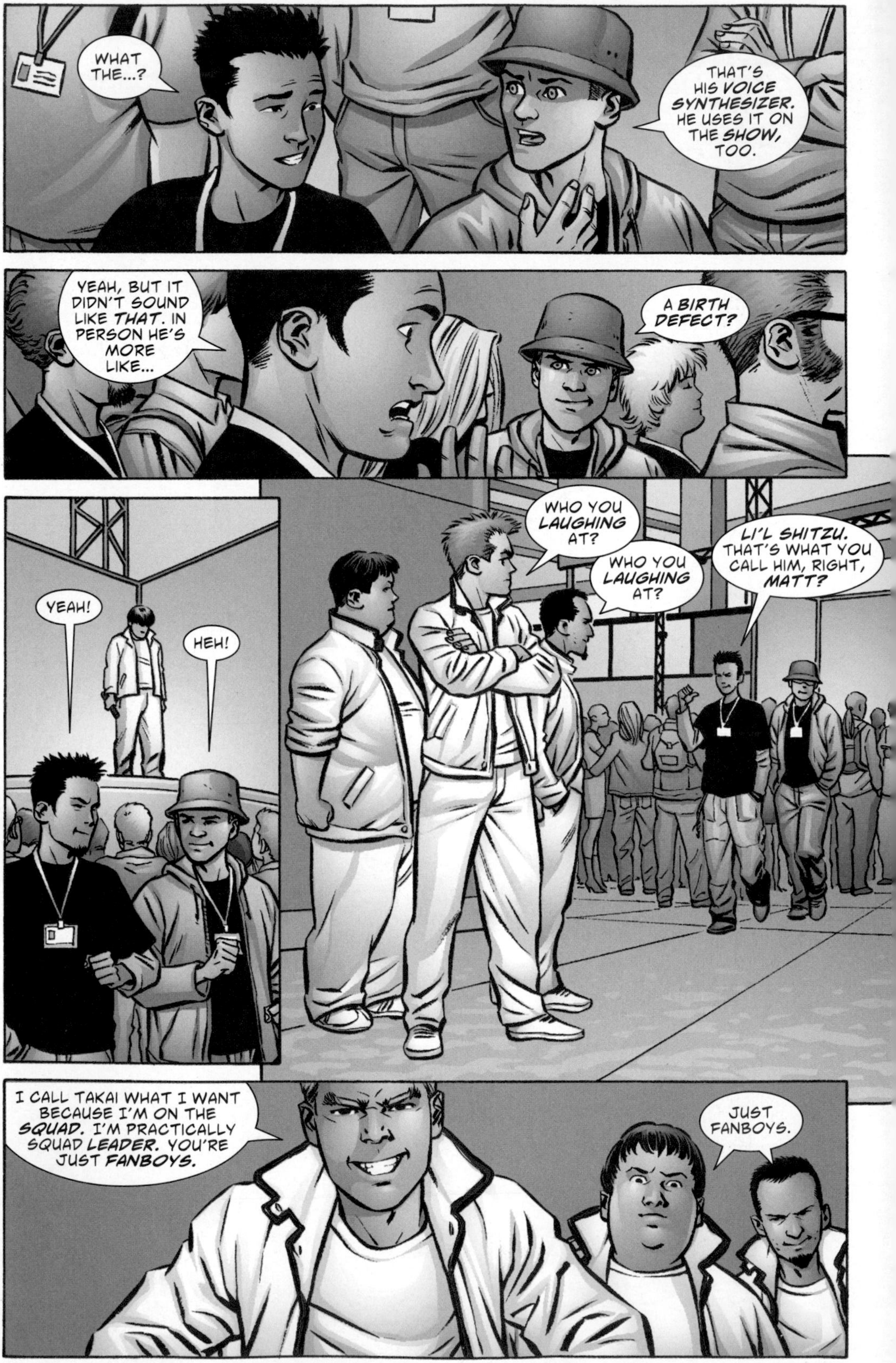
WHAT THE...?
THAT'S HIS VOICE SYNTHESIZER. HE USES IT ON THE SHOW, TOO.
YEAH, BUT IT DIDN'T SOUND LIKE THAT. IN PERSON HE'S MORE LIKE...
A BIRTH DEFECT?
YEAH!
HEH!
WHO YOU LAUGHING AT?
WHO YOU LAUGHING AT?
LI'L SHITZU. THAT'S WHAT YOU CALL HIM, RIGHT, MATT?
I CALL TAKAI WHAT I WANT BECAUSE I'M ON THE SQUAD. I'M PRACTICALLY SQUAD LEADER. YOU'RE JUST FANBOYS.
JUST FANBOYS.

YOU'RE NOT SQUAD LEADER, MATT. NOT UNTIL I GRADUATE.

OR 'TIL YOU *LOSE* TO ME TOMORROW...

'TIL YOU *LOSE* TO ME.

THIS IS FREAK CITY.

ECHOES AREN'T FRIENDS, MATT. YOU STILL SHOOTING *SHUGS?*

SHUGS? LIKE *DRUGS?*

ARE WE ON THE *SHOW?*

THIS ISN'T WORKING QUITE AS I EXPECTED, DR. WASSERMAN.

I TOLD YOU THE BOYS WOULD BE *UNPREDICTABLE,* AT BEST.

GET THEM BACK ON THE *BUS* BEFORE THEY DO ANY MORE *DAMAGE.*

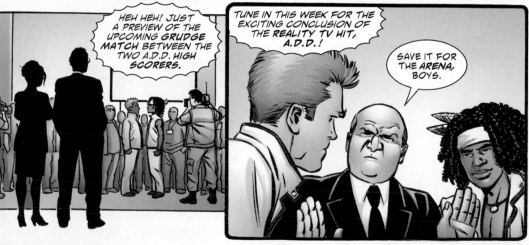

HEH HEH! JUST A PREVIEW OF THE UPCOMING *GRUDGE MATCH* BETWEEN THE TWO *A.D.D.* HIGH SCORERS.

TUNE IN THIS WEEK FOR THE EXCITING CONCLUSION OF THE REALITY TV HIT, *A.D.D.!*

SAVE IT FOR THE *ARENA,* BOYS.

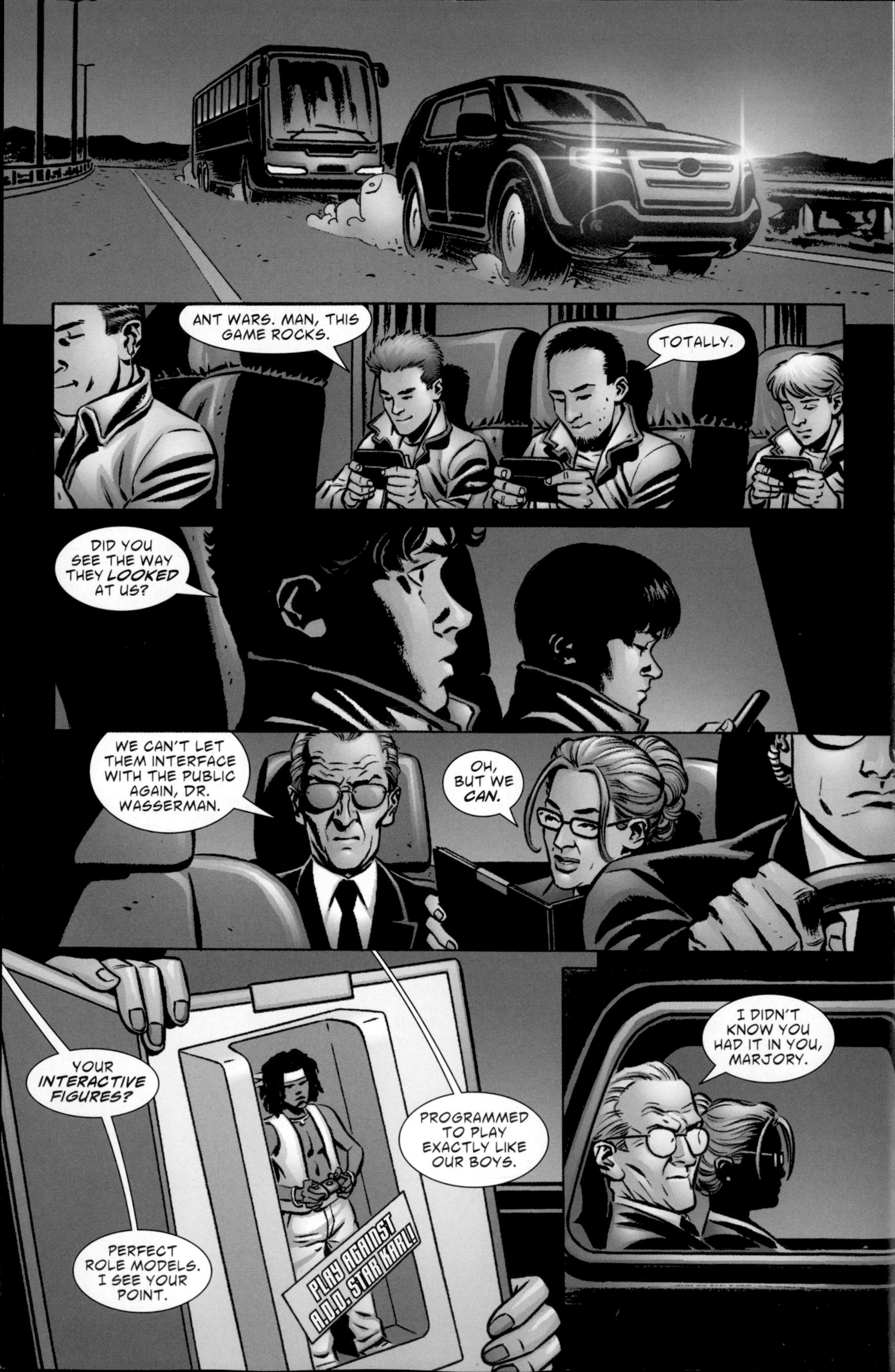
ANT WARS. MAN, THIS GAME ROCKS.
TOTALLY.
DID YOU SEE THE WAY THEY *LOOKED* AT US?
WE CAN'T LET THEM INTERFACE WITH THE PUBLIC AGAIN, DR. WASSERMAN.
OH, BUT WE *CAN.*
YOUR *INTERACTIVE FIGURES?*
PERFECT ROLE MODELS. I SEE YOUR POINT.
PROGRAMMED TO PLAY EXACTLY LIKE OUR BOYS.
PLAY AGAINST A.D.D. STAR KARL!
I DIDN'T KNOW YOU HAD IT IN YOU, MARJORY.

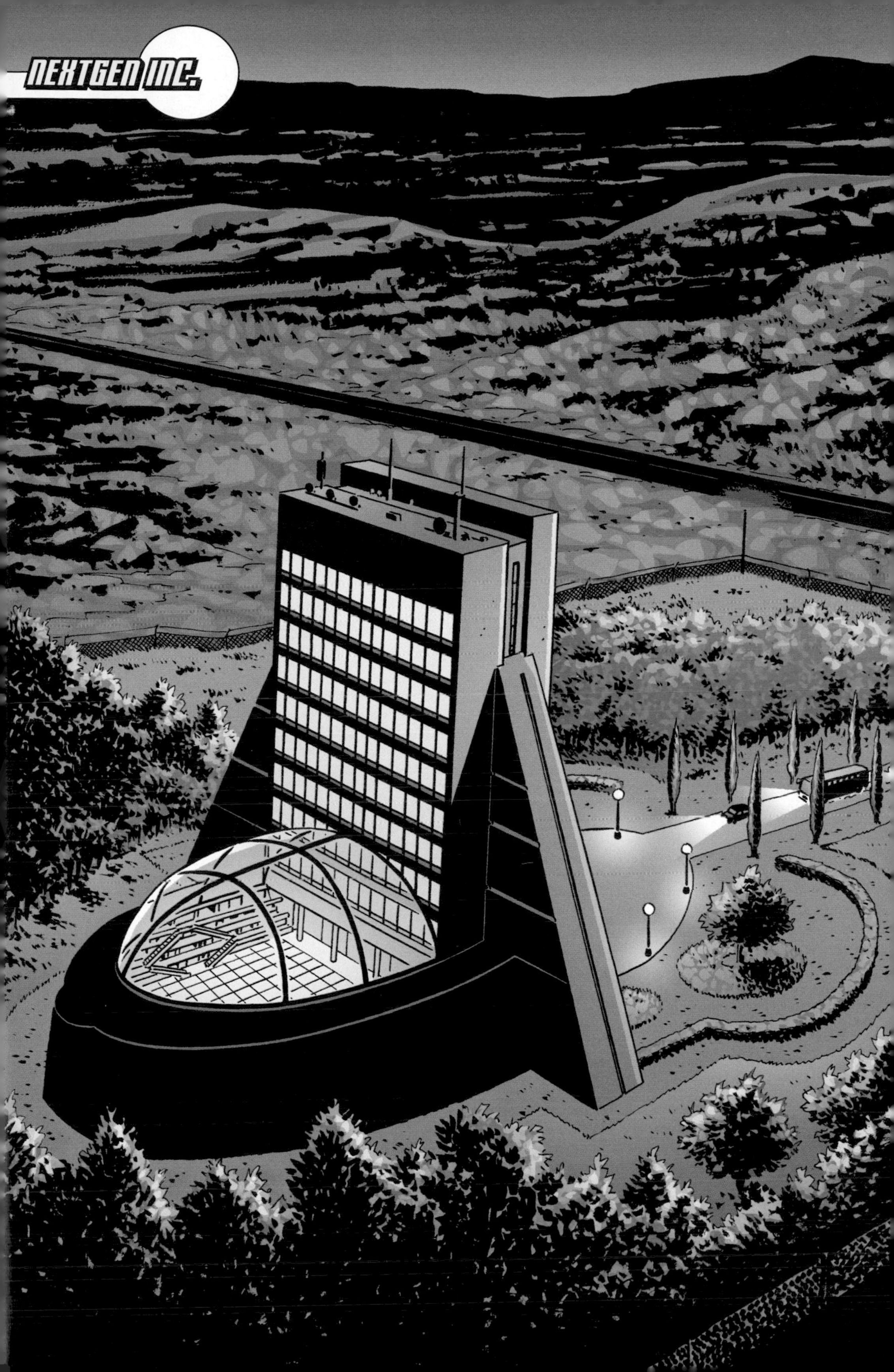
NEXTGEN INC.

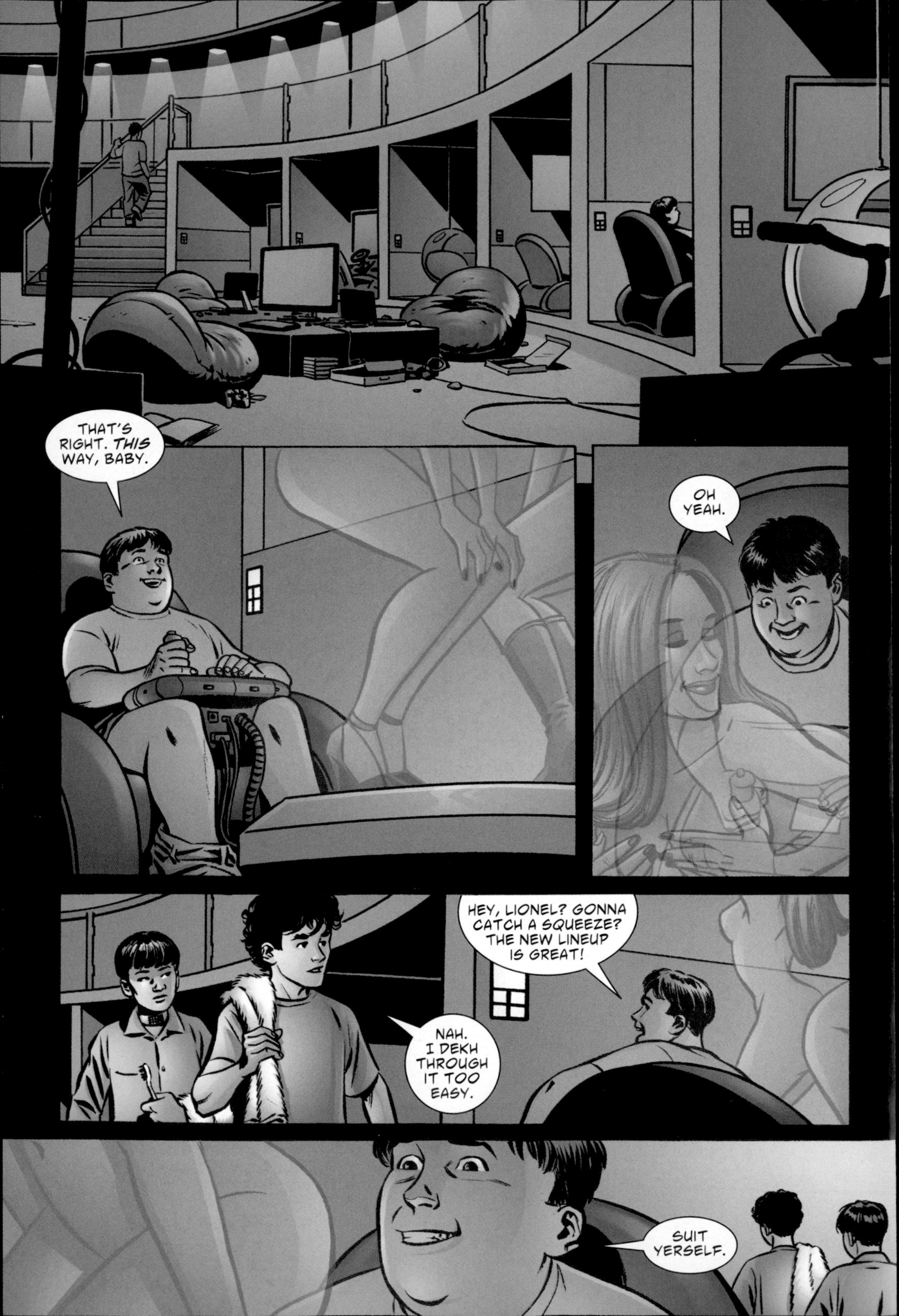
THAT'S RIGHT. THIS WAY, BABY.
OH YEAH.
HEY, LIONEL? GONNA CATCH A SQUEEZE? THE NEW LINEUP IS GREAT!
NAH. I DEKH THROUGH IT TOO EASY.
SUIT YERSELF.

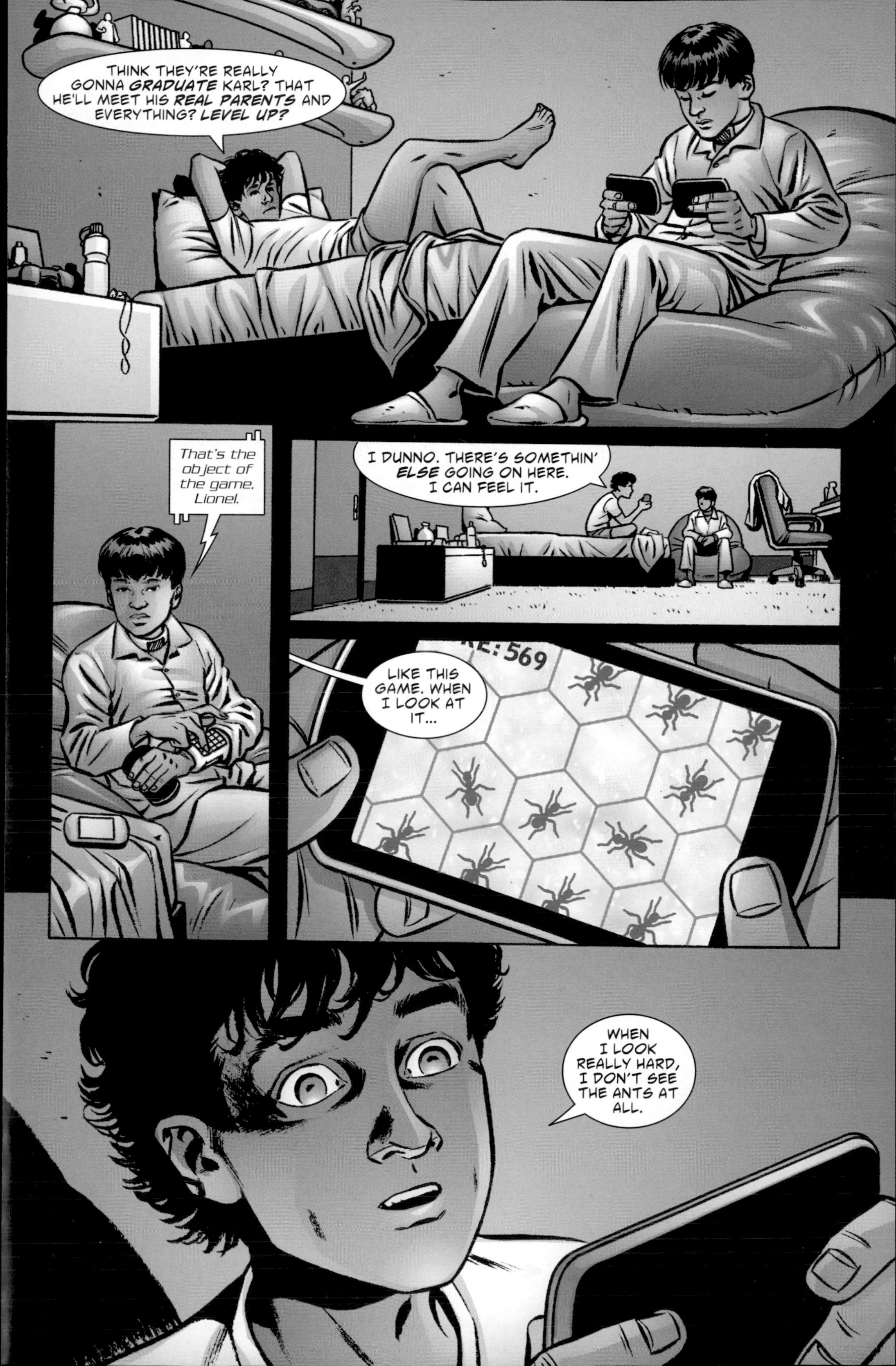
THINK THEY'RE REALLY GONNA GRADUATE KARL? THAT HE'LL MEET HIS REAL PARENTS AND EVERYTHING? LEVEL UP?
That's the object of the game. Lionel.
I DUNNO. THERE'S SOMETHIN' ELSE GOING ON HERE. I CAN FEEL IT.
RE:569
LIKE THIS GAME. WHEN I LOOK AT IT...
WHEN I LOOK REALLY HARD, I DON'T SEE THE ANTS AT ALL.

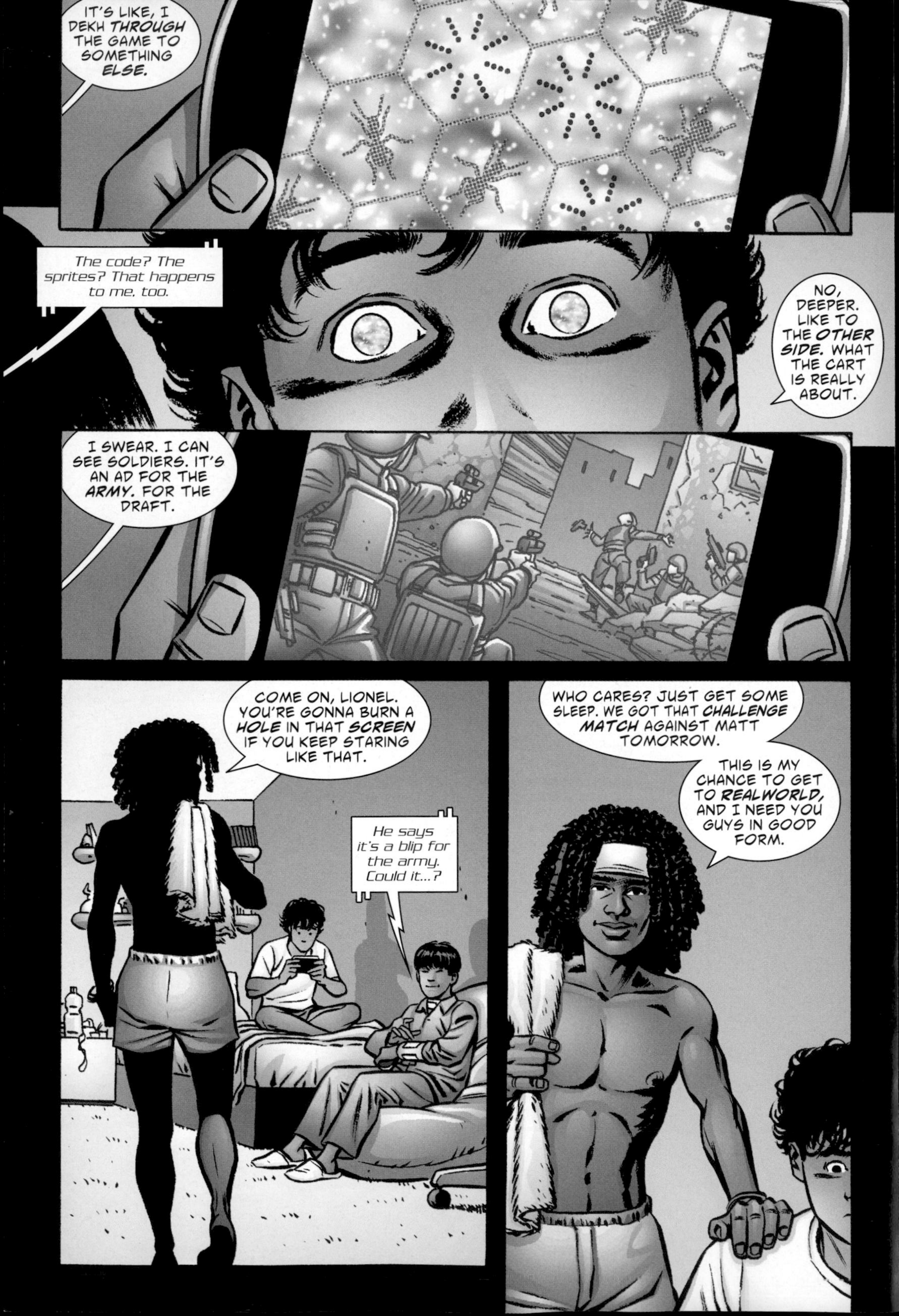
IT'S LIKE, I DEKH THROUGH THE GAME TO SOMETHING ELSE.
The code? The sprites? That happens to me, too.
NO, DEEPER. LIKE TO THE OTHER SIDE. WHAT THE CART IS REALLY ABOUT.
I SWEAR. I CAN SEE SOLDIERS. IT'S AN AD FOR THE ARMY. FOR THE DRAFT.
COME ON, LIONEL. YOU'RE GONNA BURN A HOLE IN THAT SCREEN IF YOU KEEP STARING LIKE THAT.
He says it's a blip for the army. Could it...?
WHO CARES? JUST GET SOME SLEEP. WE GOT THAT CHALLENGE MATCH AGAINST MATT TOMORROW.
THIS IS MY CHANCE TO GET TO REALWORLD, AND I NEED YOU GUYS IN GOOD FORM.

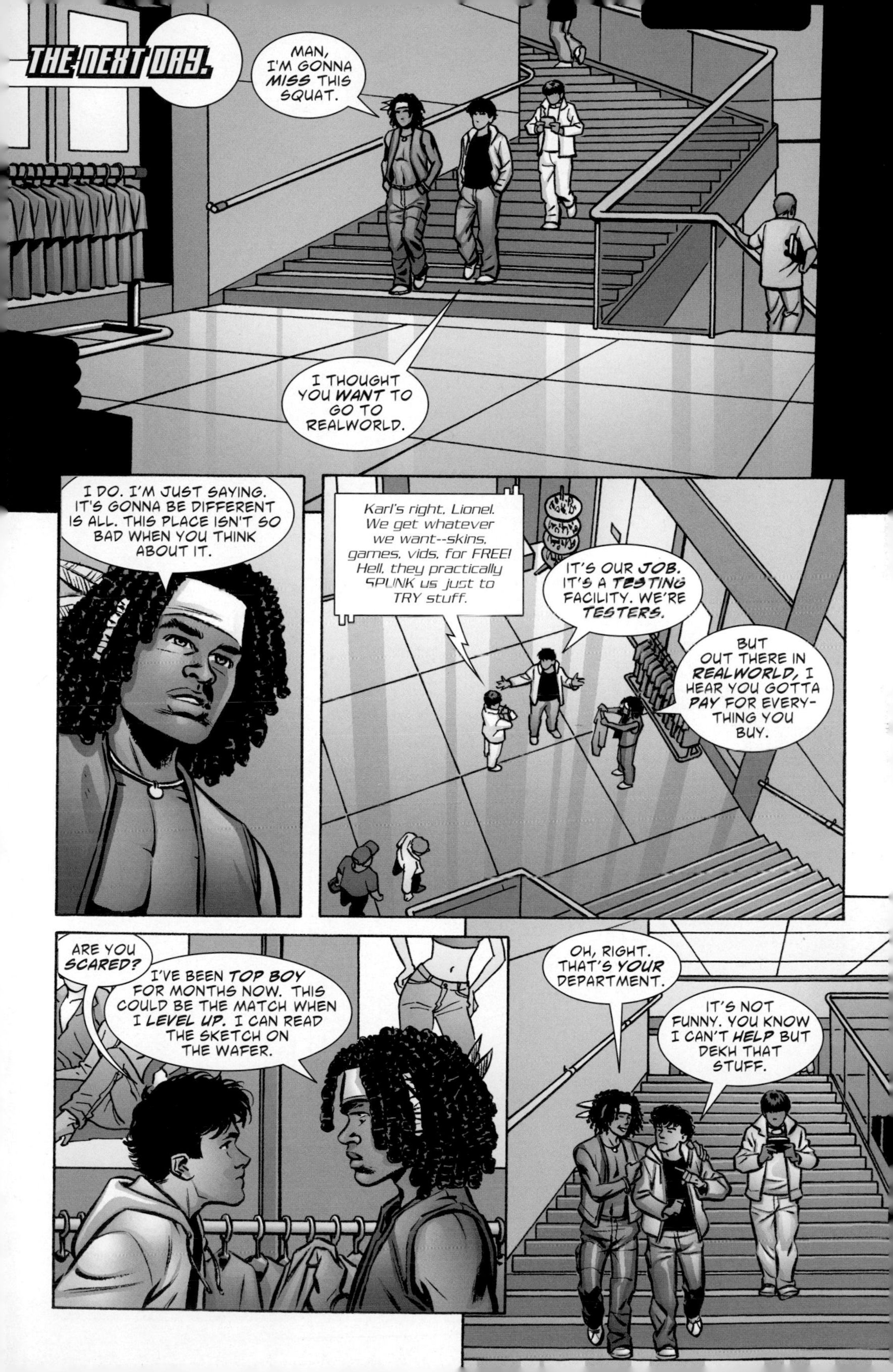
THE NEXT DAY.
MAN, I'M GONNA MISS THIS SQUAT.
I THOUGHT YOU WANT TO GO TO REALWORLD.
I DO. I'M JUST SAYING. IT'S GONNA BE DIFFERENT IS ALL. THIS PLACE ISN'T SO BAD WHEN YOU THINK ABOUT IT.
Karl's right, Lionel. We get whatever we want--skins, games, vids, for FREE! Hell, they practically SPUNK us just to TRY stuff.
IT'S OUR JOB. IT'S A TESTING FACILITY. WE'RE TESTERS.
BUT OUT THERE IN REALWORLD, I HEAR YOU GOTTA PAY FOR EVERY-THING YOU BUY.
ARE YOU SCARED?
I'VE BEEN TOP BOY FOR MONTHS NOW. THIS COULD BE THE MATCH WHEN I LEVEL UP. I CAN READ THE SKETCH ON THE WAFER.
OH, RIGHT. THAT'S YOUR DEPARTMENT.
IT'S NOT FUNNY. YOU KNOW I CAN'T HELP BUT DEKH THAT STUFF.

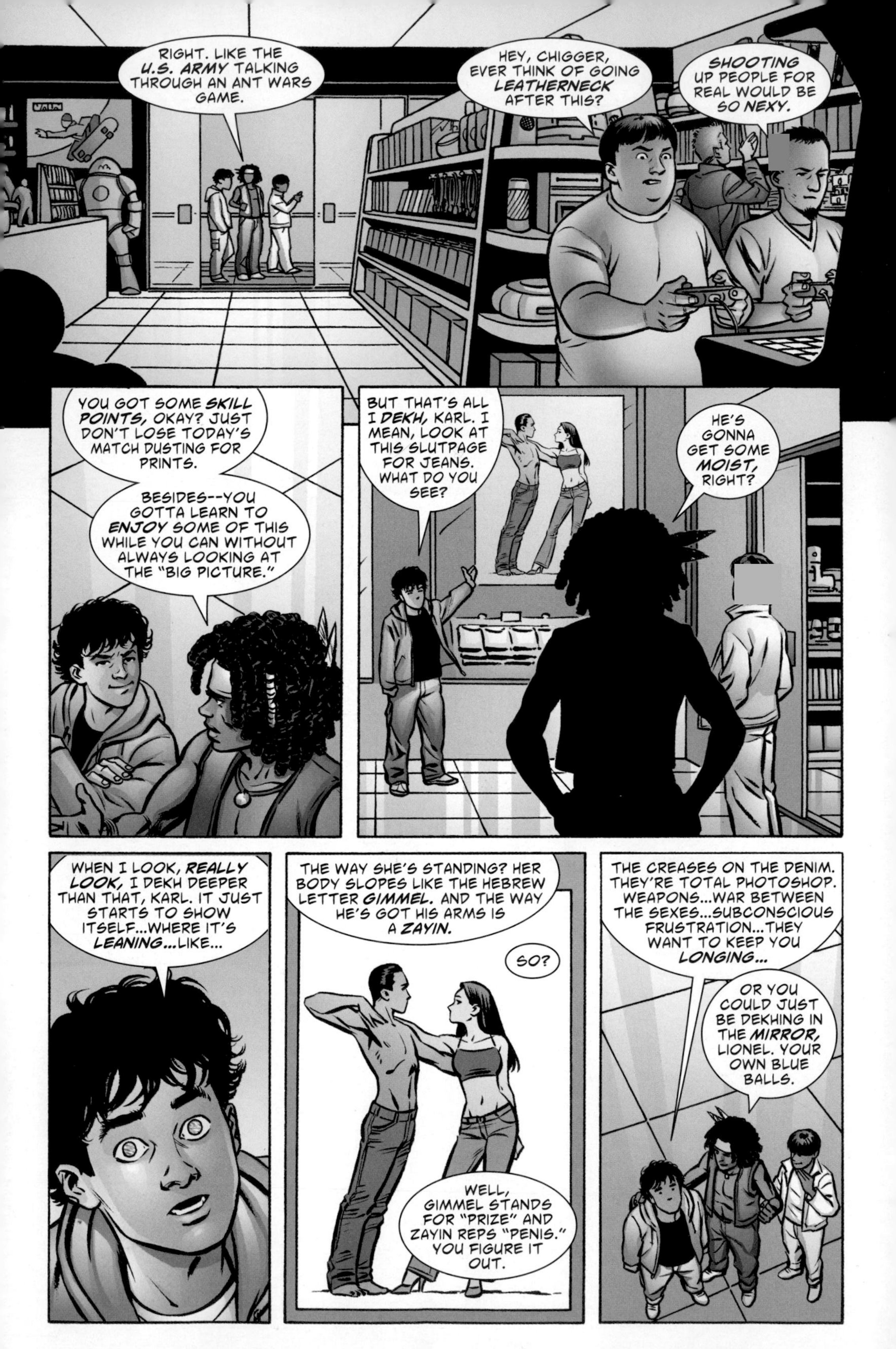
RIGHT. LIKE THE U.S. ARMY TALKING THROUGH AN ANT WARS GAME.
HEY, CHIGGER, EVER THINK OF GOING LEATHERNECK AFTER THIS?
SHOOTING UP PEOPLE FOR REAL WOULD BE SO NEXY.
YOU GOT SOME SKILL POINTS, OKAY? JUST DON'T LOSE TODAY'S MATCH DUSTING FOR PRINTS.
BESIDES--YOU GOTTA LEARN TO ENJOY SOME OF THIS WHILE YOU CAN WITHOUT ALWAYS LOOKING AT THE "BIG PICTURE."
BUT THAT'S ALL I DEKH, KARL. I MEAN, LOOK AT THIS SLUTPAGE FOR JEANS. WHAT DO YOU SEE?
HE'S GONNA GET SOME MOIST, RIGHT?
WHEN I LOOK, REALLY LOOK, I DEKH DEEPER THAN THAT, KARL. IT JUST STARTS TO SHOW ITSELF...WHERE IT'S LEANING...LIKE...
THE WAY SHE'S STANDING? HER BODY SLOPES LIKE THE HEBREW LETTER GIMMEL. AND THE WAY HE'S GOT HIS ARMS IS A ZAYIN.
SO?
WELL, GIMMEL STANDS FOR "PRIZE" AND ZAYIN REPS "PENIS." YOU FIGURE IT OUT.
THE CREASES ON THE DENIM. THEY'RE TOTAL PHOTOSHOP. WEAPONS...WAR BETWEEN THE SEXES...SUBCONSCIOUS FRUSTRATION...THEY WANT TO KEEP YOU LONGING...
OR YOU COULD JUST BE DEKHING IN THE MIRROR, LIONEL. YOUR OWN BLUE BALLS.

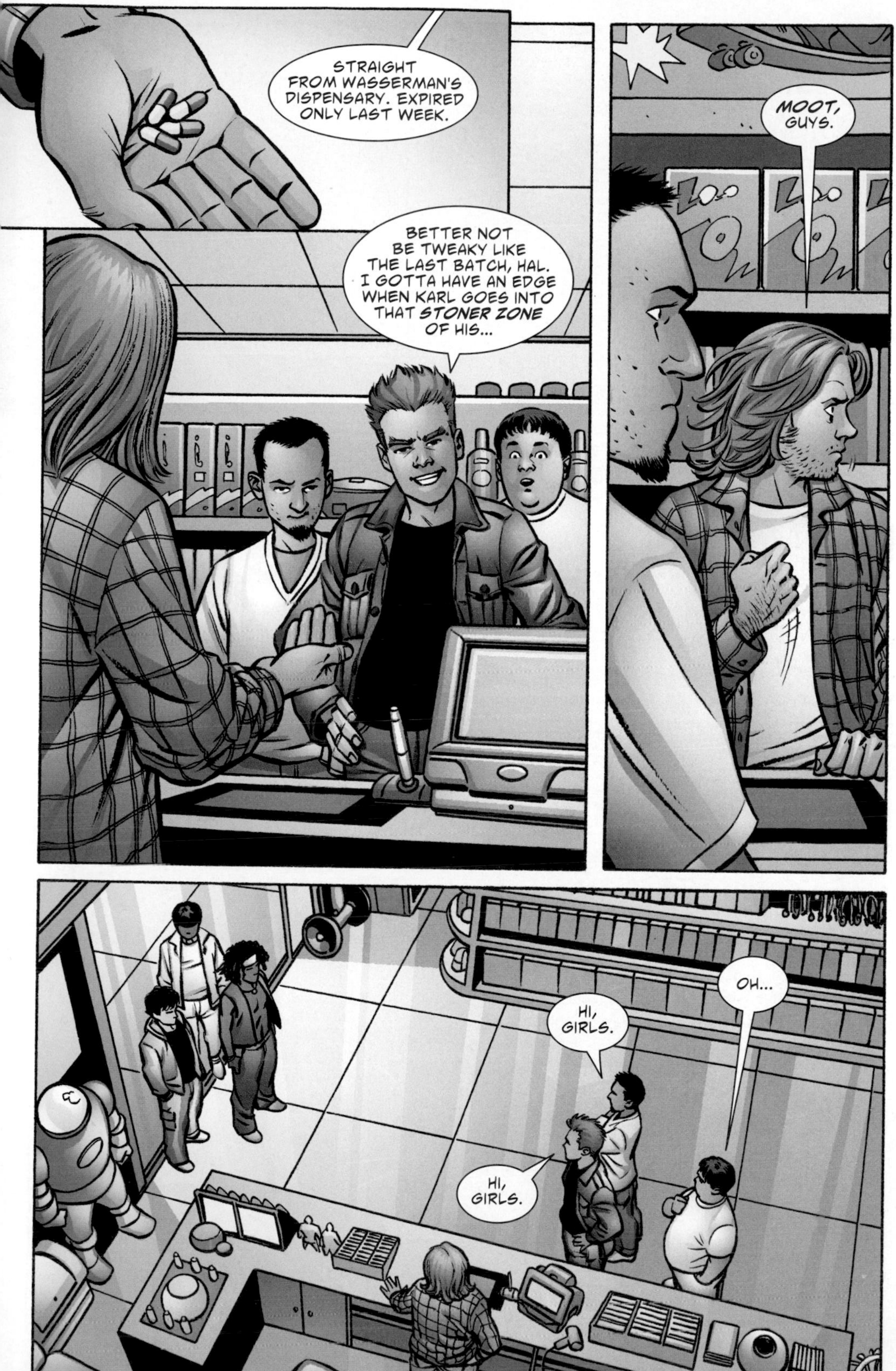
STRAIGHT FROM WASSERMAN'S DISPENSARY. EXPIRED ONLY LAST WEEK.
BETTER NOT BE TWEAKY LIKE THE LAST BATCH, HAL. I GOTTA HAVE AN EDGE WHEN KARL GOES INTO THAT STONER ZONE OF HIS...
MOOT, GUYS.
HI, GIRLS.
HI, GIRLS.
OH...

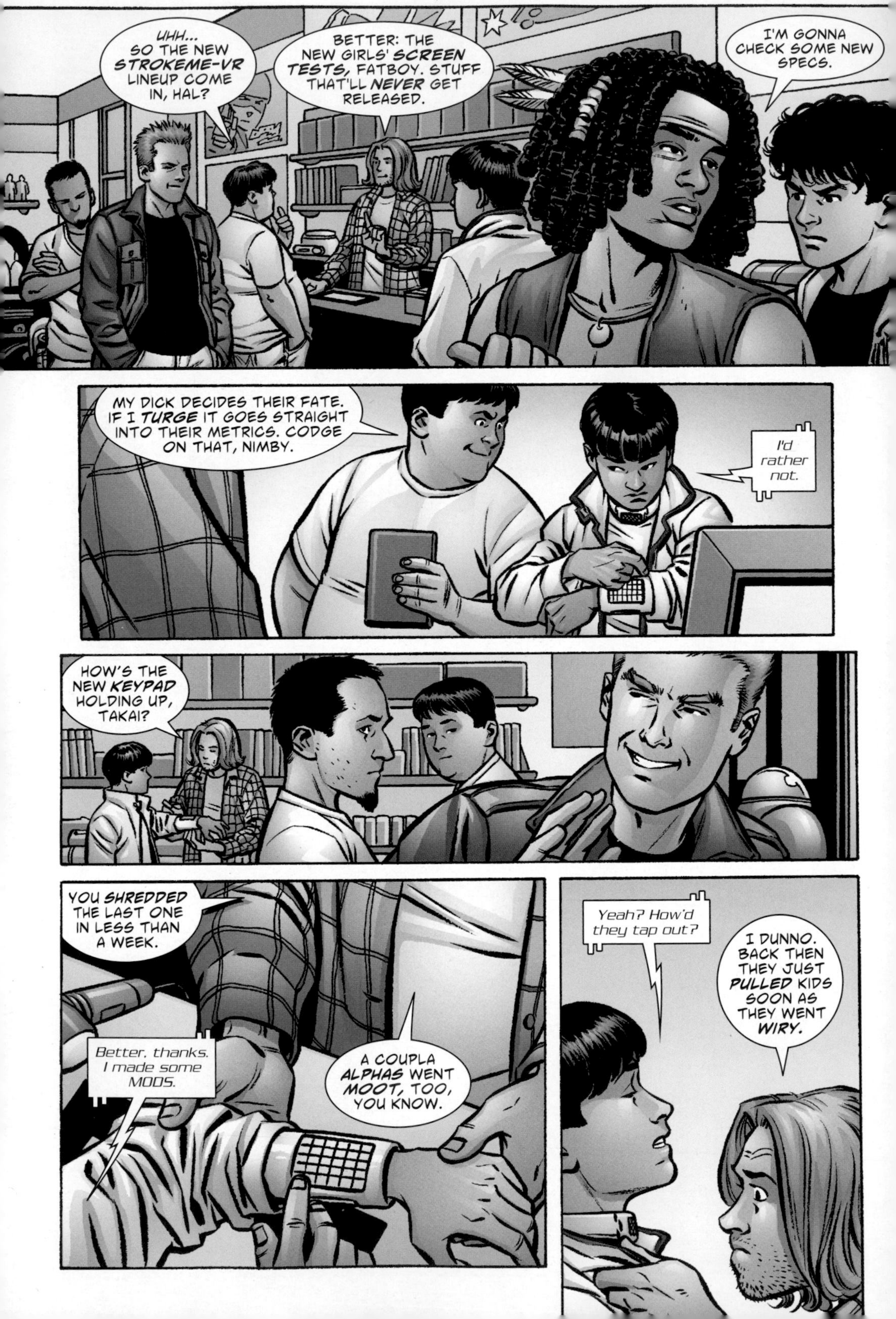
UHH... SO THE NEW STROKEME-VR LINEUP COME IN, HAL?
BETTER: THE NEW GIRLS' SCREEN TESTS, FATBOY. STUFF THAT'LL NEVER GET RELEASED.
I'M GONNA CHECK SOME NEW SPECS.
MY DICK DECIDES THEIR FATE. IF I TURGE IT GOES STRAIGHT INTO THEIR METRICS. CODGE ON THAT, NIMBY.
I'd rather not.
HOW'S THE NEW KEYPAD HOLDING UP, TAKAI?
YOU SHREDDED THE LAST ONE IN LESS THAN A WEEK.
Better, thanks. I made some MODS.
A COUPLA ALPHAS WENT MOOT, TOO, YOU KNOW.
Yeah? How'd they tap out?
I DUNNO. BACK THEN THEY JUST PULLED KIDS SOON AS THEY WENT WIRY.

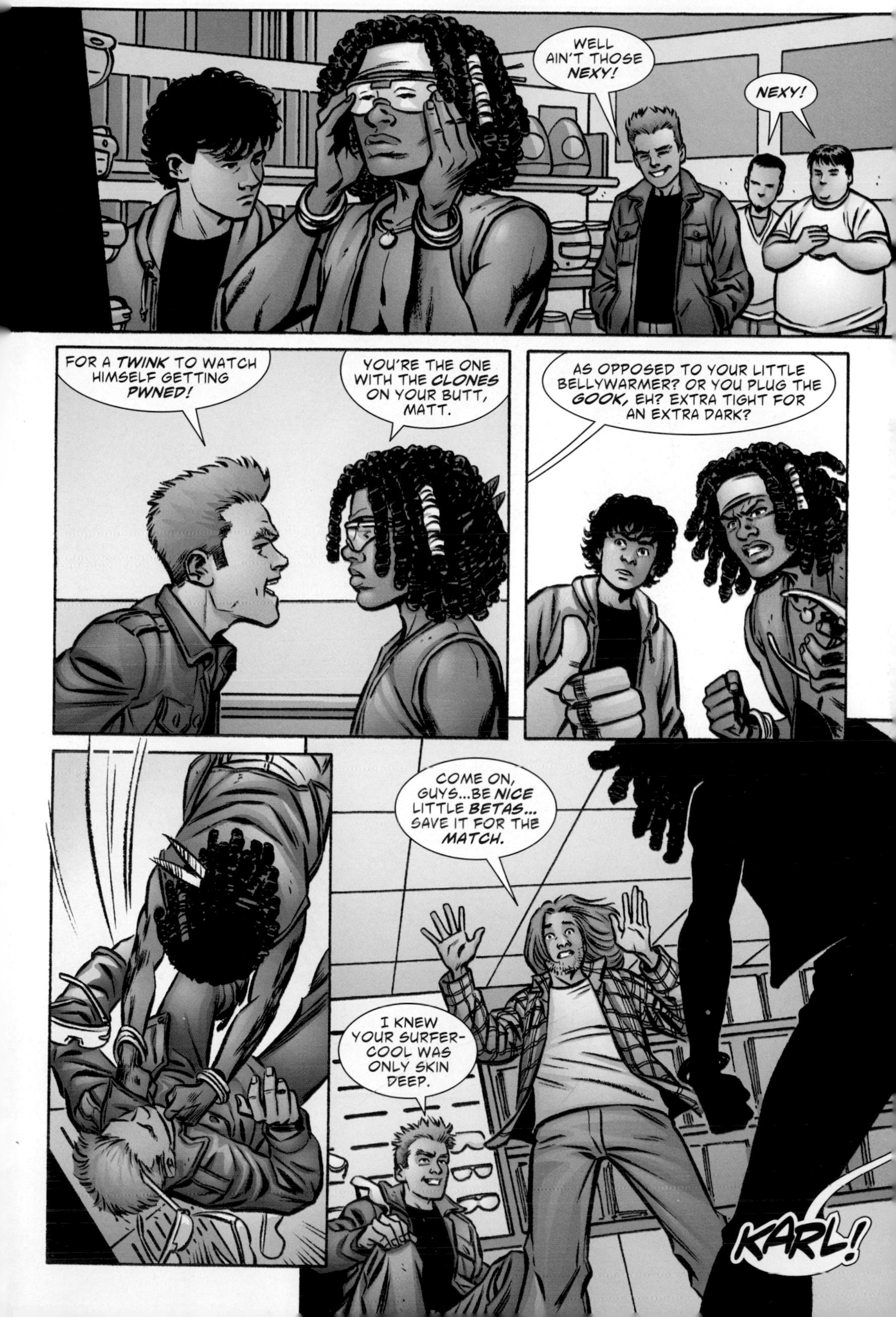
WELL AIN'T THOSE NEXY!
NEXY!
FOR A TWINK TO WATCH HIMSELF GETTING PWNED!
YOU'RE THE ONE WITH THE CLONES ON YOUR BUTT, MATT.
AS OPPOSED TO YOUR LITTLE BELLYWARMER? OR YOU PLUG THE GOOK, EH? EXTRA TIGHT FOR AN EXTRA DARK?
COME ON, GUYS...BE NICE LITTLE BETAS... SAVE IT FOR THE MATCH.
I KNEW YOUR SURFER-COOL WAS ONLY SKIN DEEP.
KARL!

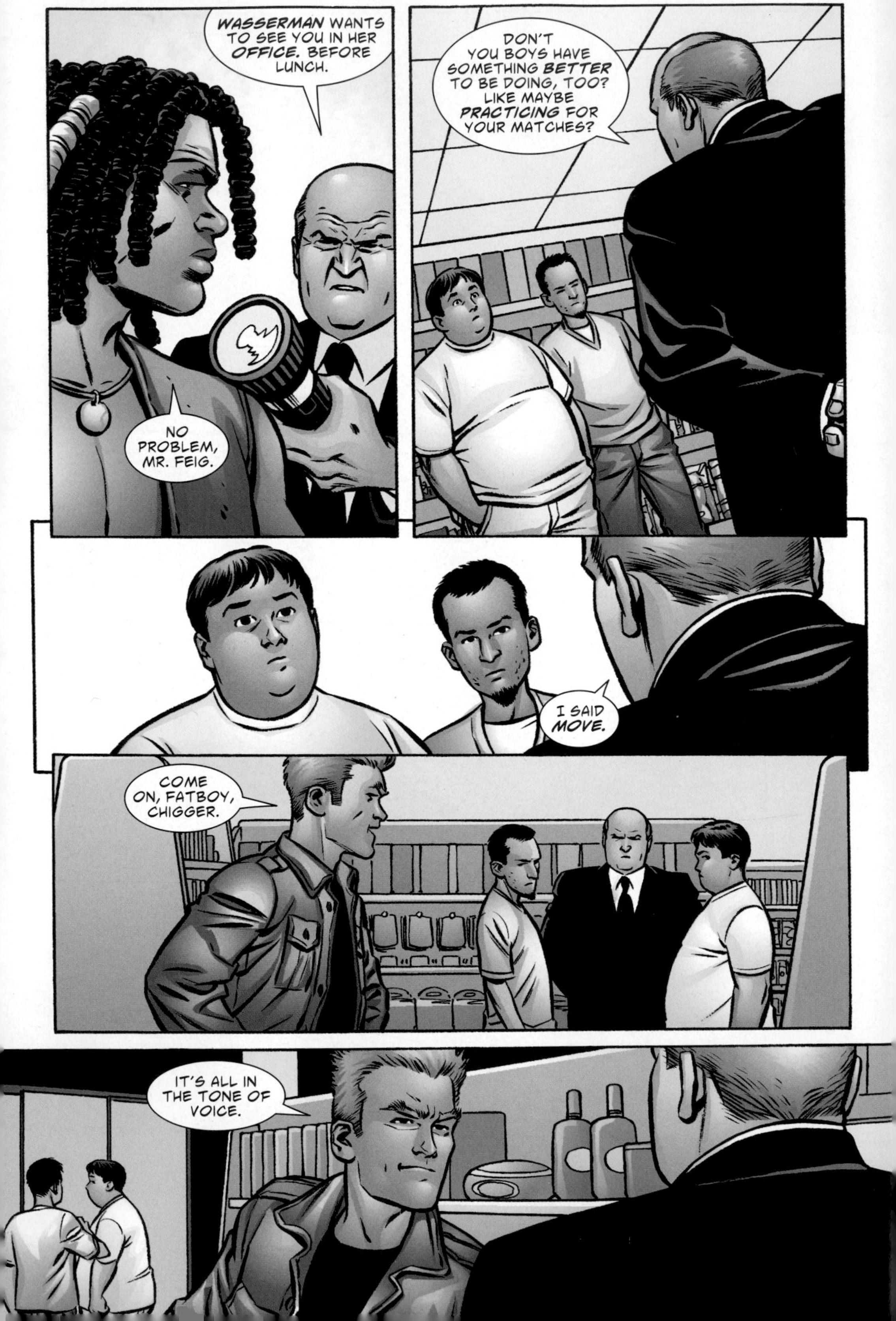

WASSERMAN WANTS TO SEE YOU IN HER OFFICE. BEFORE LUNCH.
NO PROBLEM, MR. FEIG.
DON'T YOU BOYS HAVE SOMETHING BETTER TO BE DOING, TOO? LIKE MAYBE PRACTICING FOR YOUR MATCHES?
I SAID MOVE.
COME ON, FATBOY, CHIGGER.
IT'S ALL IN THE TONE OF VOICE.

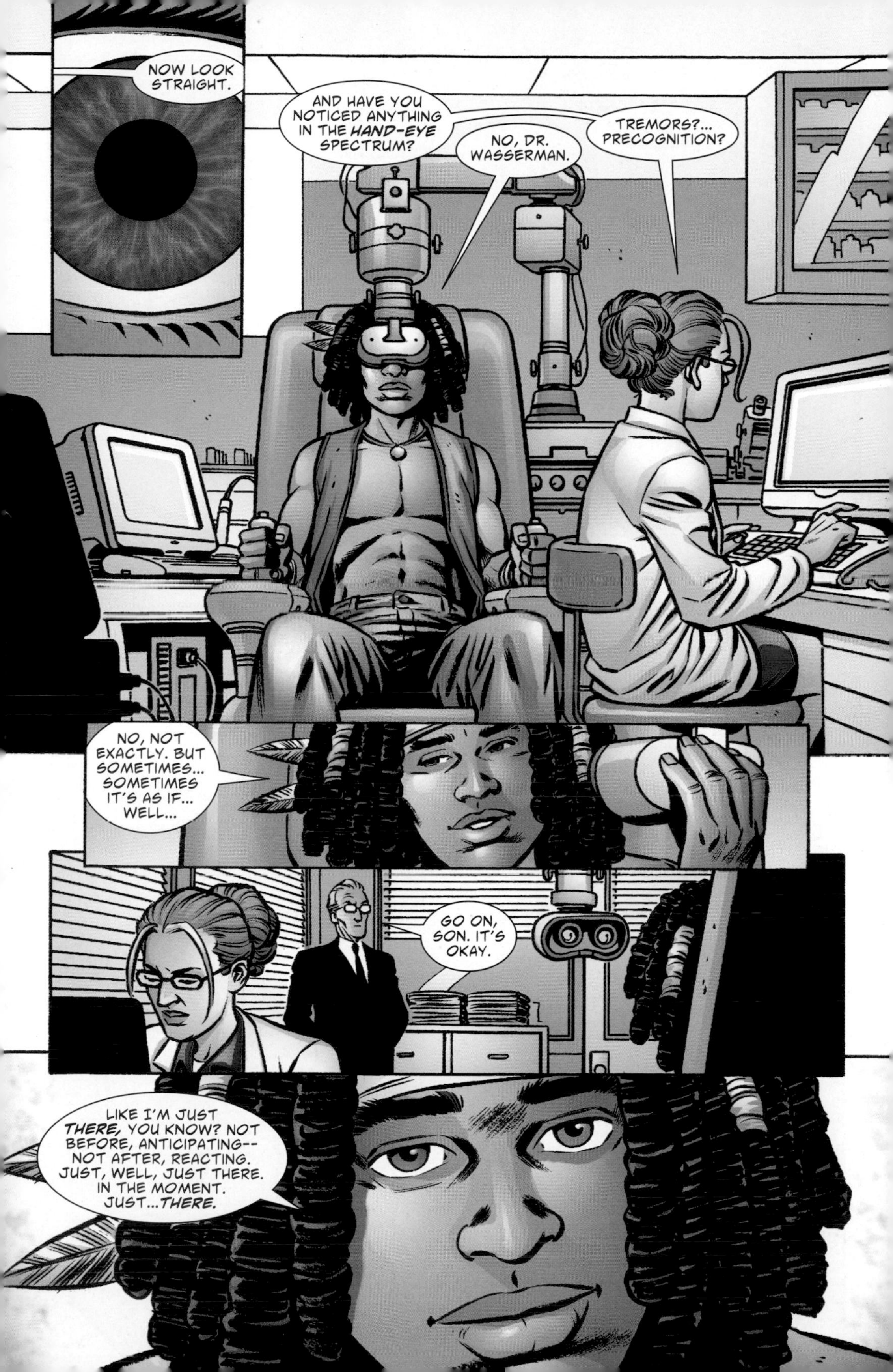
NOW LOOK STRAIGHT.
AND HAVE YOU NOTICED ANYTHING IN THE *HAND-EYE* SPECTRUM?
TREMORS?... PRECOGNITION?
NO, DR. WASSERMAN.
NO, NOT EXACTLY. BUT SOMETIMES... SOMETIMES IT'S AS IF... WELL...
GO ON, SON. IT'S OKAY.
LIKE I'M JUST *THERE,* YOU KNOW? NOT BEFORE, ANTICIPATING-- NOT AFTER, REACTING. JUST, WELL, JUST THERE. IN THE MOMENT. JUST...*THERE.*

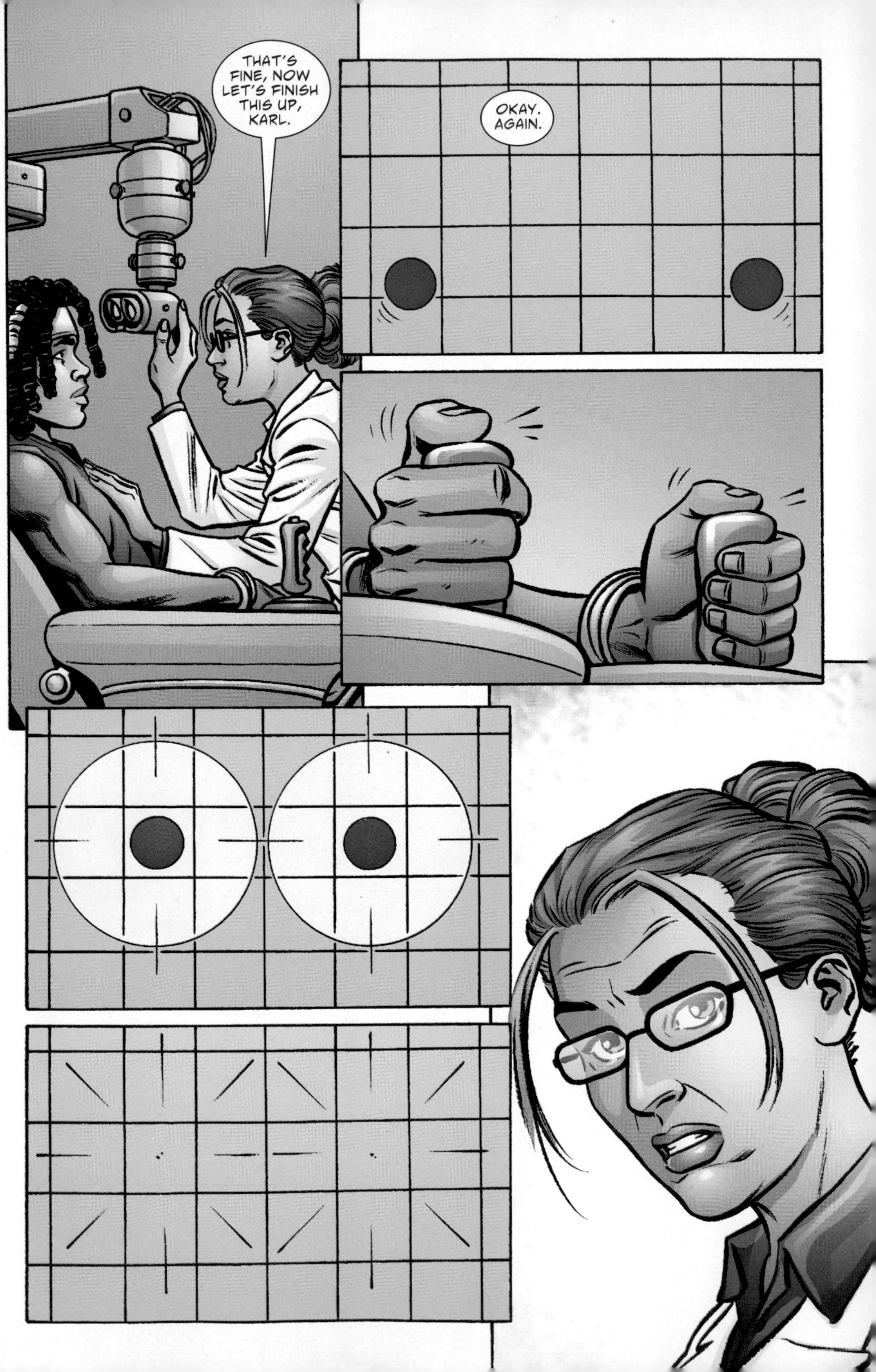
THAT'S FINE, NOW LET'S FINISH THIS UP, KARL.
OKAY. AGAIN.

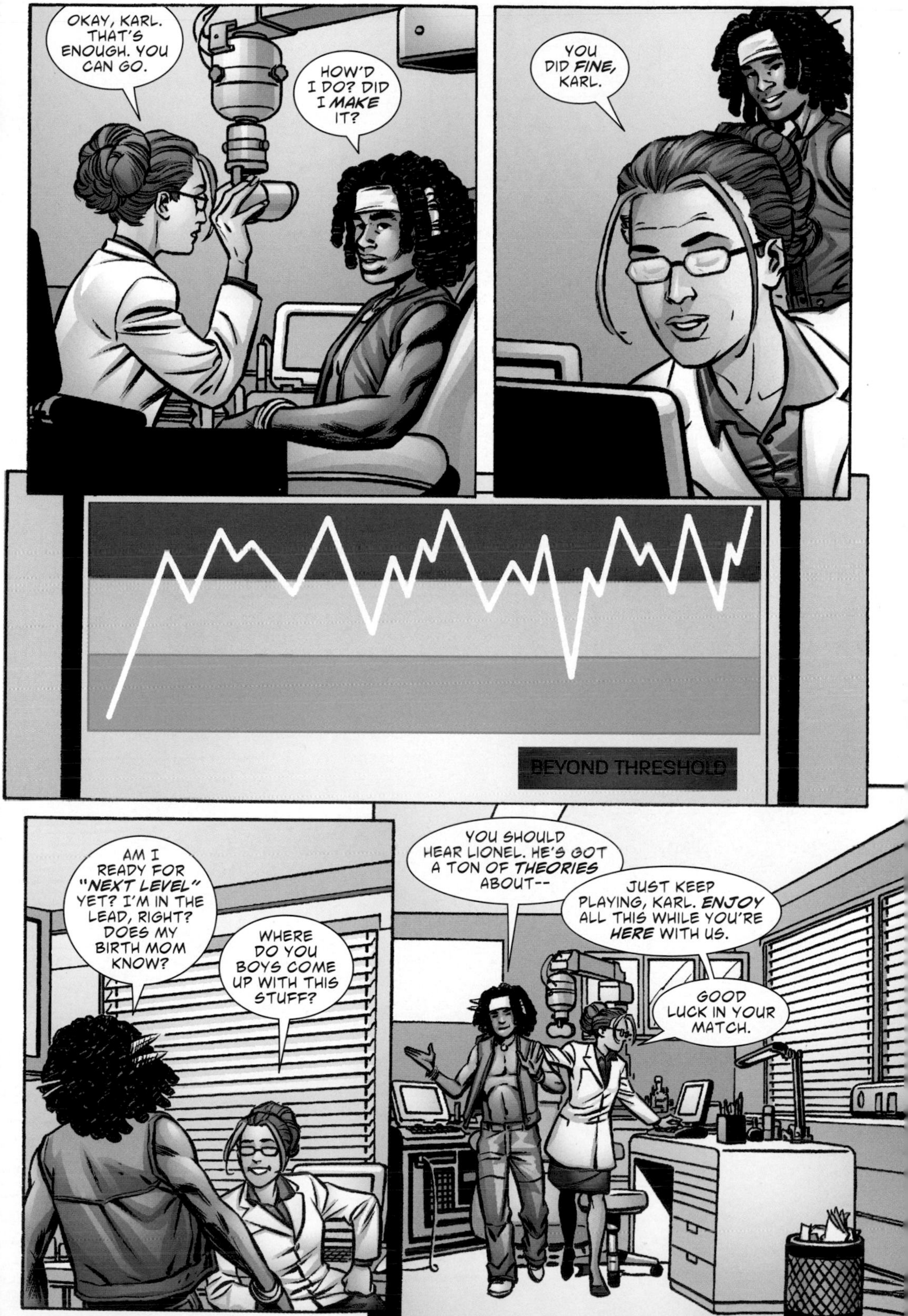
OKAY, KARL. THAT'S ENOUGH. YOU CAN GO.
HOW'D I DO? DID I *MAKE* IT?
YOU DID *FINE,* KARL.
BEYOND THRESHOLD
AM I READY FOR *"NEXT LEVEL"* YET? I'M IN THE LEAD, RIGHT? DOES MY BIRTH MOM KNOW?
WHERE DO YOU BOYS COME UP WITH THIS STUFF?
YOU SHOULD HEAR LIONEL. HE'S GOT A TON OF *THEORIES* ABOUT--
JUST KEEP PLAYING, KARL. *ENJOY* ALL THIS WHILE YOU'RE *HERE* WITH US.
GOOD LUCK IN YOUR MATCH.

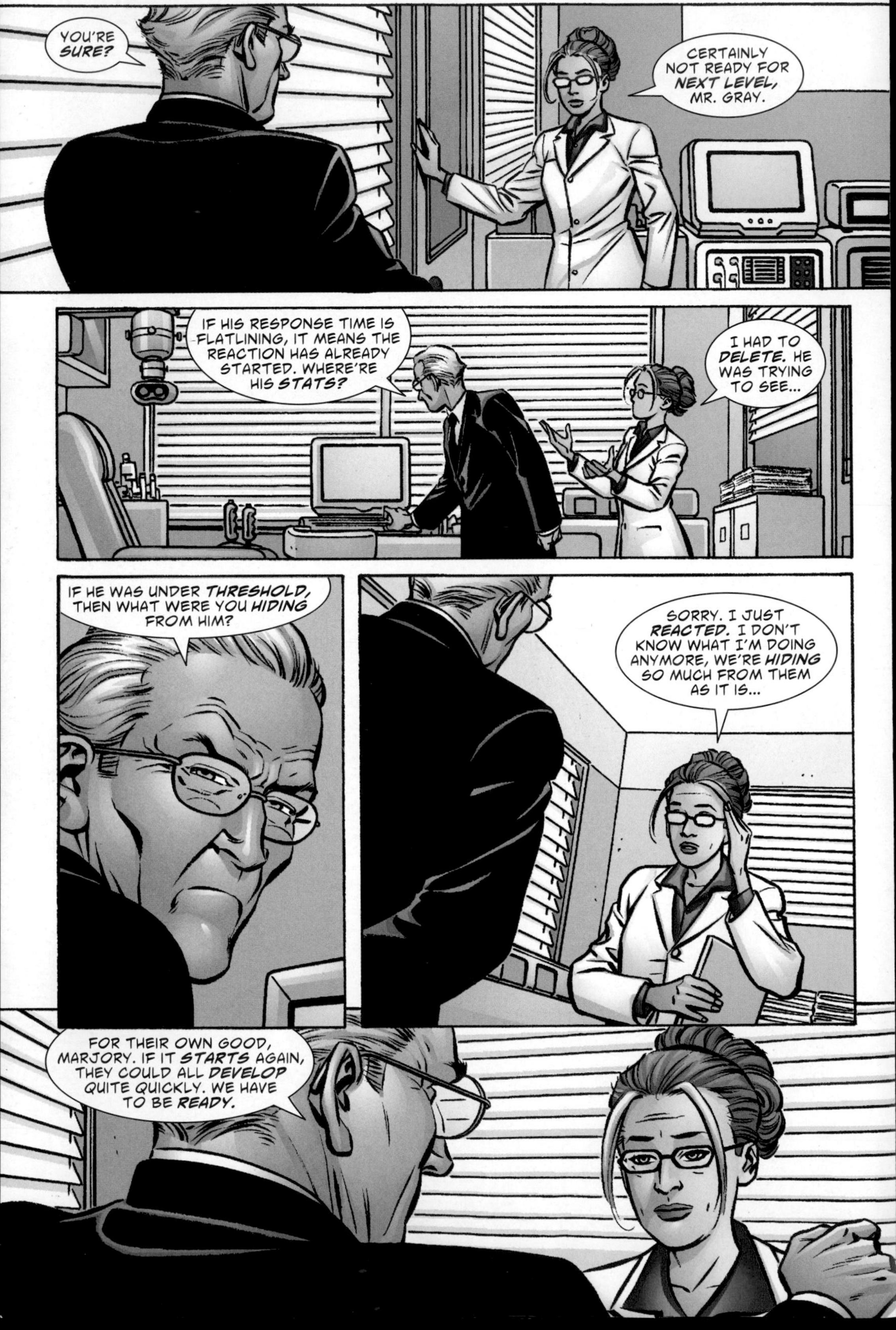
YOU'RE SURE?
CERTAINLY NOT READY FOR NEXT LEVEL, MR. GRAY.
IF HIS RESPONSE TIME IS FLATLINING, IT MEANS THE REACTION HAS ALREADY STARTED. WHERE'RE HIS STATS?
I HAD TO DELETE. HE WAS TRYING TO SEE...
IF HE WAS UNDER THRESHOLD, THEN WHAT WERE YOU HIDING FROM HIM?
SORRY. I JUST REACTED. I DON'T KNOW WHAT I'M DOING ANYMORE, WE'RE HIDING SO MUCH FROM THEM AS IT IS...
FOR THEIR OWN GOOD, MARJORY. IF IT STARTS AGAIN, THEY COULD ALL DEVELOP QUITE QUICKLY. WE HAVE TO BE READY.

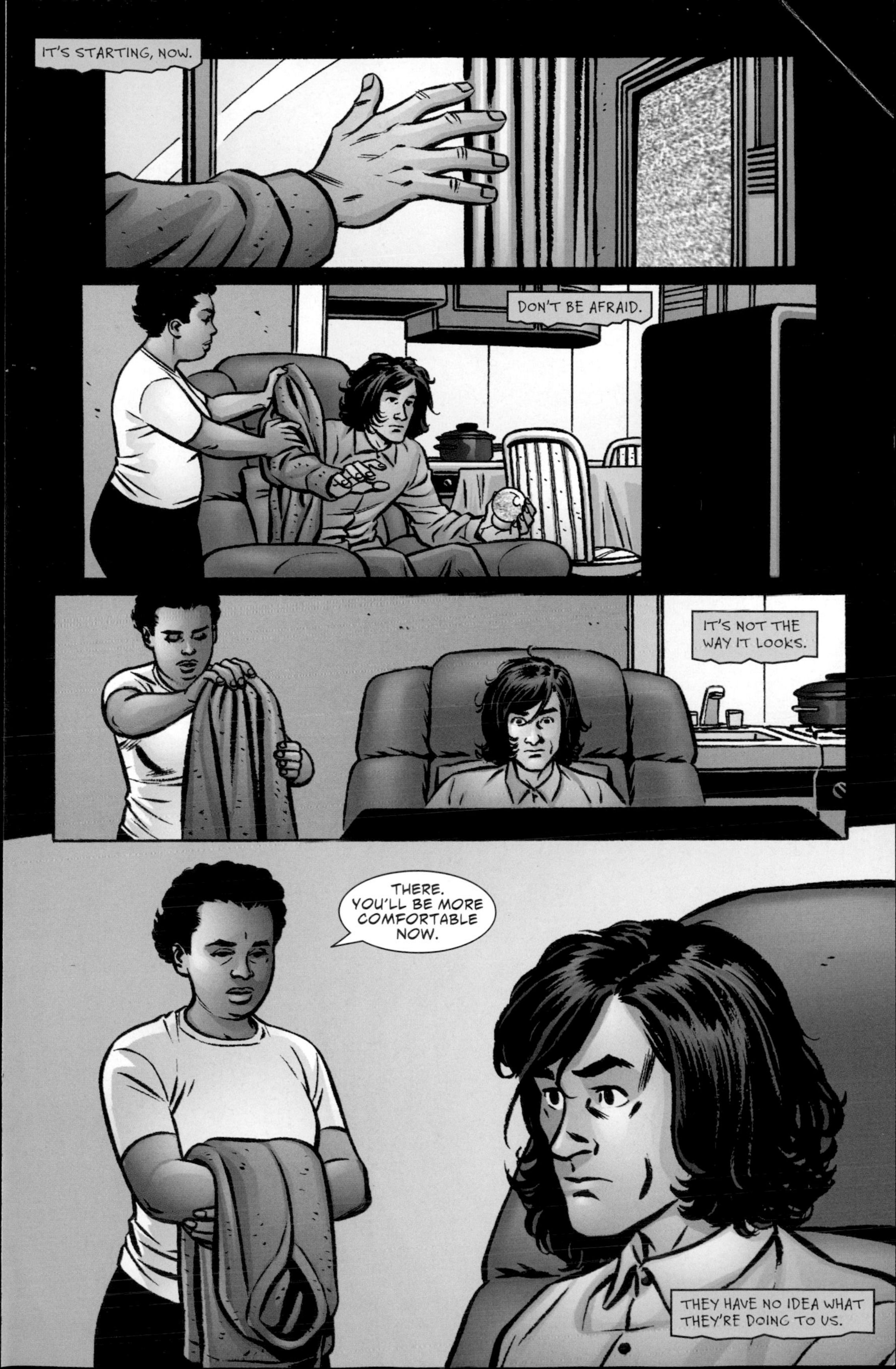
IT'S STARTING, NOW.
DON'T BE AFRAID.
IT'S NOT THE WAY IT LOOKS.
THERE. YOU'LL BE MORE COMFORTABLE NOW.
THEY HAVE NO IDEA WHAT THEY'RE DOING TO US.

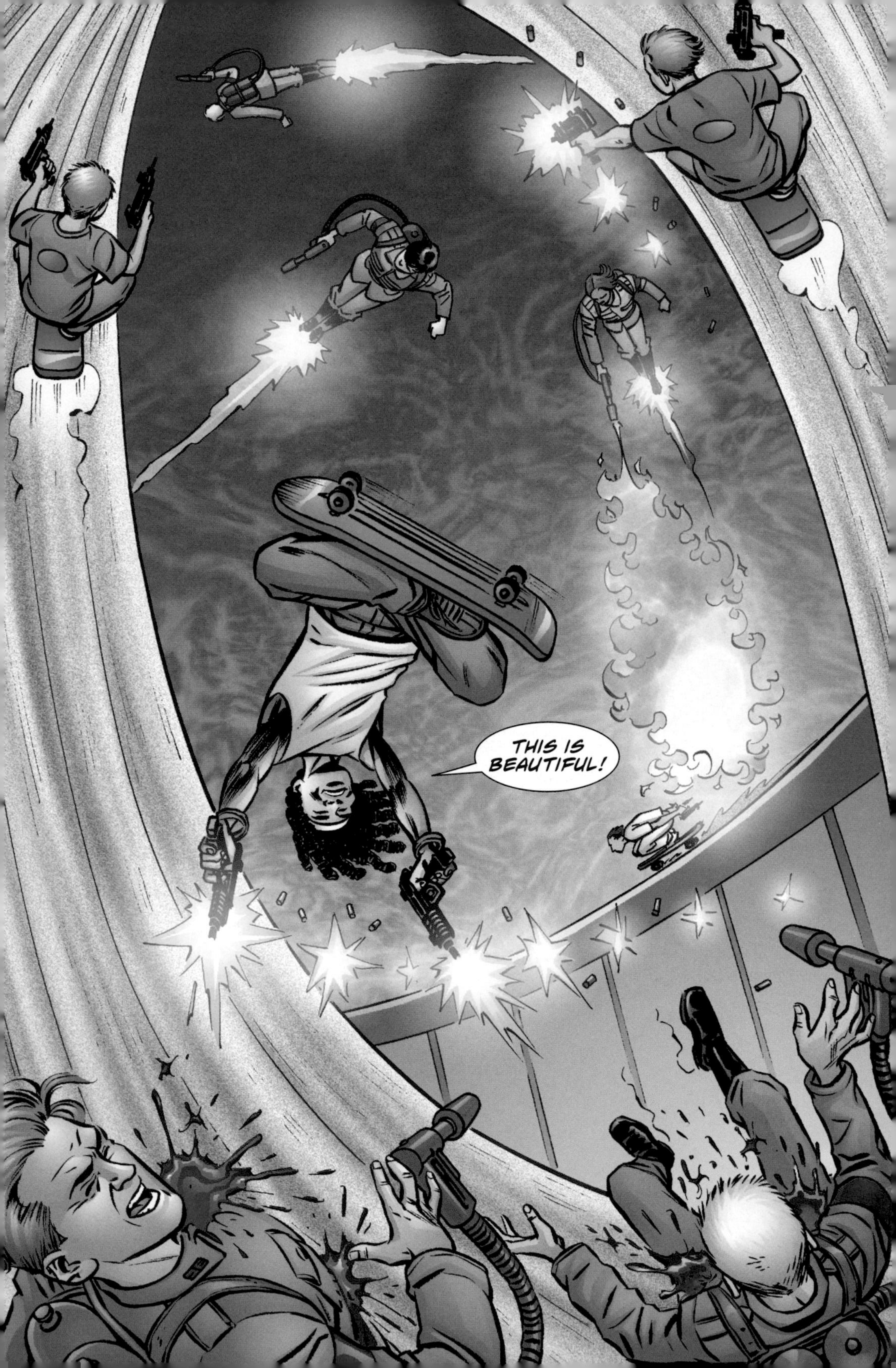
THIS IS BEAUTIFUL!

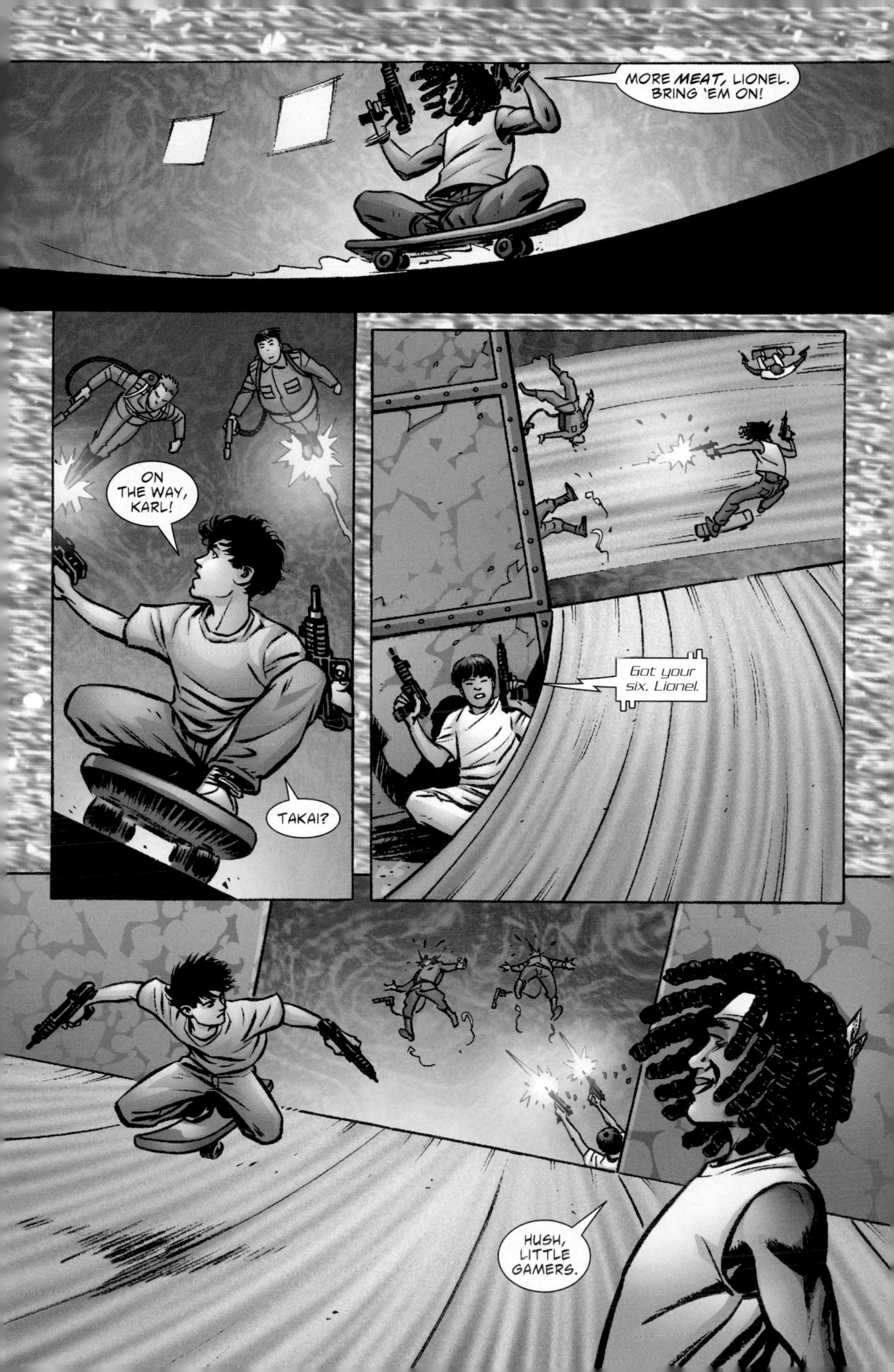
MORE MEAT, LIONEL. BRING 'EM ON!
ON THE WAY, KARL!
TAKAI?
Got your six, Lionel.
HUSH, LITTLE GAMERS.

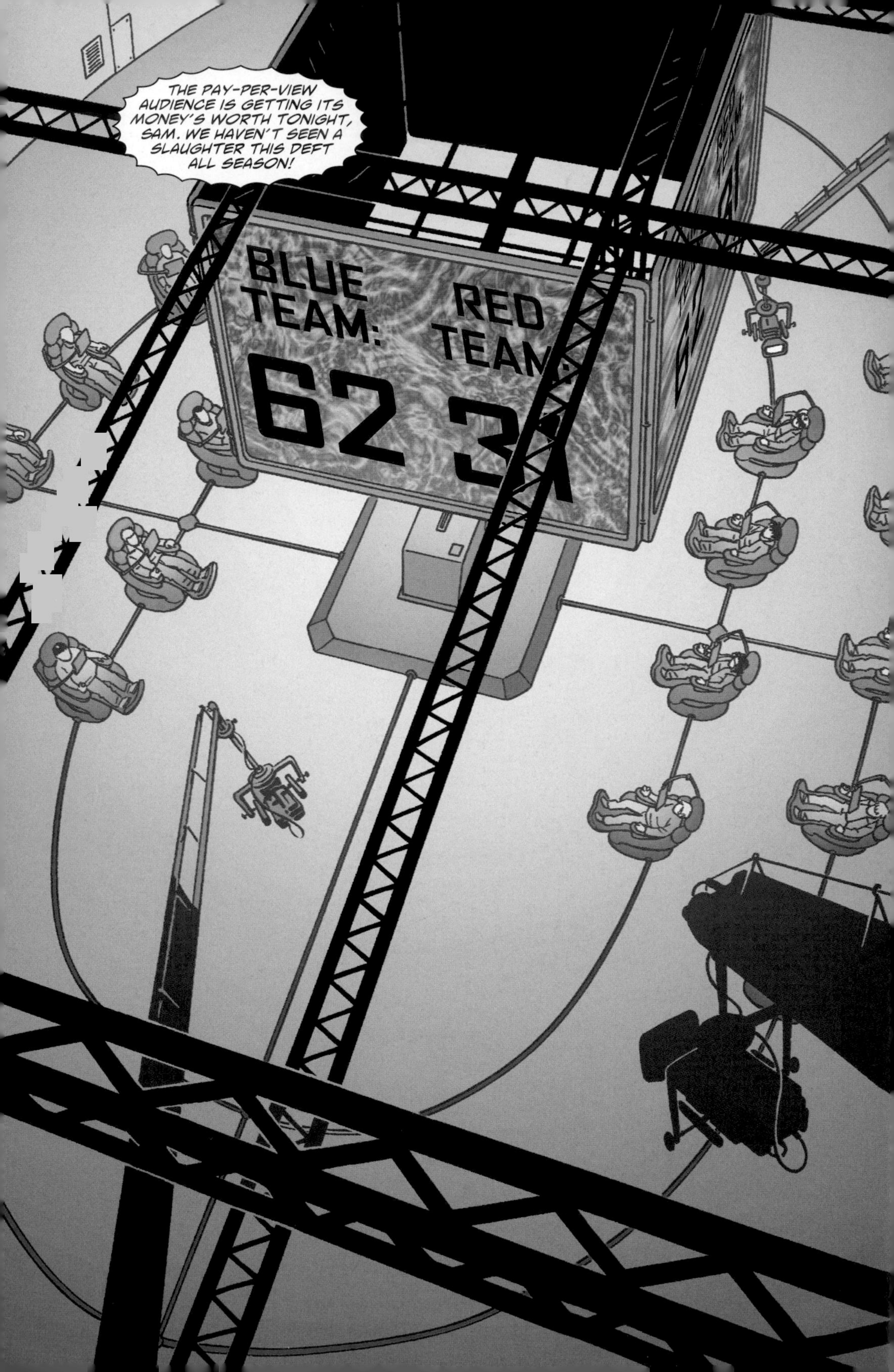
THE PAY-PER-VIEW AUDIENCE IS GETTING ITS MONEY'S WORTH TONIGHT, SAM. WE HAVEN'T SEEN A SLAUGHTER THIS DEFT ALL SEASON!
BLUE TEAM: 62
RED TEAM: 31

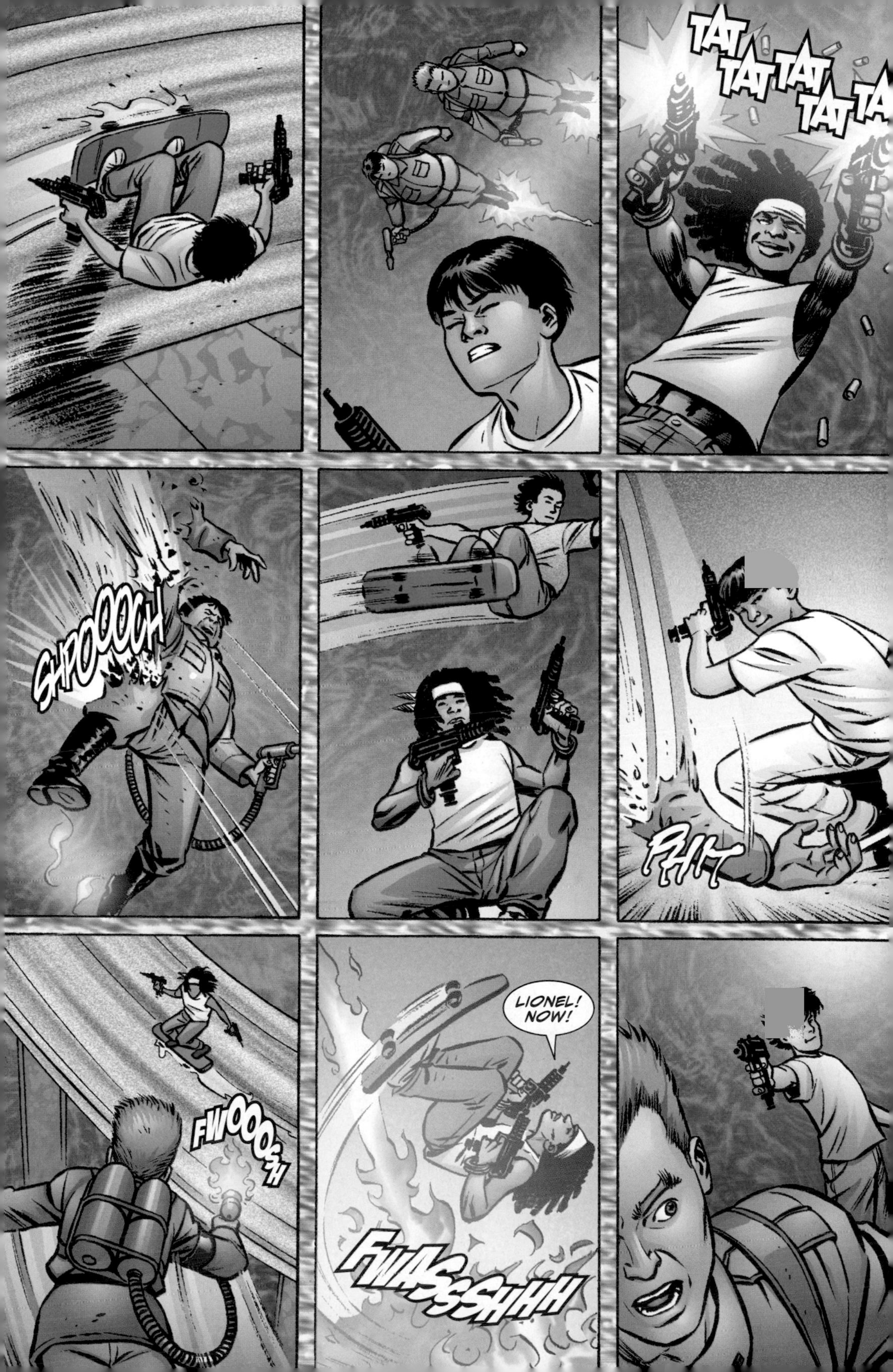
TAT TAT TAT TAT TA
SHPOOOCH
PHIT
FWOOOSH
LIONEL! NOW!
FWASSSHHH

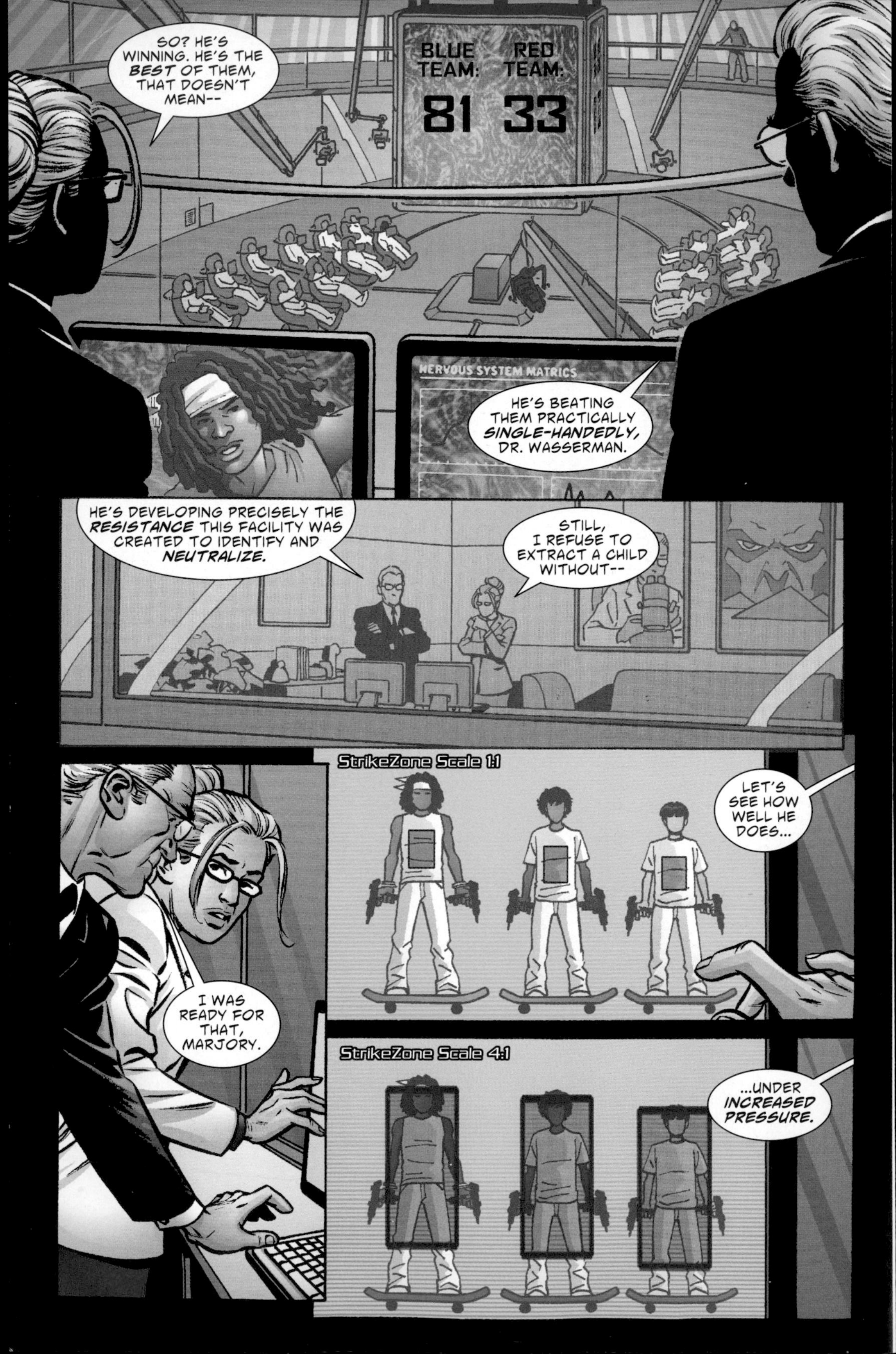
BLUE TEAM: RED TEAM:
81 33
SO? HE'S WINNING. HE'S THE BEST OF THEM, THAT DOESN'T MEAN--
NERVOUS SYSTEM MATRICS
HE'S BEATING THEM PRACTICALLY SINGLE-HANDEDLY, DR. WASSERMAN.
HE'S DEVELOPING PRECISELY THE RESISTANCE THIS FACILITY WAS CREATED TO IDENTIFY AND NEUTRALIZE.
STILL, I REFUSE TO EXTRACT A CHILD WITHOUT--
StrikeZone Scale 1:1
LET'S SEE HOW WELL HE DOES...
I WAS READY FOR THAT, MARJORY.
StrikeZone Scale 4:1
...UNDER INCREASED PRESSURE.

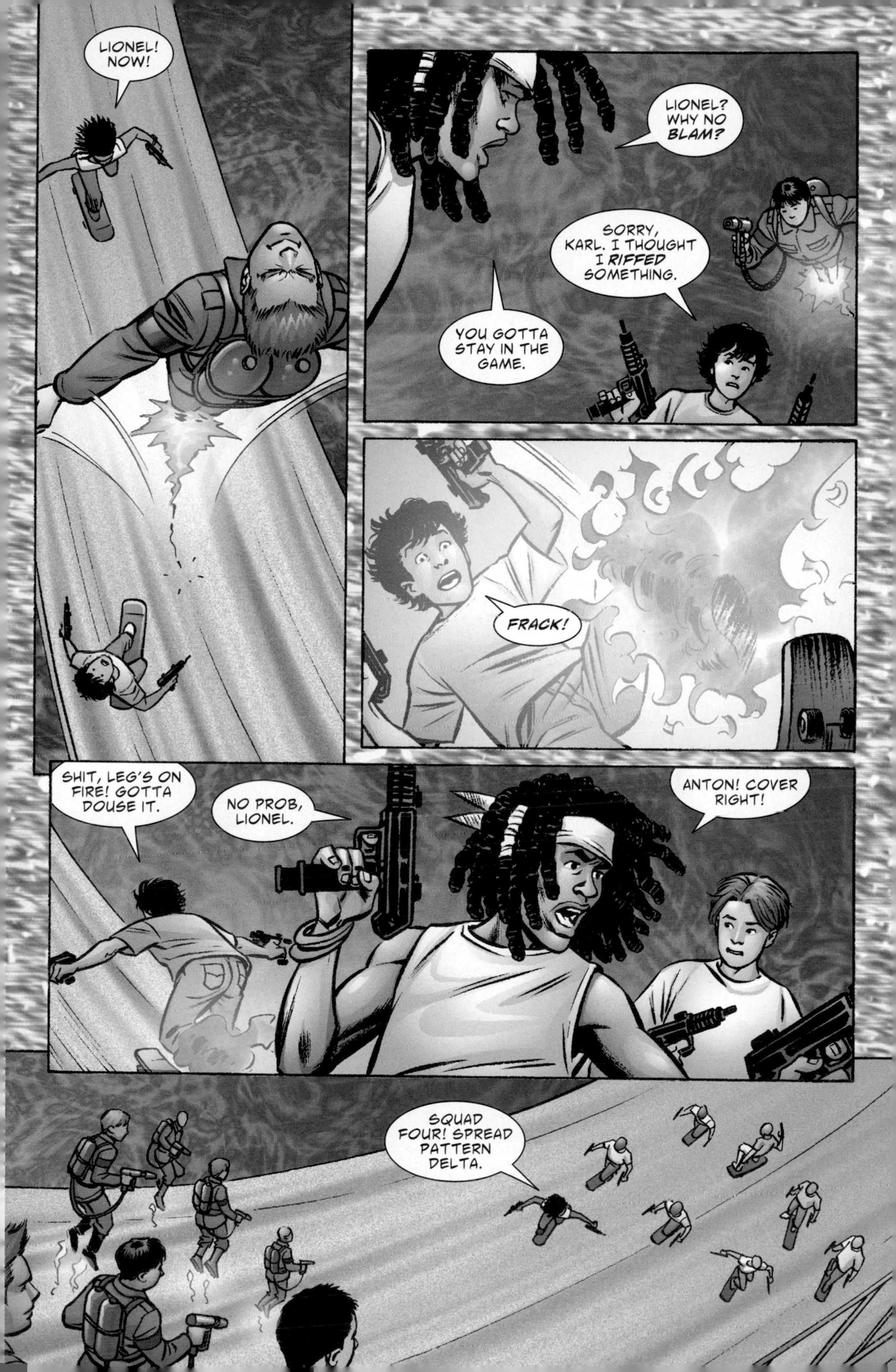
LIONEL! NOW!
LIONEL? WHY NO BLAM?
SORRY, KARL. I THOUGHT I RIFFED SOMETHING.
YOU GOTTA STAY IN THE GAME.
FRACK!
SHIT, LEG'S ON FIRE! GOTTA DOUSE IT.
NO PROB, LIONEL.
ANTON! COVER RIGHT!
SQUAD FOUR! SPREAD PATTERN DELTA.

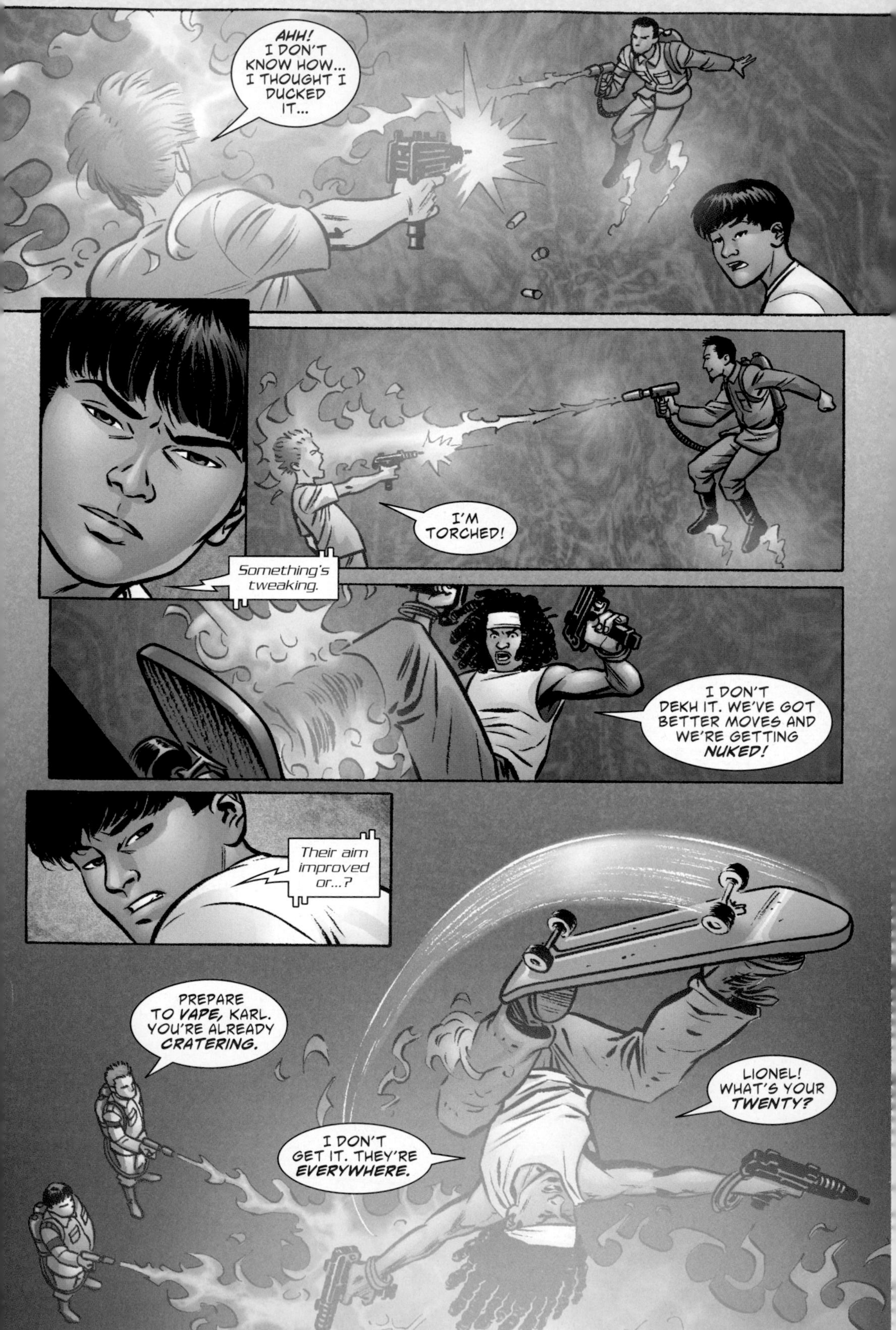
AHH! I DON'T KNOW HOW... I THOUGHT I DUCKED IT...
I'M TORCHED!
Something's tweaking.
I DON'T DEKH IT. WE'VE GOT BETTER MOVES AND WE'RE GETTING NUKED!
Their aim improved or...?
PREPARE TO VAPE, KARL. YOU'RE ALREADY CRATERING.
LIONEL! WHAT'S YOUR TWENTY?
I DON'T GET IT. THEY'RE EVERYWHERE.

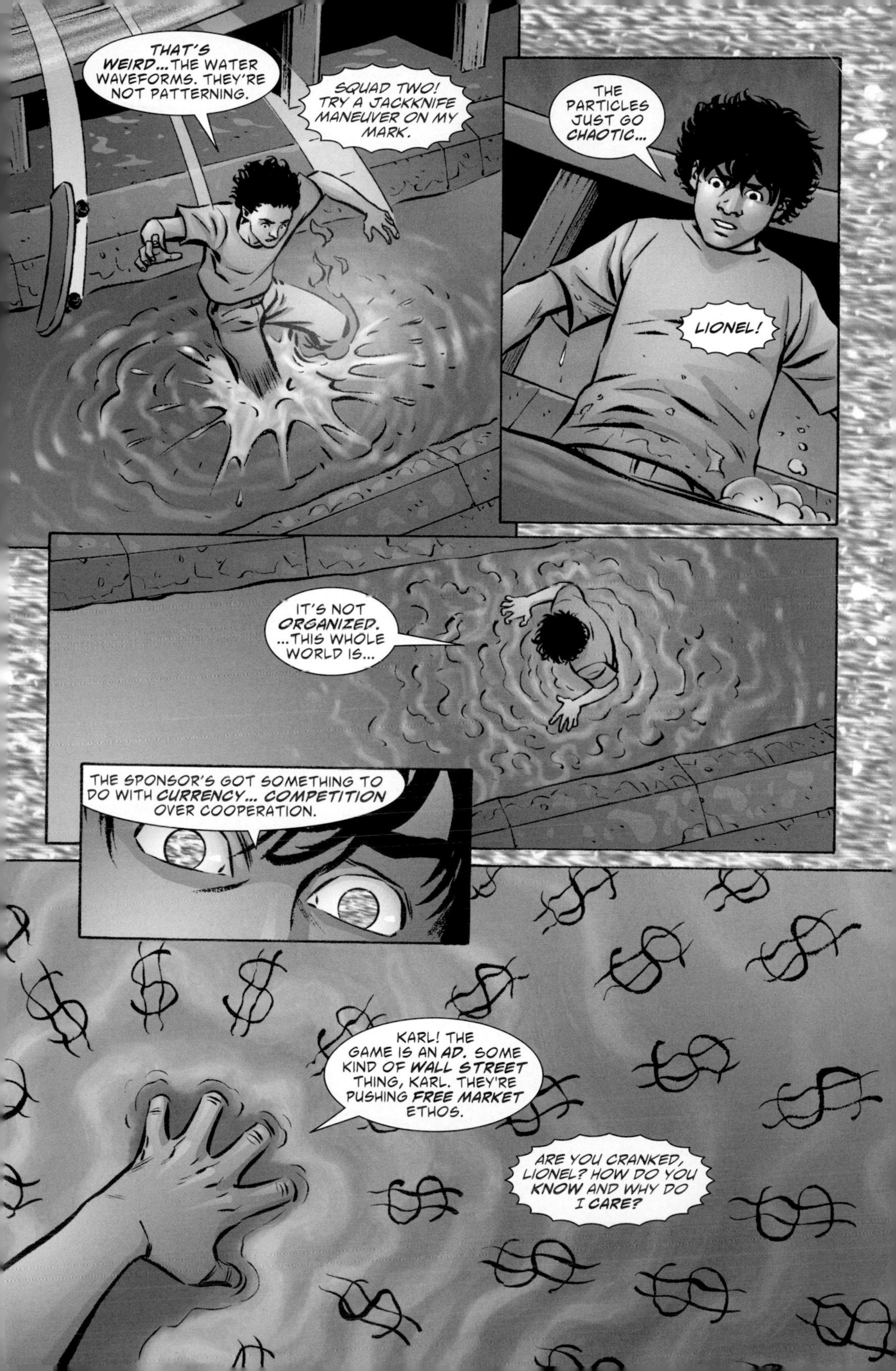
THAT'S WEIRD... THE WATER WAVEFORMS. THEY'RE NOT PATTERNING.
SQUAD TWO! TRY A JACKKNIFE MANEUVER ON MY MARK.
THE PARTICLES JUST GO CHAOTIC...
LIONEL!
IT'S NOT ORGANIZED. ...THIS WHOLE WORLD IS...
THE SPONSOR'S GOT SOMETHING TO DO WITH CURRENCY... COMPETITION OVER COOPERATION.
KARL! THE GAME IS AN AD. SOME KIND OF WALL STREET THING, KARL. THEY'RE PUSHING FREE MARKET ETHOS.
ARE YOU CRANKED, LIONEL? HOW DO YOU KNOW AND WHY DO I CARE?

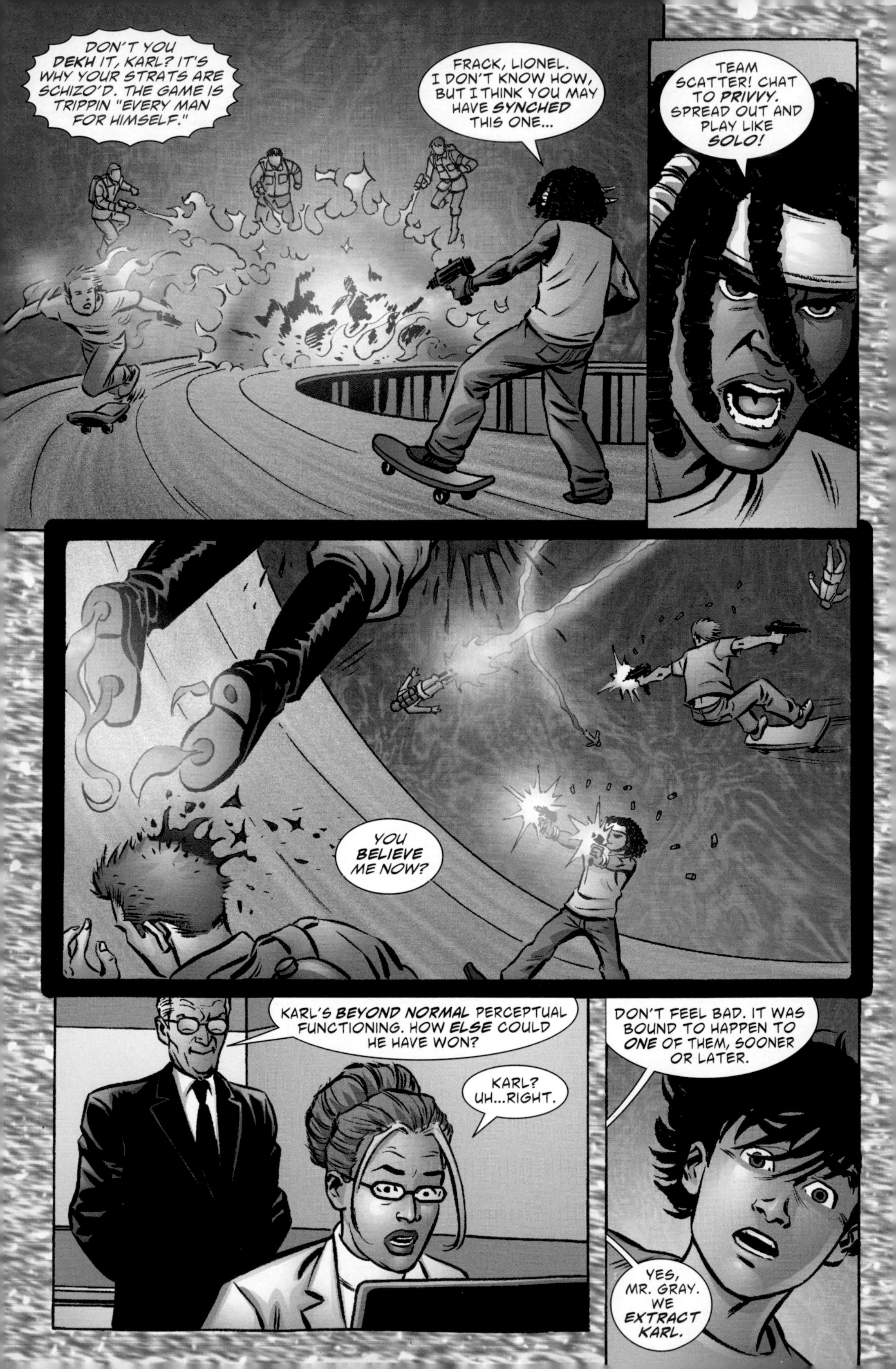
DON'T YOU DEKH IT, KARL? IT'S WHY YOUR STRATS ARE SCHIZO'D. THE GAME IS TRIPPIN "EVERY MAN FOR HIMSELF."
FRACK, LIONEL. I DON'T KNOW HOW, BUT I THINK YOU MAY HAVE SYNCHED THIS ONE...
TEAM SCATTER! CHAT TO PRIVVY. SPREAD OUT AND PLAY LIKE SOLO!
YOU BELIEVE ME NOW?
KARL'S BEYOND NORMAL PERCEPTUAL FUNCTIONING. HOW ELSE COULD HE HAVE WON?
KARL? UH...RIGHT.
DON'T FEEL BAD. IT WAS BOUND TO HAPPEN TO ONE OF THEM, SOONER OR LATER.
YES, MR. GRAY. WE EXTRACT KARL.

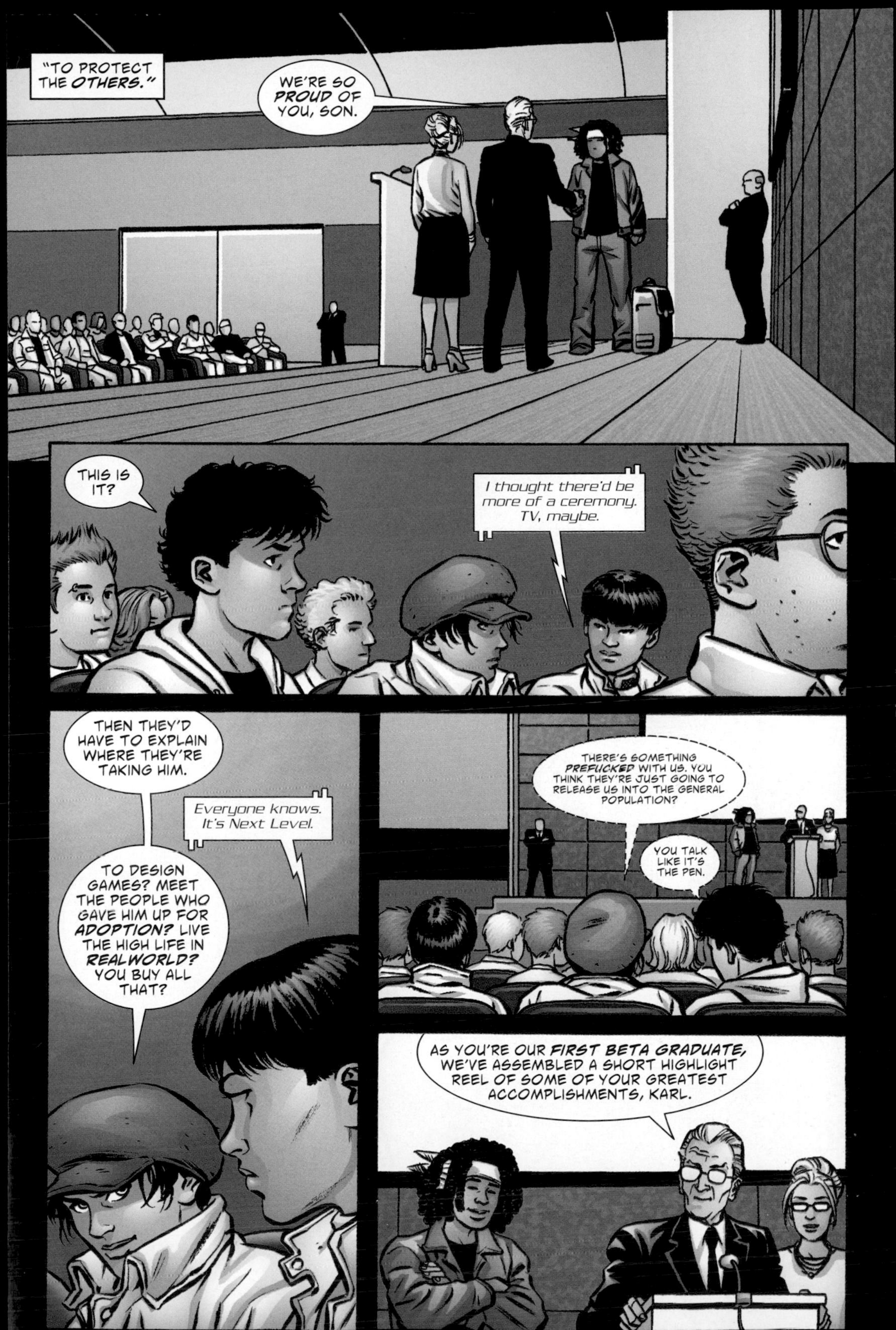
"TO PROTECT THE OTHERS."
WE'RE SO PROUD OF YOU, SON.
THIS IS IT?
I thought there'd be more of a ceremony. TV, maybe.
THEN THEY'D HAVE TO EXPLAIN WHERE THEY'RE TAKING HIM.
Everyone knows. It's Next Level.
TO DESIGN GAMES? MEET THE PEOPLE WHO GAVE HIM UP FOR ADOPTION? LIVE THE HIGH LIFE IN REALWORLD? YOU BUY ALL THAT?
THERE'S SOMETHING PREFUCKED WITH US. YOU THINK THEY'RE JUST GOING TO RELEASE US INTO THE GENERAL POPULATION?
YOU TALK LIKE IT'S THE PEN.
AS YOU'RE OUR FIRST BETA GRADUATE, WE'VE ASSEMBLED A SHORT HIGHLIGHT REEL OF SOME OF YOUR GREATEST ACCOMPLISHMENTS, KARL.

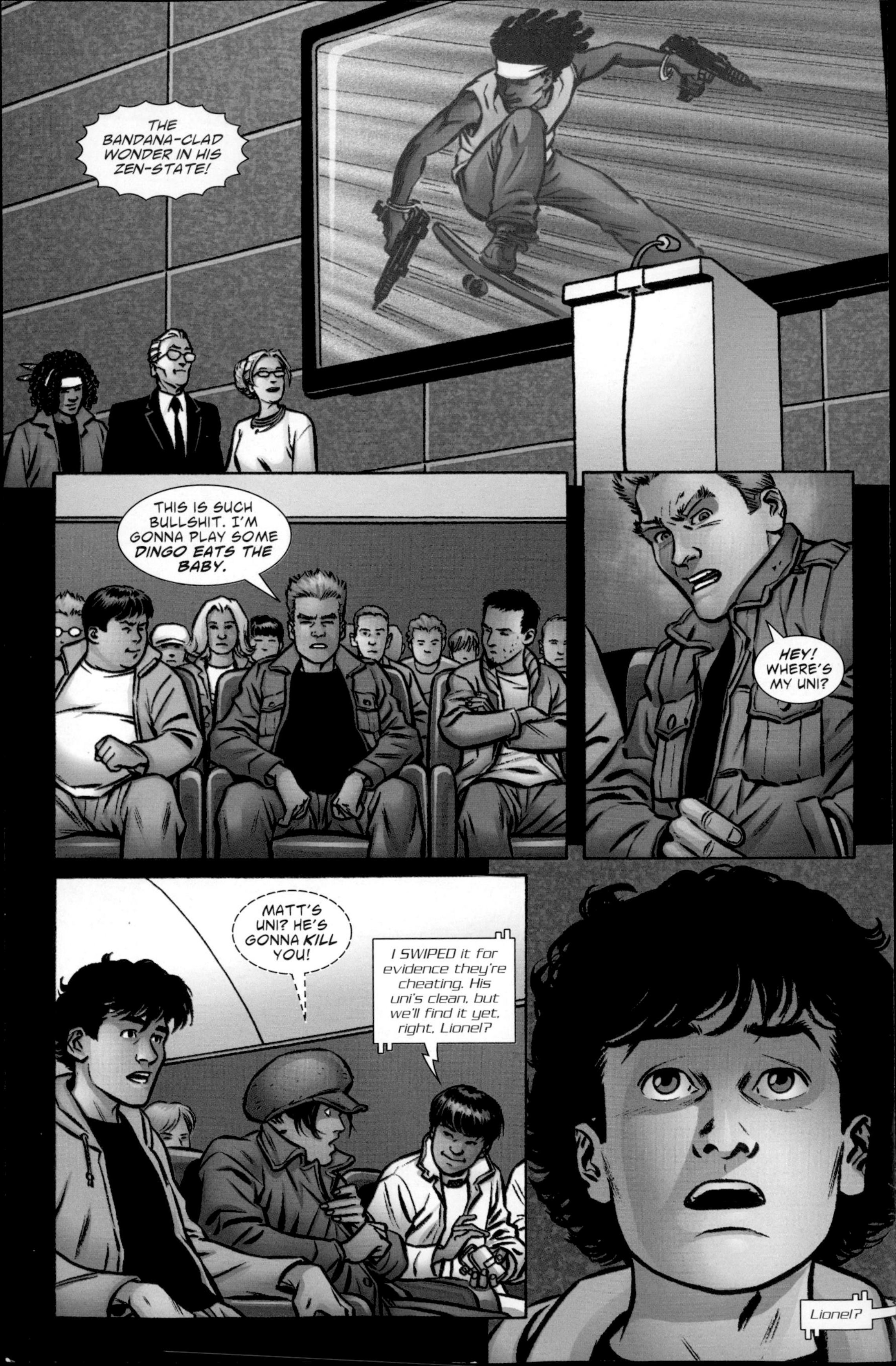
THE BANDANA-CLAD WONDER IN HIS ZEN-STATE!
THIS IS SUCH BULLSHIT. I'M GONNA PLAY SOME DINGO EATS THE BABY.
HEY! WHERE'S MY UNI?
MATT'S UNI? HE'S GONNA KILL YOU!
I SWIPED it for evidence they're cheating. His uni's clean, but we'll find it yet, right, Lionel?
Lionel?

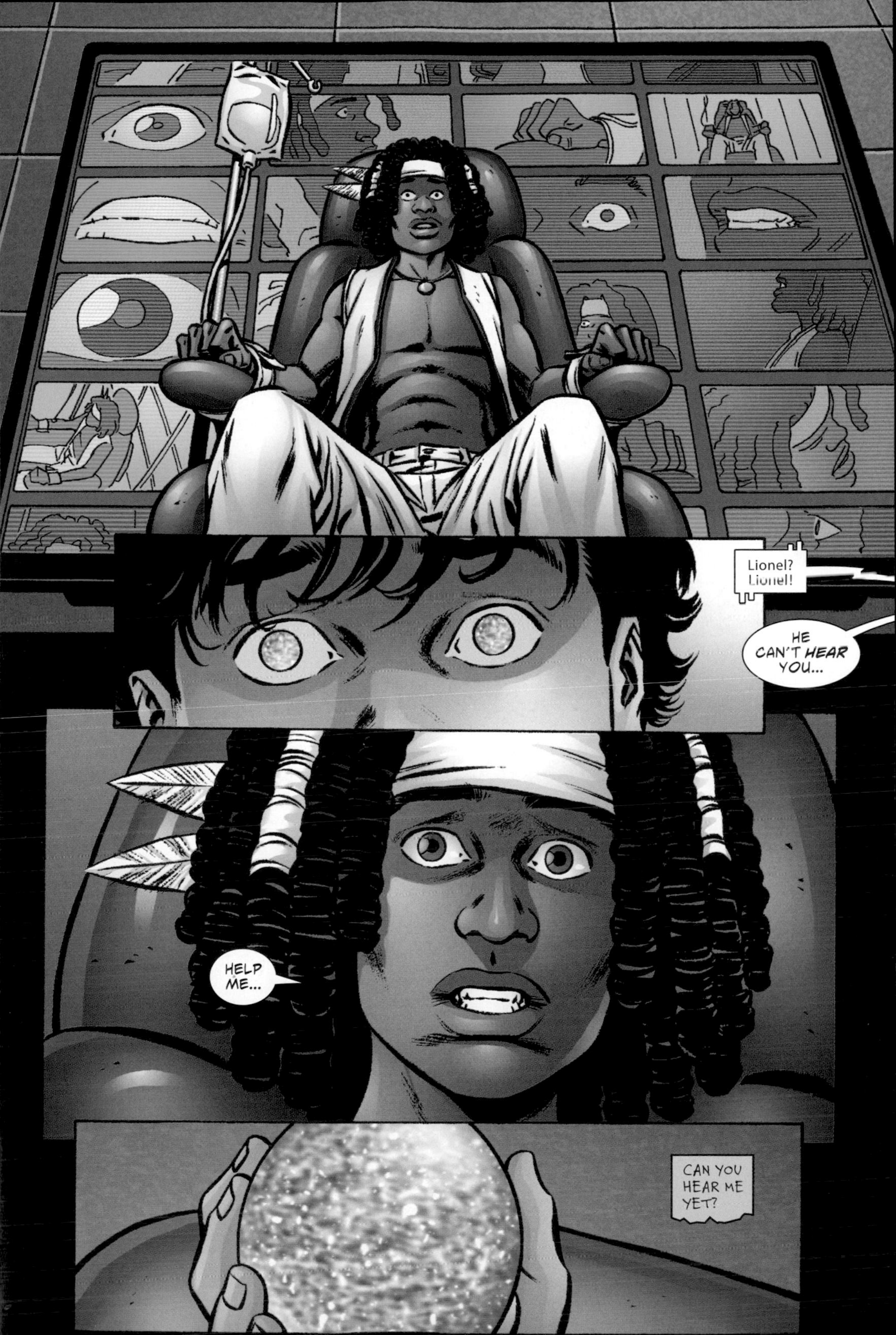
Lionel? Lionel!
HE CAN'T HEAR YOU...
HELP ME...
CAN YOU HEAR ME YET?

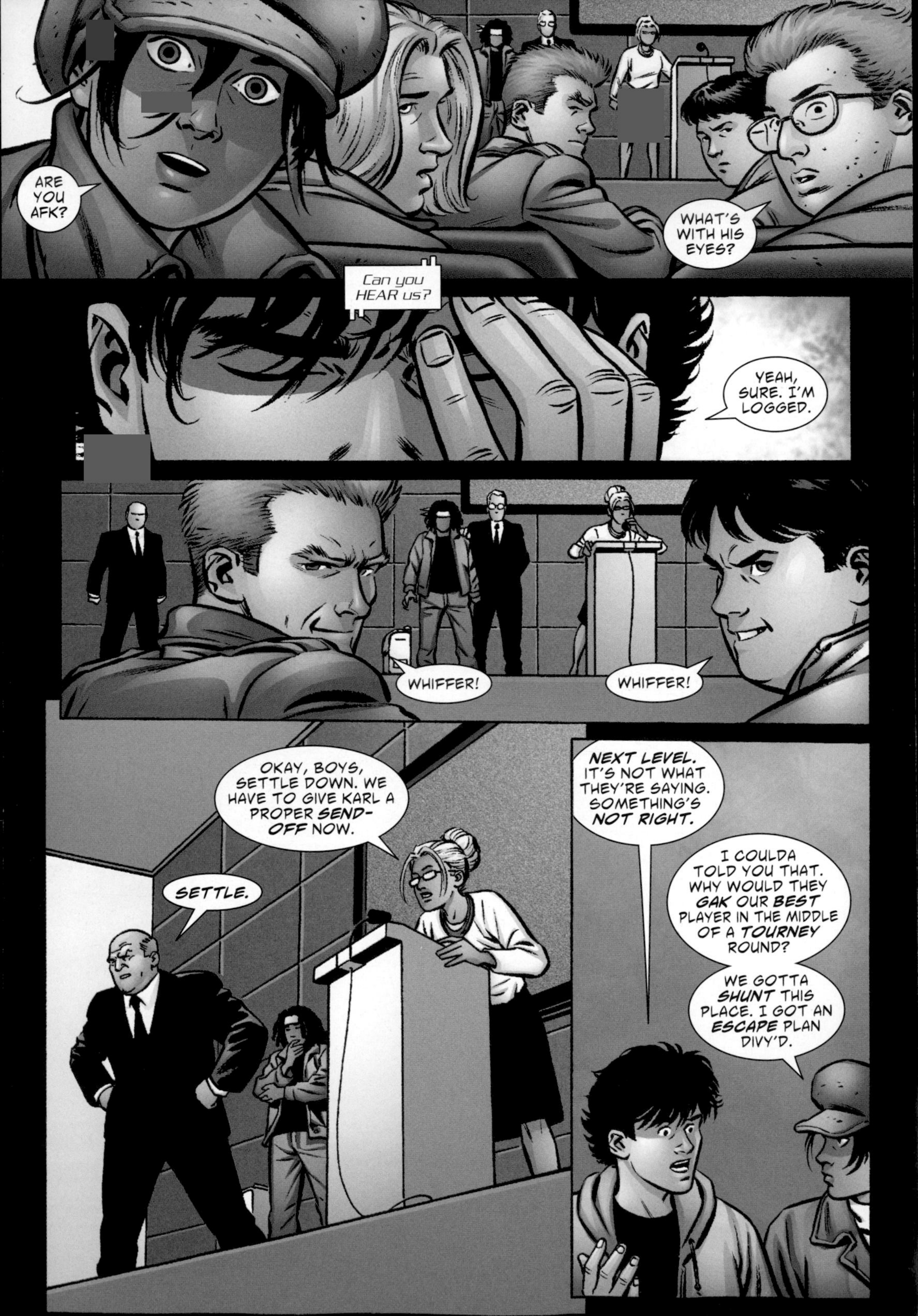
ARE YOU AFK?
WHAT'S WITH HIS EYES?
Can you HEAR us?
YEAH, SURE. I'M LOGGED.
WHIFFER!
WHIFFER!
OKAY, BOYS, SETTLE DOWN. WE HAVE TO GIVE KARL A PROPER SEND-OFF NOW.
SETTLE.
NEXT LEVEL. IT'S NOT WHAT THEY'RE SAYING. SOMETHING'S NOT RIGHT.
I COULDA TOLD YOU THAT. WHY WOULD THEY GAK OUR BEST PLAYER IN THE MIDDLE OF A TOURNEY ROUND?
WE GOTTA SHUNT THIS PLACE. I GOT AN ESCAPE PLAN DIVY'D.

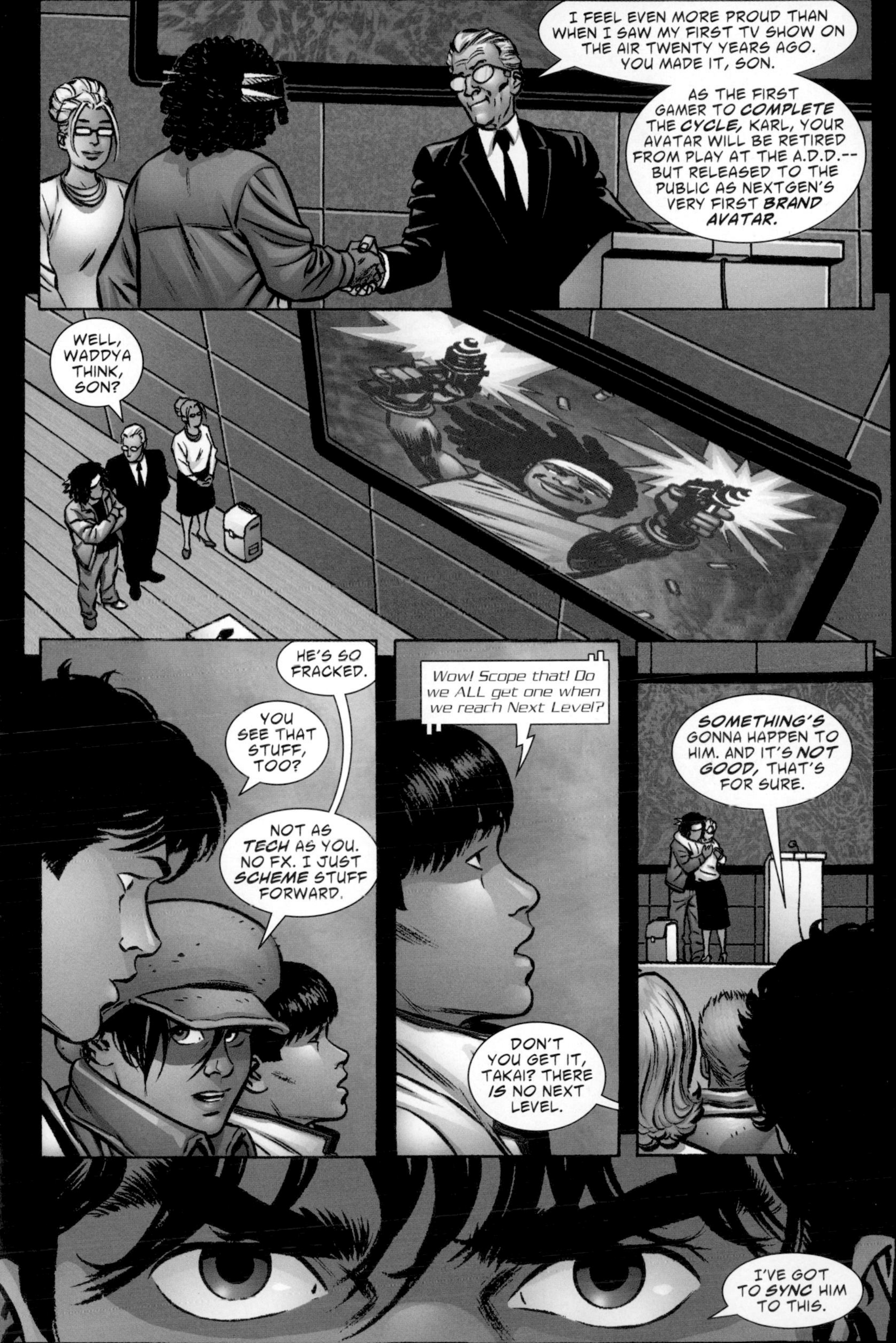
I FEEL EVEN MORE PROUD THAN WHEN I SAW MY FIRST TV SHOW ON THE AIR TWENTY YEARS AGO. YOU MADE IT, SON.
AS THE FIRST GAMER TO COMPLETE THE CYCLE, KARL, YOUR AVATAR WILL BE RETIRED FROM PLAY AT THE A.D.D.-- BUT RELEASED TO THE PUBLIC AS NEXTGEN'S VERY FIRST BRAND AVATAR.
WELL, WADDYA THINK, SON?
HE'S SO FRACKED.
YOU SEE THAT STUFF, TOO?
NOT AS TECH AS YOU. NO FX. I JUST SCHEME STUFF FORWARD.
Wow! Scope that! Do we ALL get one when we reach Next Level?
DON'T YOU GET IT, TAKAI? THERE IS NO NEXT LEVEL.
SOMETHING'S GONNA HAPPEN TO HIM. AND IT'S NOT GOOD, THAT'S FOR SURE.
I'VE GOT TO SYNC HIM TO THIS.

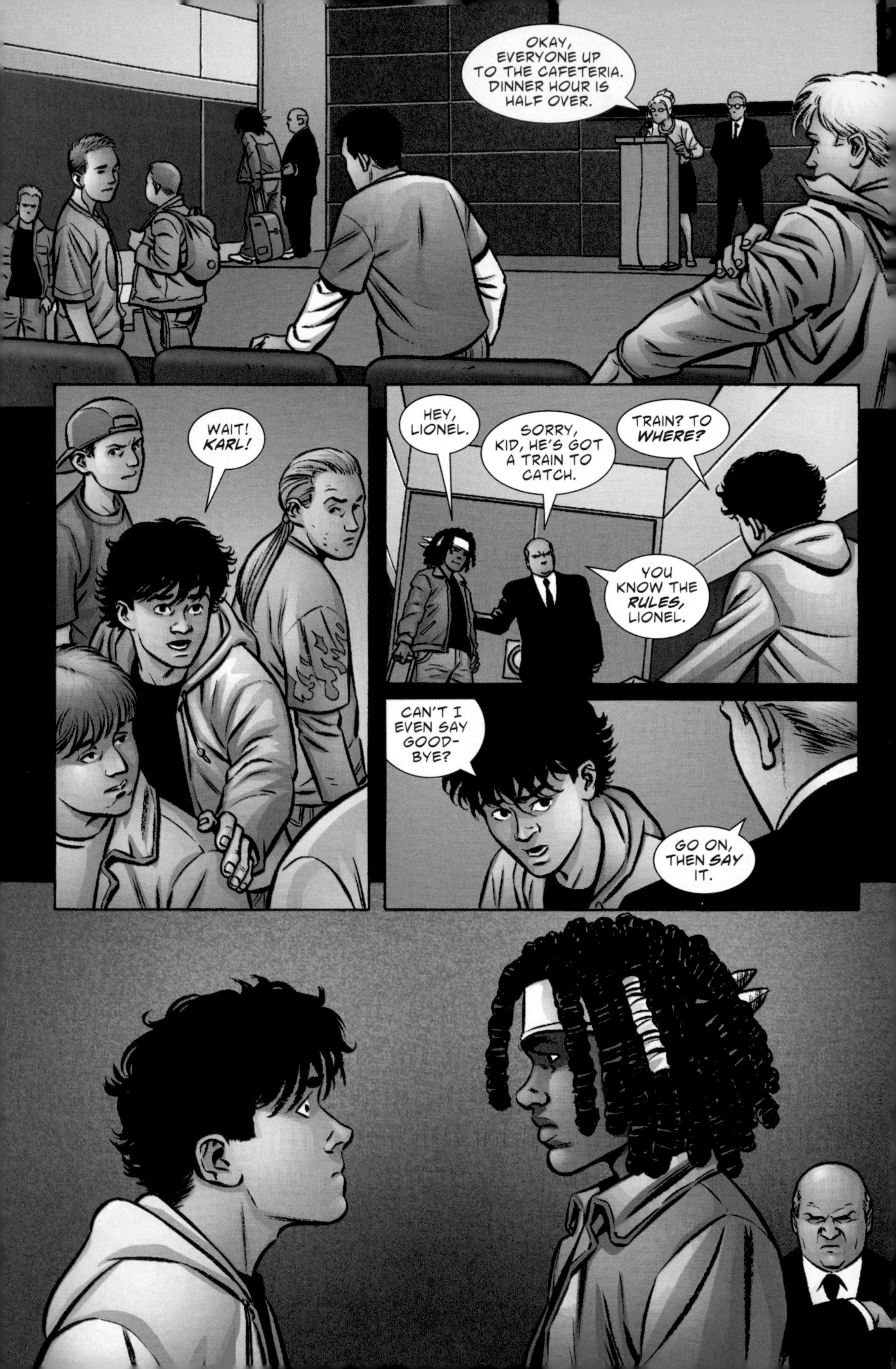
OKAY, EVERYONE UP TO THE CAFETERIA. DINNER HOUR IS HALF OVER.
WAIT! KARL!
HEY, LIONEL.
SORRY, KID, HE'S GOT A TRAIN TO CATCH.
TRAIN? TO WHERE?
YOU KNOW THE RULES, LIONEL.
CAN'T I EVEN SAY GOOD-BYE?
GO ON, THEN SAY IT.

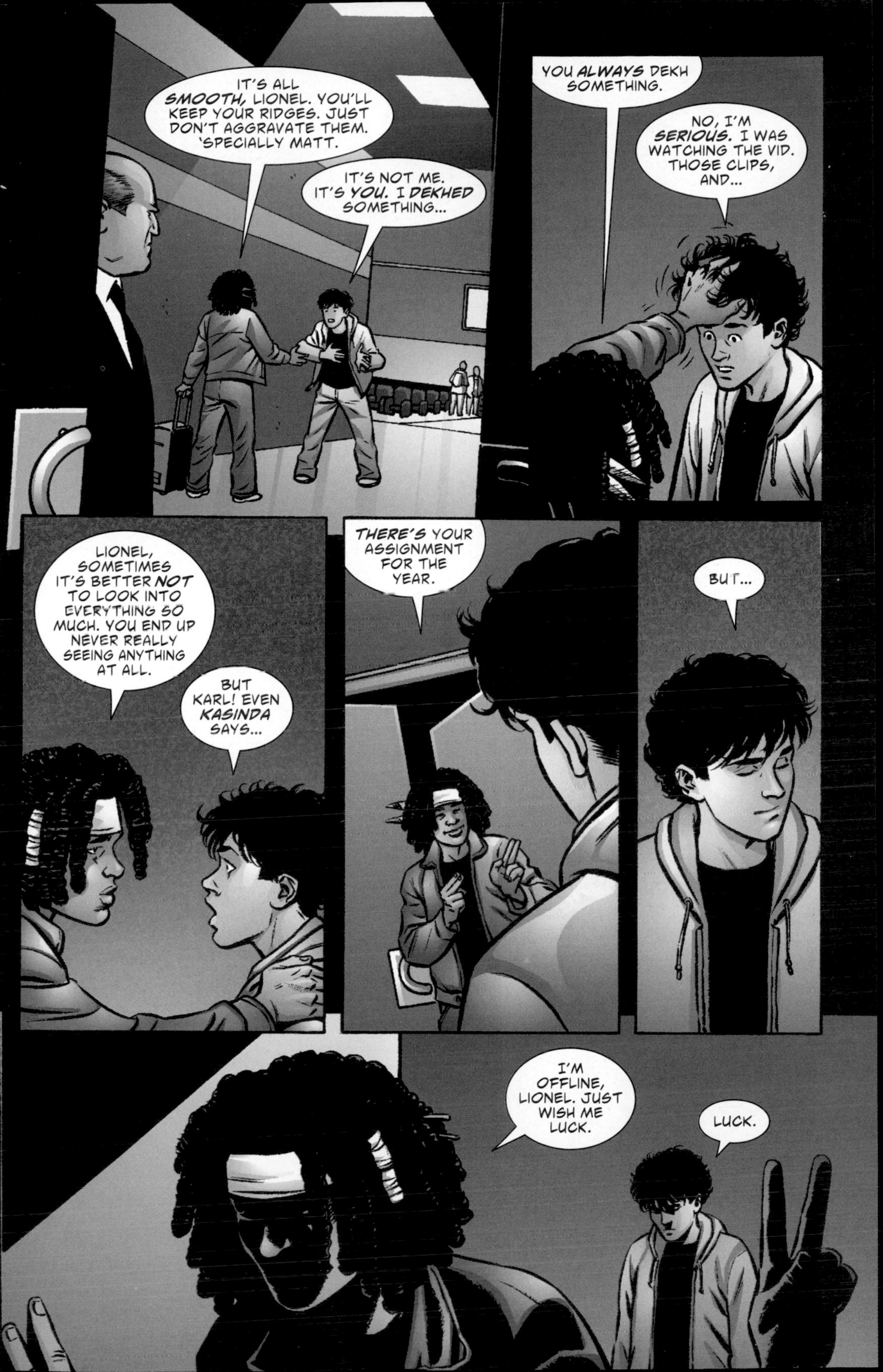
IT'S ALL SMOOTH, LIONEL. YOU'LL KEEP YOUR RIDGES. JUST DON'T AGGRAVATE THEM. 'SPECIALLY MATT.
IT'S NOT ME. IT'S YOU. I DEKHED SOMETHING...
YOU ALWAYS DEKH SOMETHING.
NO, I'M SERIOUS. I WAS WATCHING THE VID. THOSE CLIPS, AND...
LIONEL, SOMETIMES IT'S BETTER NOT TO LOOK INTO EVERYTHING SO MUCH. YOU END UP NEVER REALLY SEEING ANYTHING AT ALL.
BUT KARL! EVEN KASINDA SAYS...
THERE'S YOUR ASSIGNMENT FOR THE YEAR.
BUT...
I'M OFFLINE, LIONEL. JUST WISH ME LUCK.
LUCK.

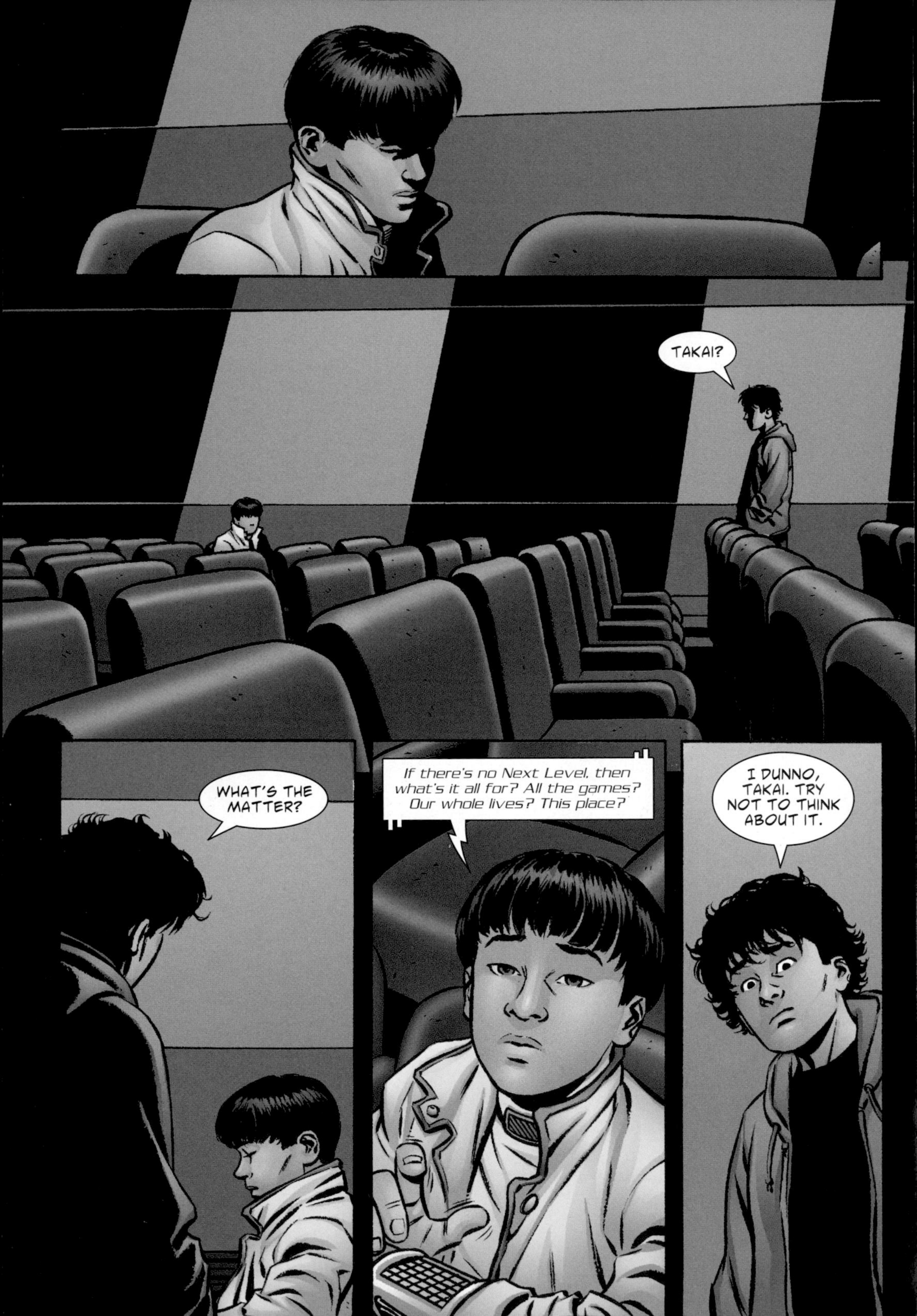
TAKAI?
WHAT'S THE MATTER?
If there's no Next Level, then what's it all for? All the games? Our whole lives? This place?
I DUNNO, TAKAI. TRY NOT TO THINK ABOUT IT.

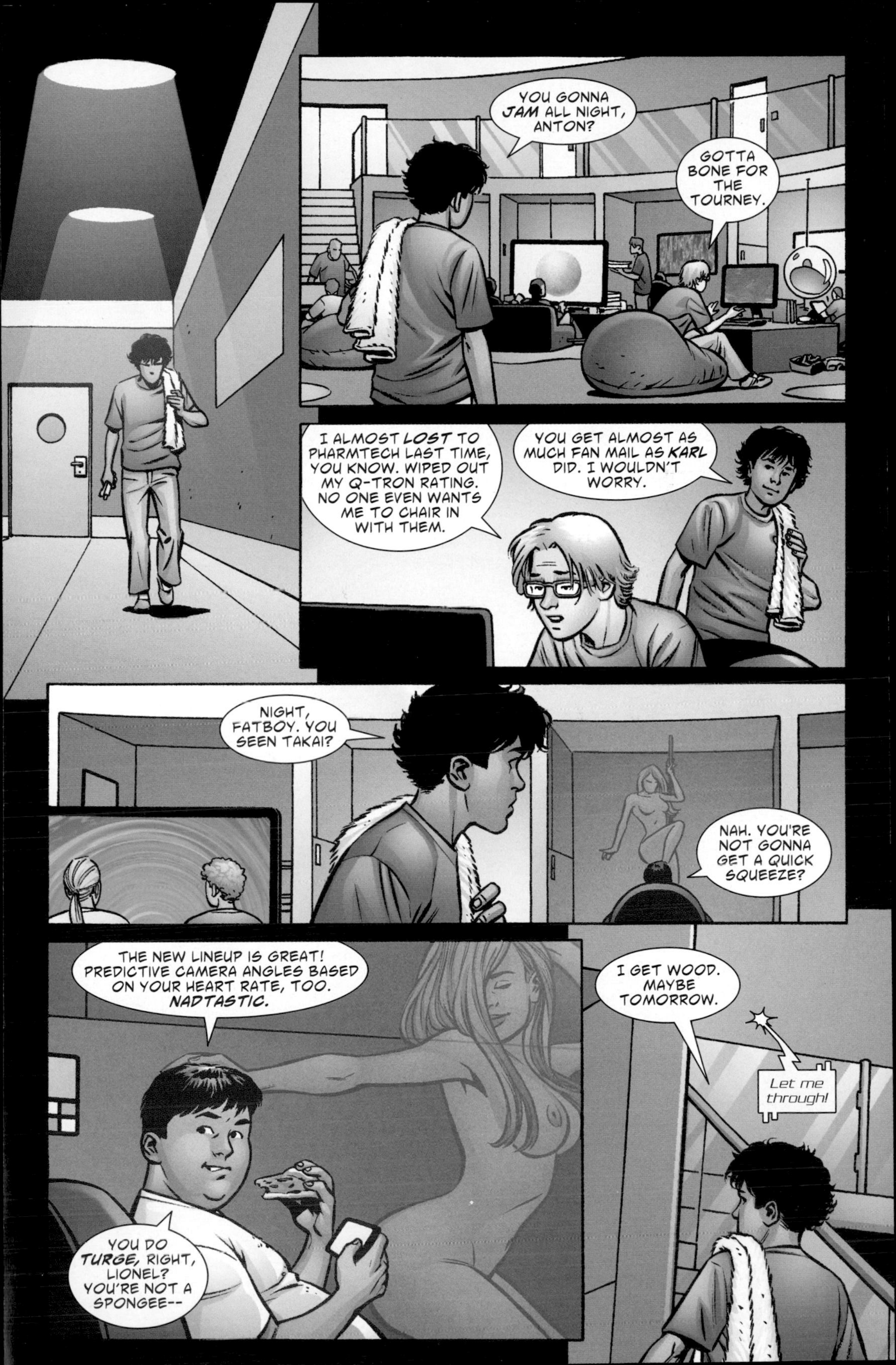
YOU GONNA JAM ALL NIGHT, ANTON?
GOTTA BONE FOR THE TOURNEY.
I ALMOST LOST TO PHARMTECH LAST TIME, YOU KNOW. WIPED OUT MY Q-TRON RATING. NO ONE EVEN WANTS ME TO CHAIR IN WITH THEM.
YOU GET ALMOST AS MUCH FAN MAIL AS KARL DID. I WOULDN'T WORRY.
NIGHT, FATBOY. YOU SEEN TAKAI?
NAH. YOU'RE NOT GONNA GET A QUICK SQUEEZE?
THE NEW LINEUP IS GREAT! PREDICTIVE CAMERA ANGLES BASED ON YOUR HEART RATE, TOO. NADTASTIC.
I GET WOOD. MAYBE TOMORROW.
Let me through!
YOU DO TURGE, RIGHT, LIONEL? YOU'RE NOT A SPONGEE--

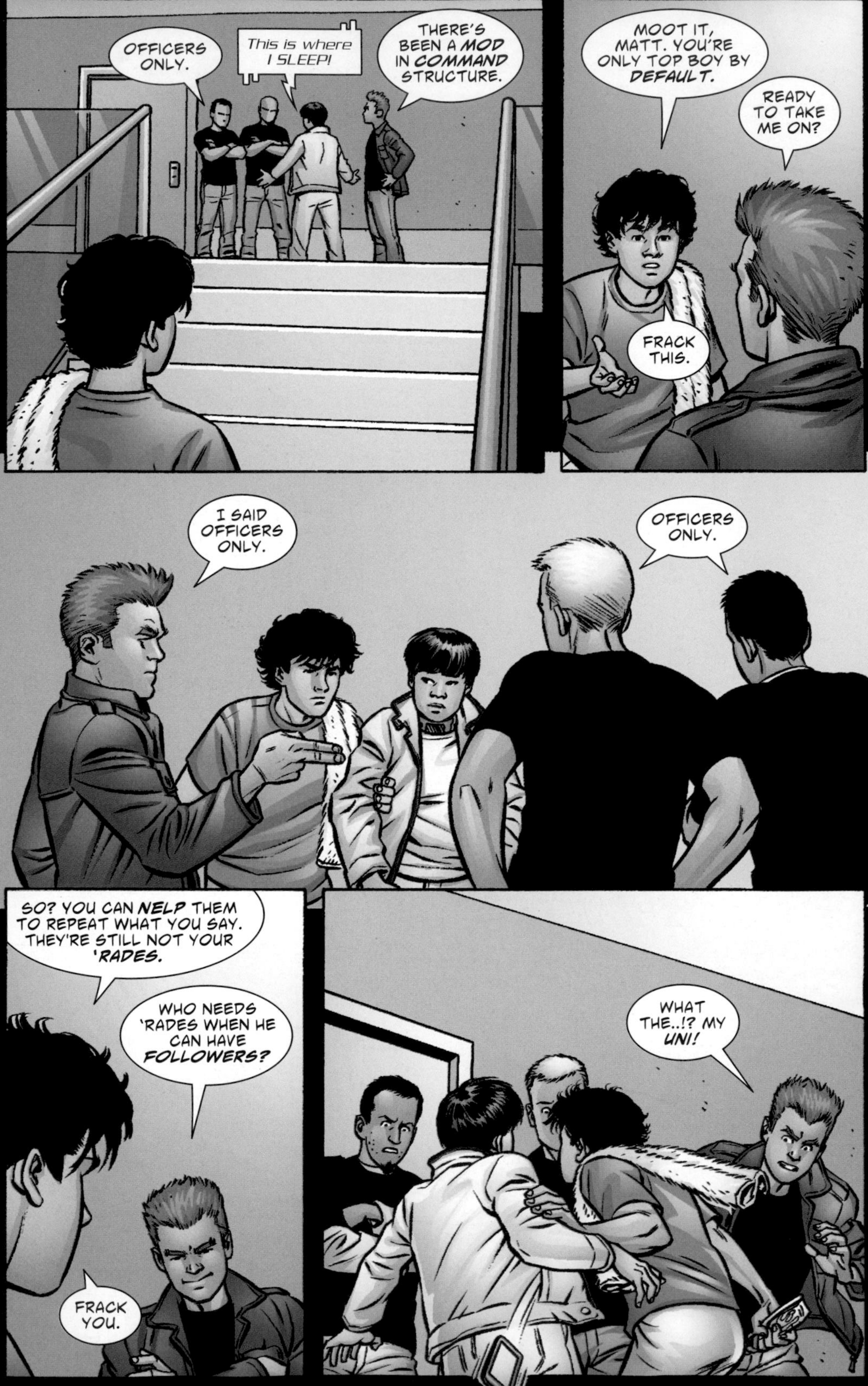
OFFICERS ONLY.
This is where I SLEEP!
THERE'S BEEN A MOD IN COMMAND STRUCTURE.
MOOT IT, MATT. YOU'RE ONLY TOP BOY BY DEFAULT.
READY TO TAKE ME ON?
FRACK THIS.
I SAID OFFICERS ONLY.
OFFICERS ONLY.
SO? YOU CAN NELP THEM TO REPEAT WHAT YOU SAY. THEY'RE STILL NOT YOUR 'RADES.
WHO NEEDS 'RADES WHEN HE CAN HAVE FOLLOWERS?
FRACK YOU.
WHAT THE..!? MY UNI!

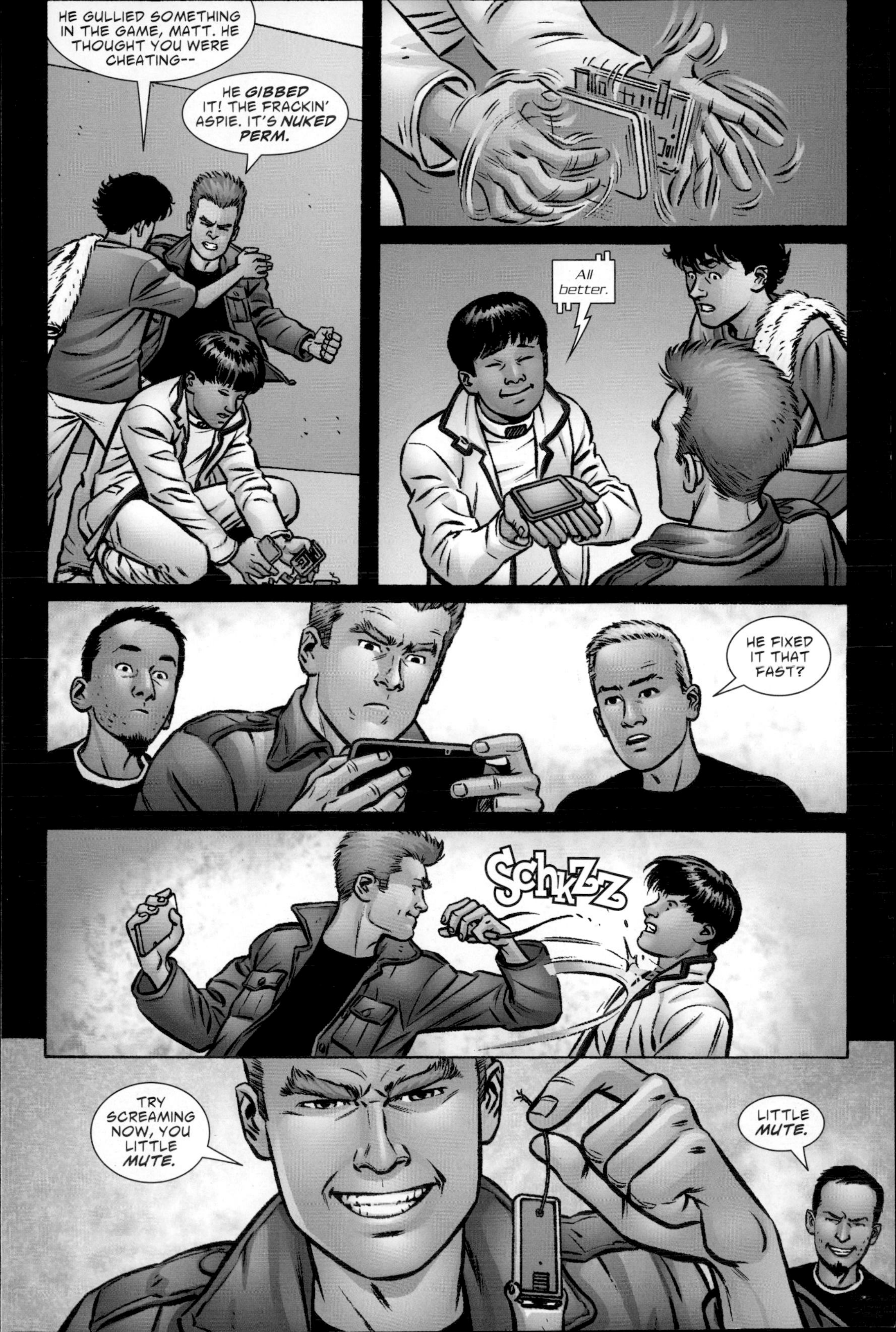
HE GULLIED SOMETHING IN THE GAME, MATT. HE THOUGHT YOU WERE CHEATING--
HE GIBBED IT! THE FRACKIN' ASPIE. IT'S NUKED PERM.
All better.
HE FIXED IT THAT FAST?
SCHKZZZ
TRY SCREAMING NOW, YOU LITTLE MUTE.
LITTLE MUTE.

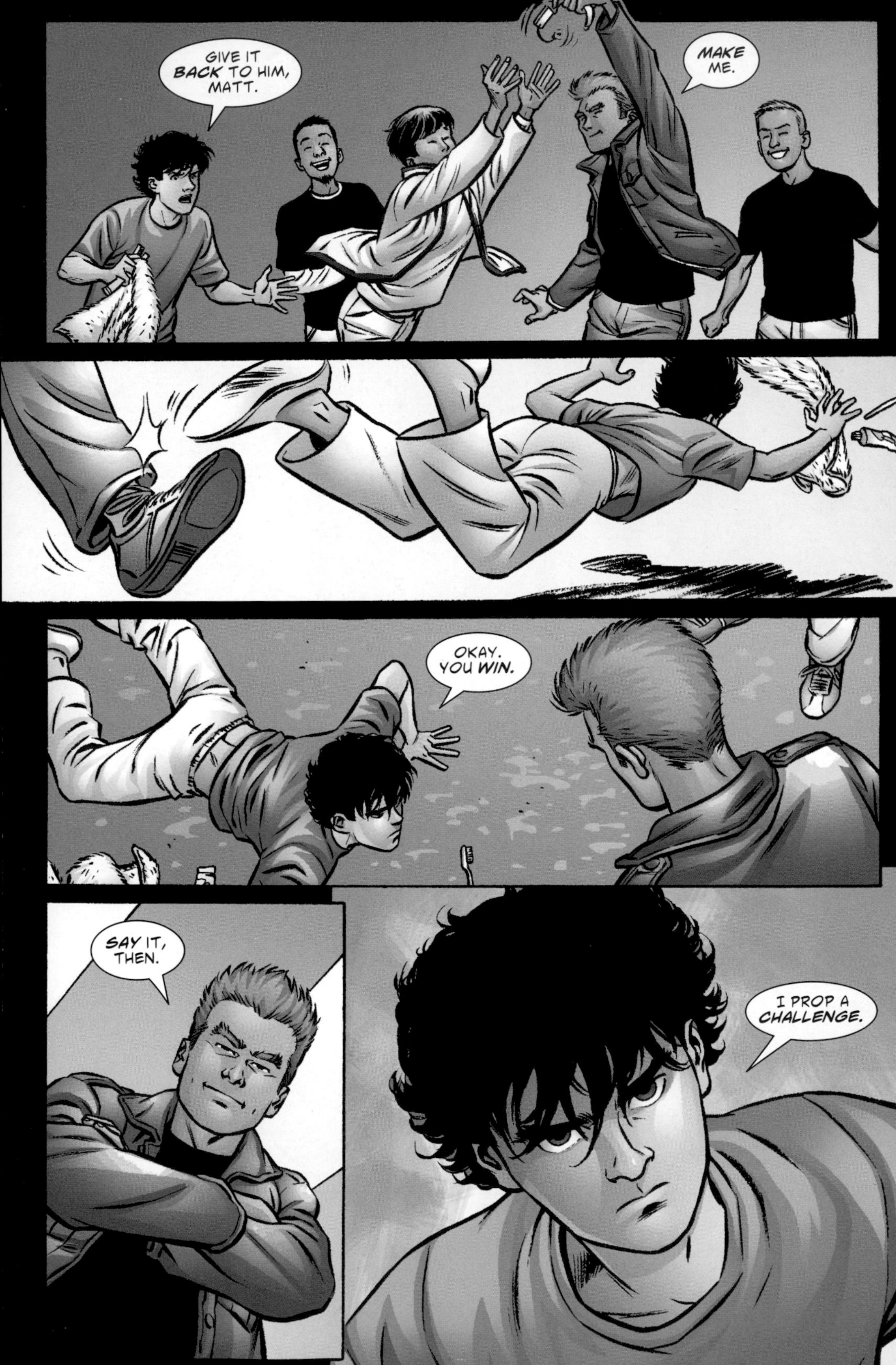
GIVE IT BACK TO HIM, MATT.
MAKE ME.
OKAY. YOU WIN.
SAY IT, THEN.
I PROP A CHALLENGE.

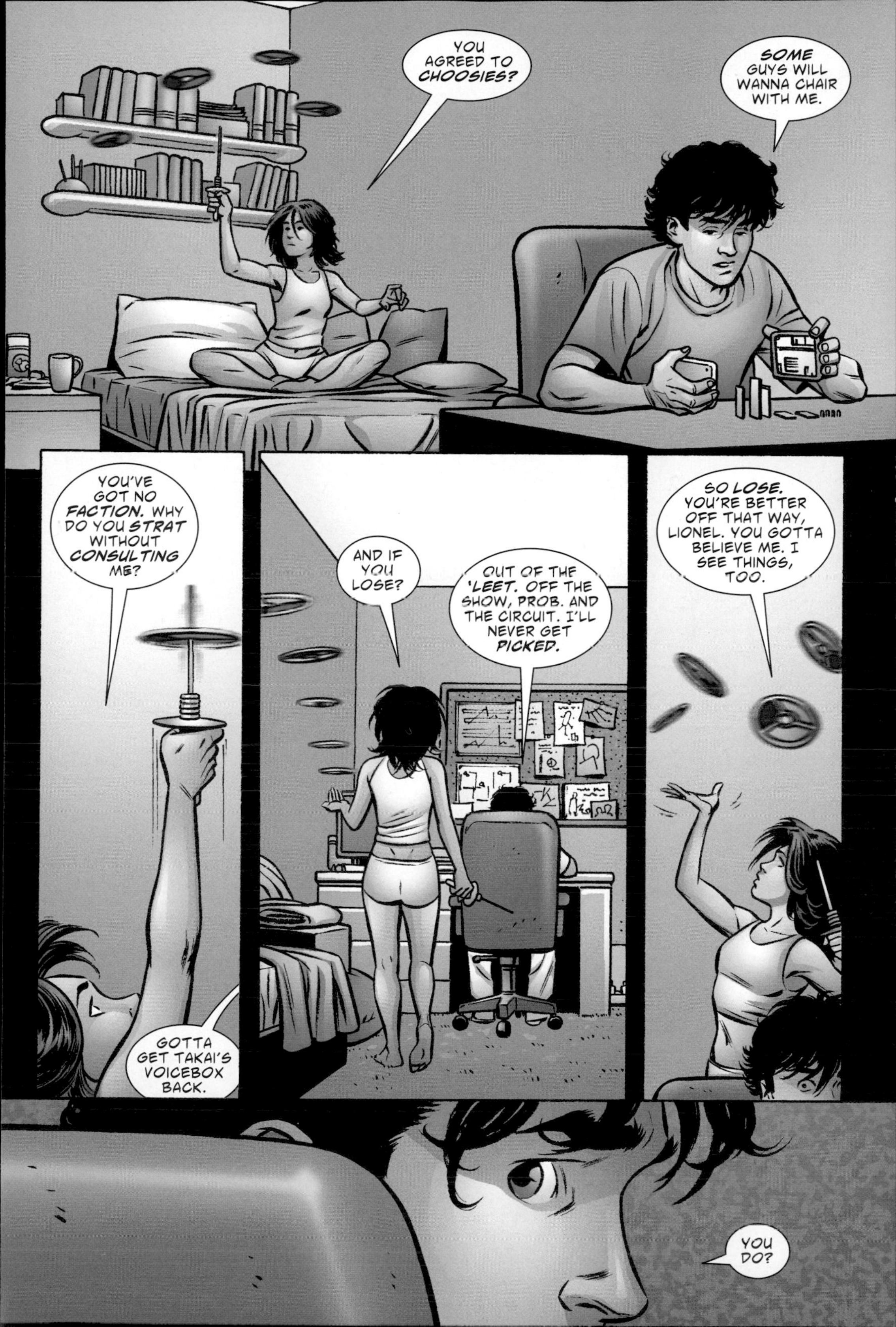
YOU AGREED TO CHOOSIES?
SOME GUYS WILL WANNA CHAIR WITH ME.
YOU'VE GOT NO FACTION. WHY DO YOU STRAT WITHOUT CONSULTING ME?
GOTTA GET TAKAI'S VOICEBOX BACK.
AND IF YOU LOSE?
OUT OF THE 'LEET. OFF THE SHOW, PROB. AND THE CIRCUIT. I'LL NEVER GET PICKED.
SO LOSE. YOU'RE BETTER OFF THAT WAY, LIONEL. YOU GOTTA BELIEVE ME. I SEE THINGS, TOO.
YOU DO?

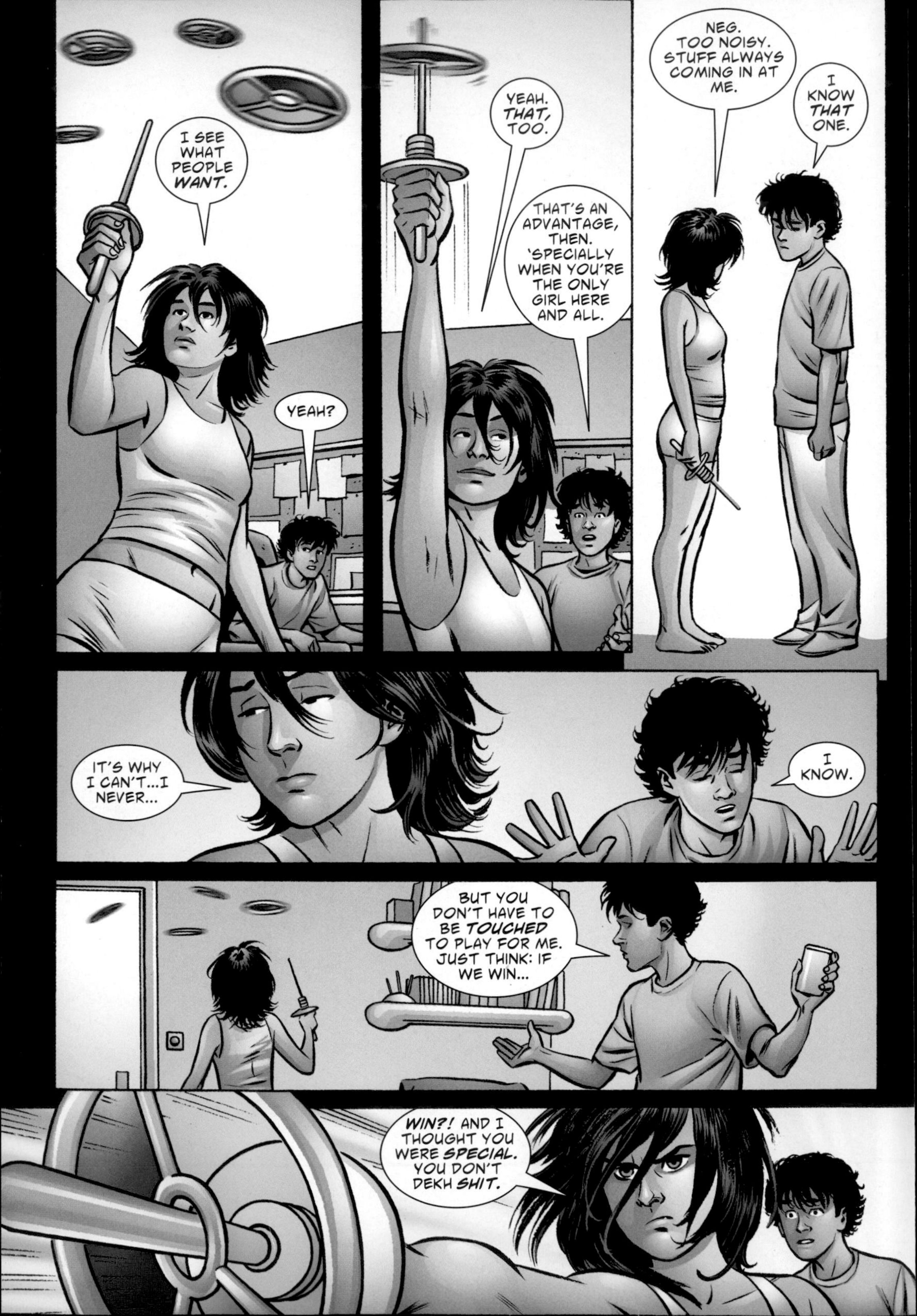
I SEE WHAT PEOPLE WANT.
YEAH?
YEAH. THAT, TOO.
THAT'S AN ADVANTAGE, THEN. 'SPECIALLY WHEN YOU'RE THE ONLY GIRL HERE AND ALL.
NEG. TOO NOISY. STUFF ALWAYS COMING IN AT ME.
I KNOW THAT ONE.
IT'S WHY I CAN'T...I NEVER...
I KNOW.
BUT YOU DON'T HAVE TO BE TOUCHED TO PLAY FOR ME. JUST THINK: IF WE WIN...
WIN?! AND I THOUGHT YOU WERE SPECIAL. YOU DON'T DEKH SHIT.

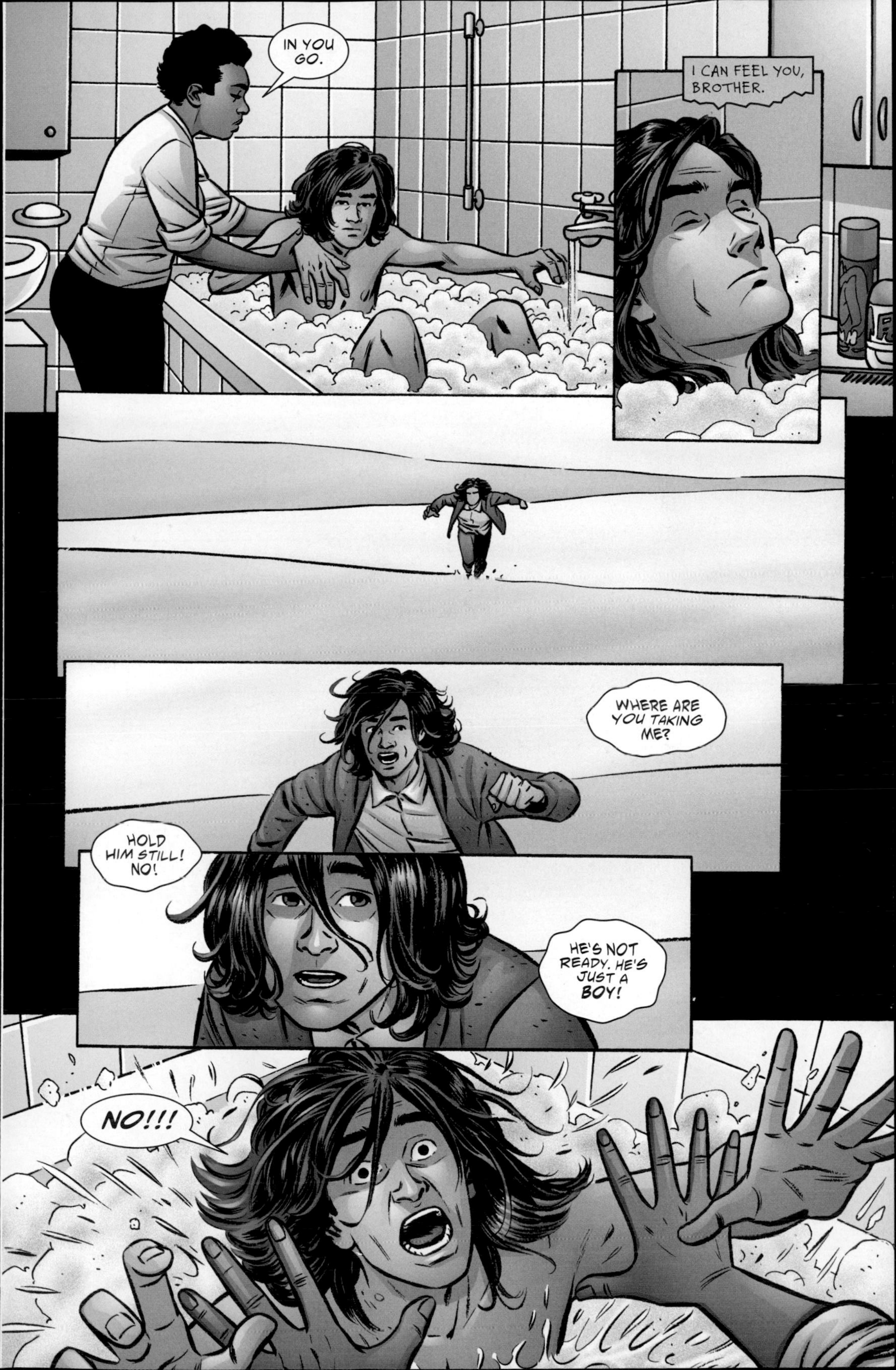

IN YOU GO.
I CAN FEEL YOU, BROTHER.
WHERE ARE YOU TAKING ME?
HOLD HIM STILL! NO!
HE'S NOT READY. HE'S JUST A BOY!
NO!!!

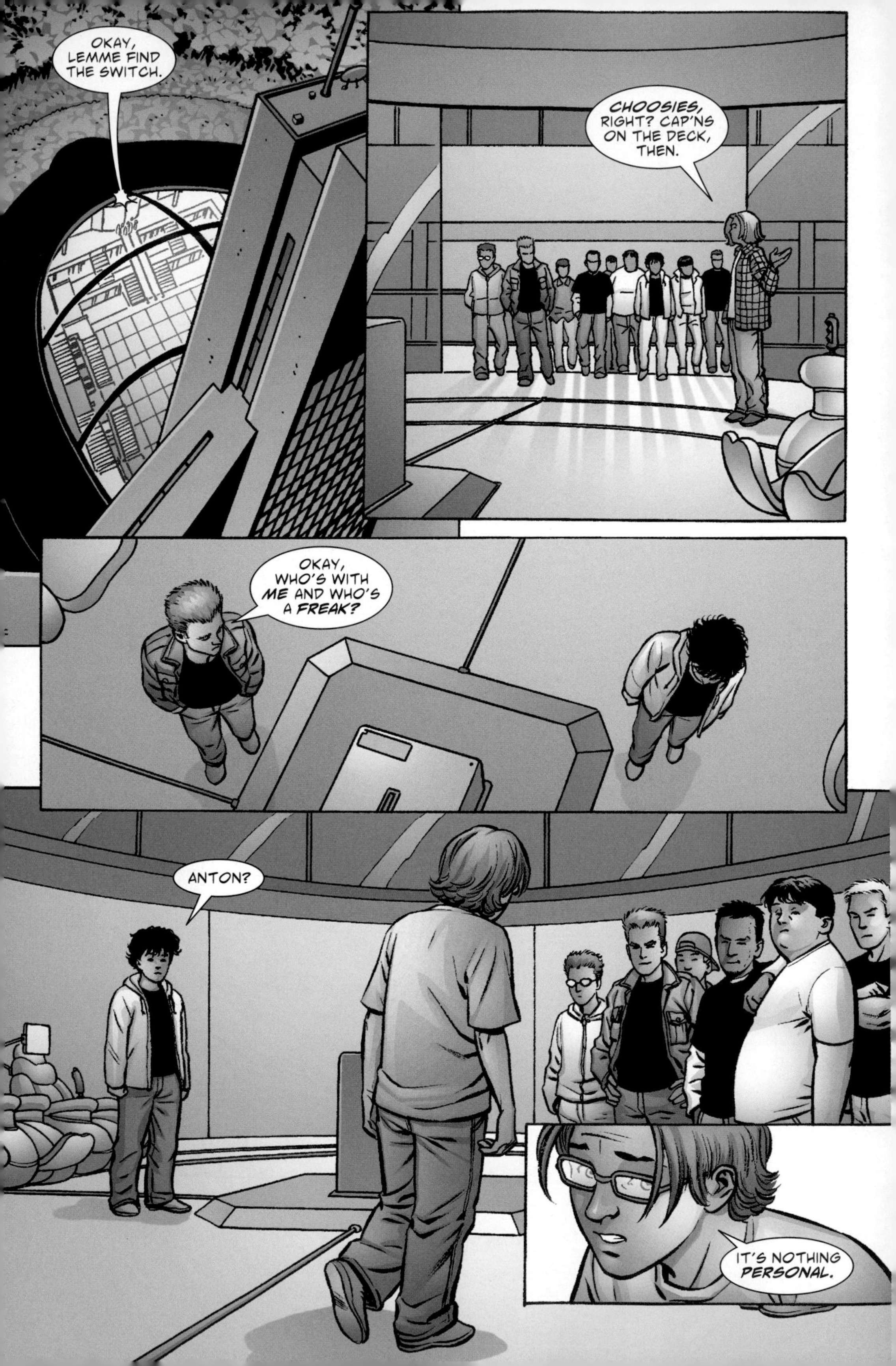
OKAY, LEMME FIND THE SWITCH.
CHOOSIES, RIGHT? CAP'NS ON THE DECK, THEN.
OKAY, WHO'S WITH ME AND WHO'S A FREAK?
ANTON?
IT'S NOTHING PERSONAL.

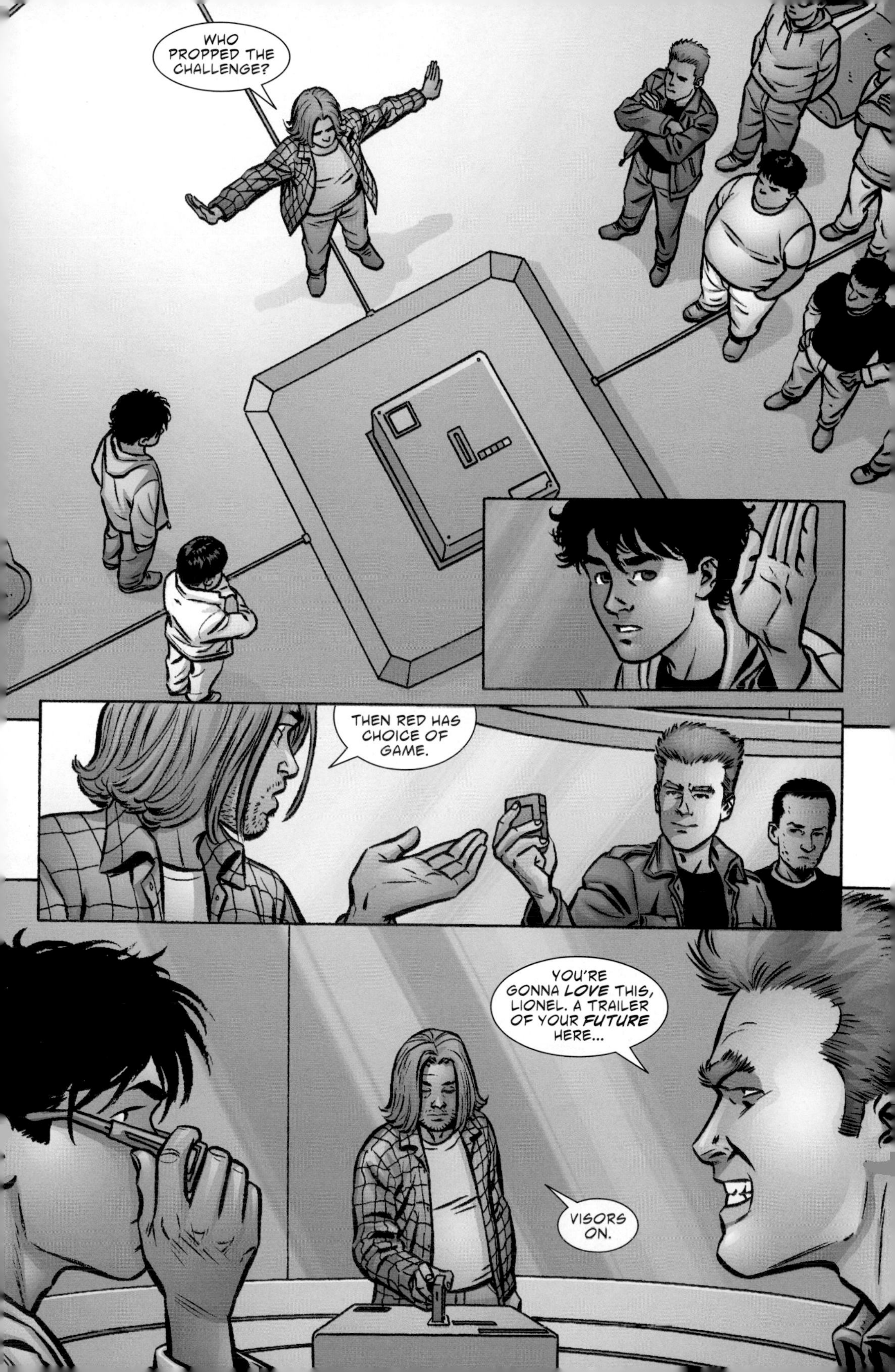
WHO PROPPED THE CHALLENGE?
THEN RED HAS CHOICE OF GAME.
YOU'RE GONNA LOVE THIS, LIONEL. A TRAILER OF YOUR FUTURE HERE...
VISORS ON.

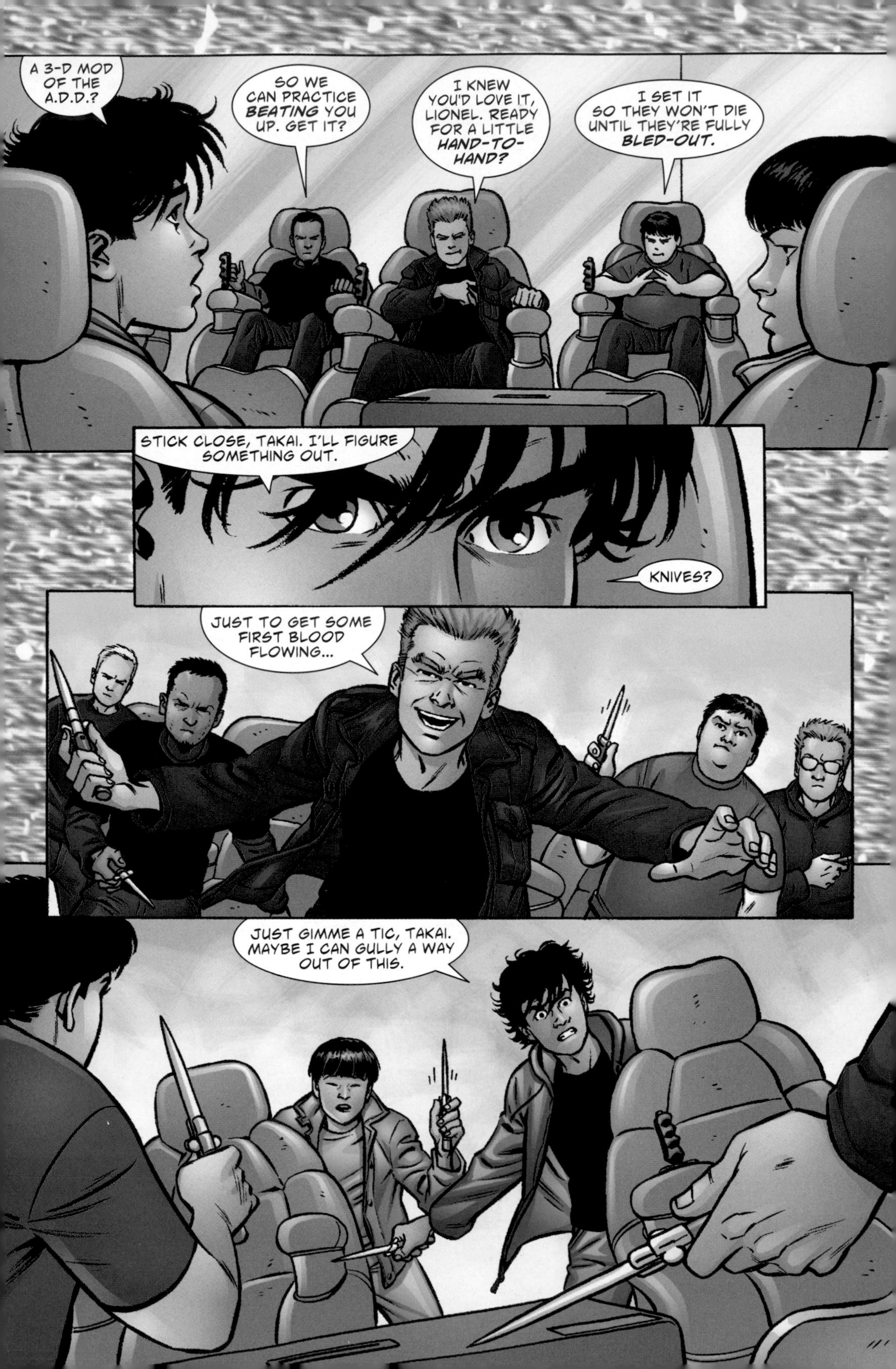
A 3-D MOD OF THE A.D.D.?
SO WE CAN PRACTICE BEATING YOU UP. GET IT?
I KNEW YOU'D LOVE IT, LIONEL. READY FOR A LITTLE HAND-TO-HAND?
I SET IT SO THEY WON'T DIE UNTIL THEY'RE FULLY BLED-OUT.
STICK CLOSE, TAKAI. I'LL FIGURE SOMETHING OUT.
KNIVES?
JUST TO GET SOME FIRST BLOOD FLOWING...
JUST GIMME A TIC, TAKAI. MAYBE I CAN GULLY A WAY OUT OF THIS.

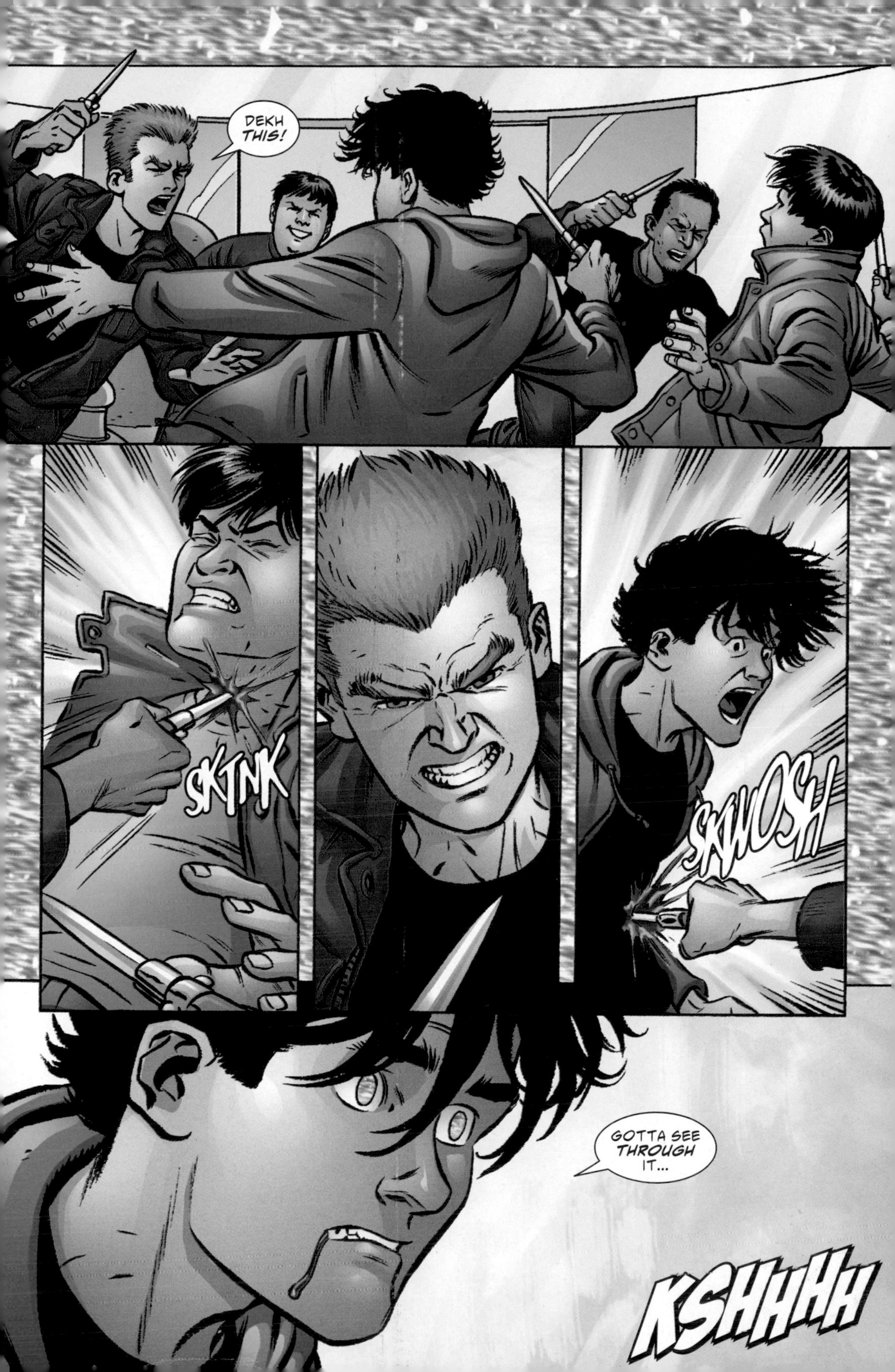
DEKH THIS!
SKTNK
SKWOSH
GOTTA SEE THROUGH IT...
KSHHHH

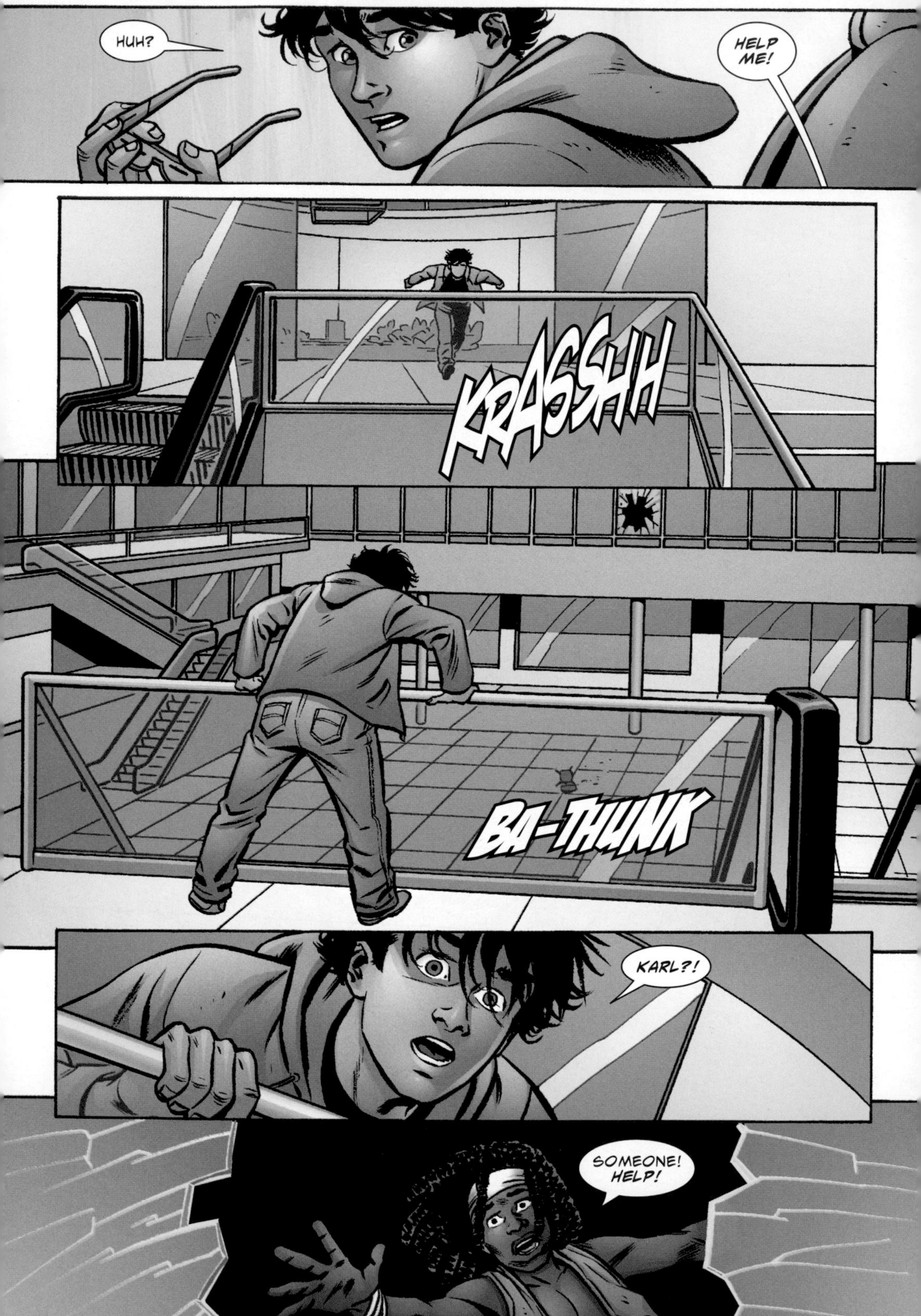
HUH?
HELP ME!
KRASSHH
BA-THUNK
KARL?!
SOMEONE! HELP!

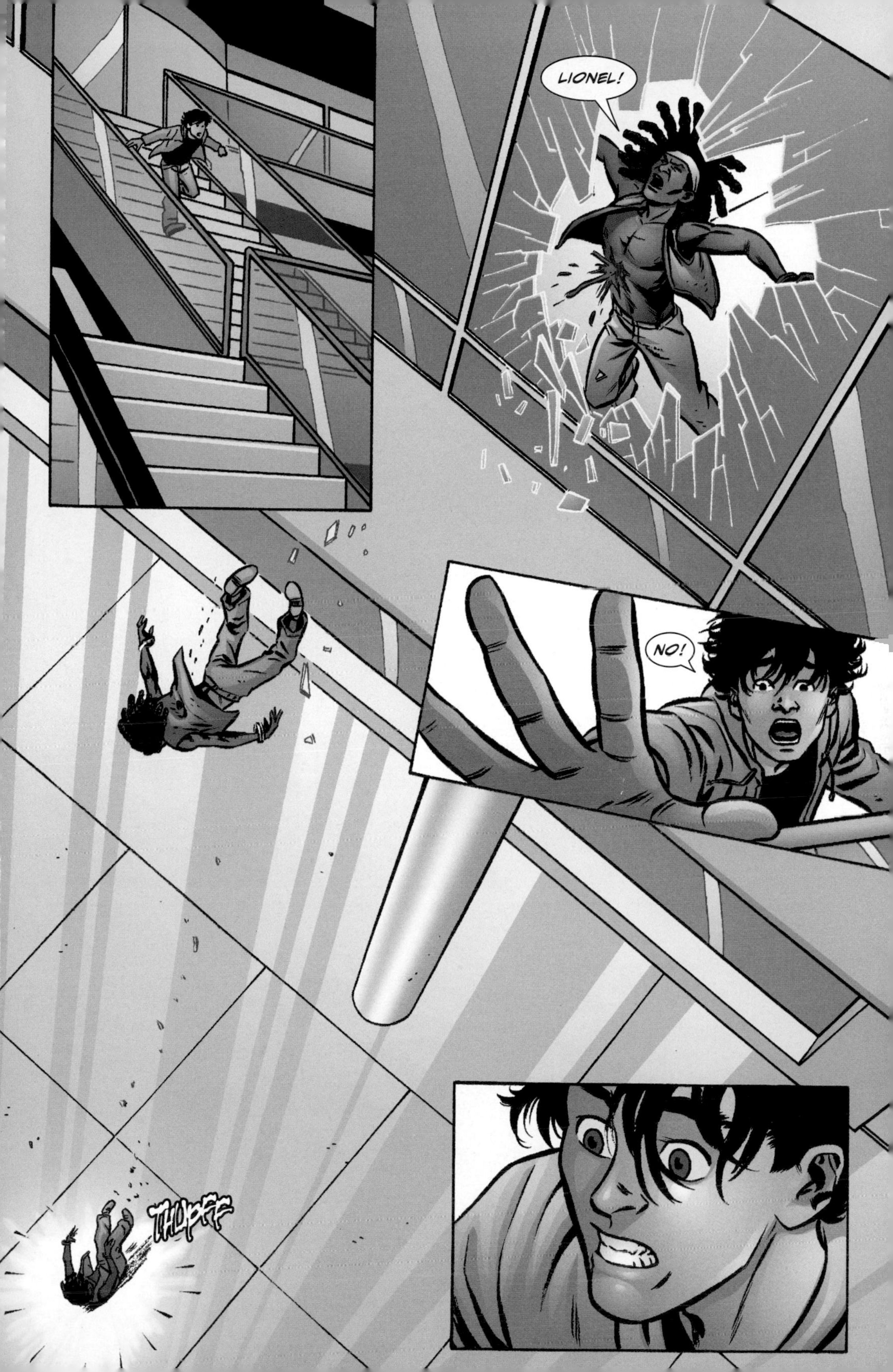
LIONEL!
NO!
THUDFF

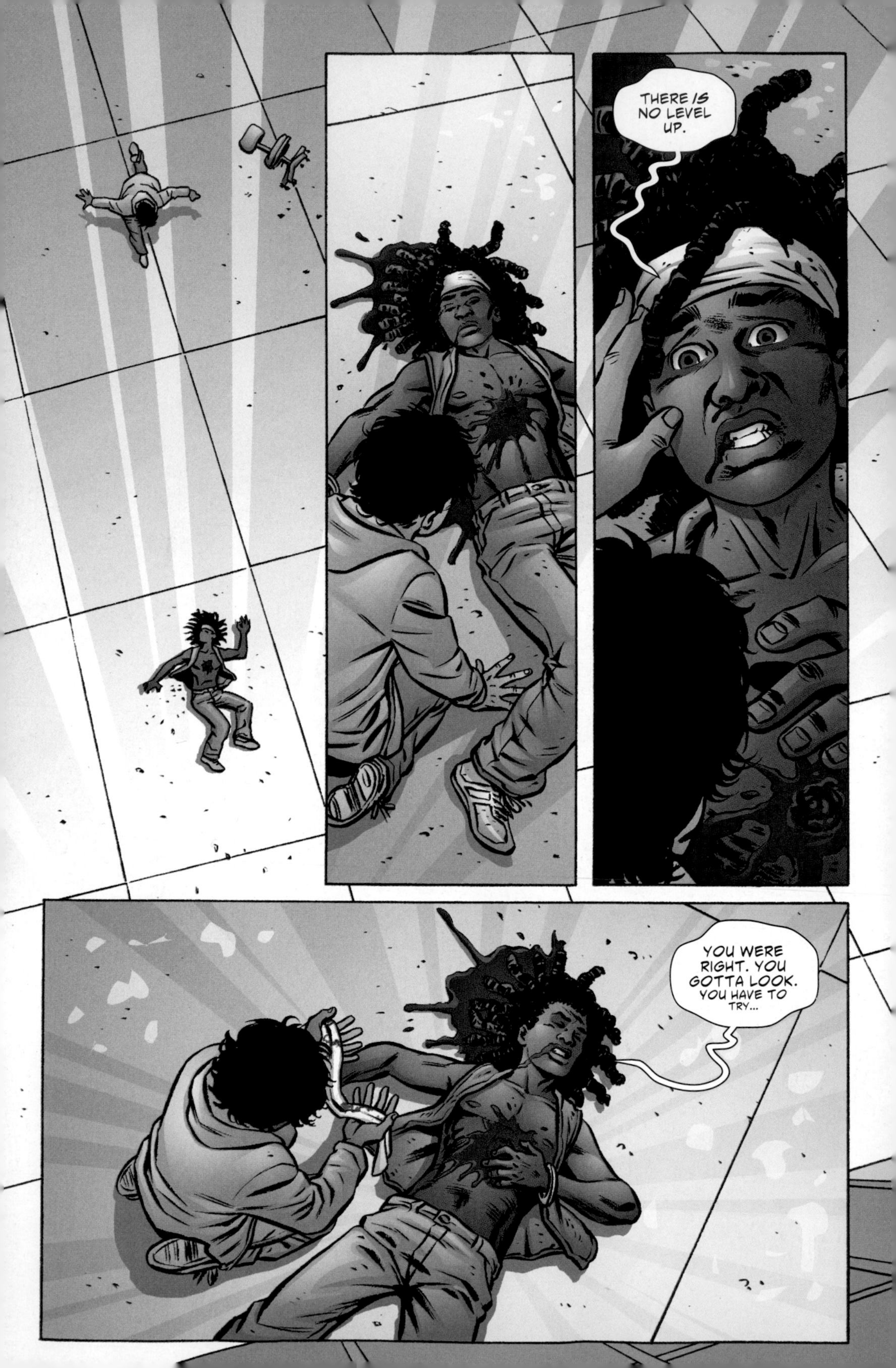
THERE IS NO LEVEL UP.
YOU WERE RIGHT. YOU GOTTA LOOK. YOU HAVE TO TRY...

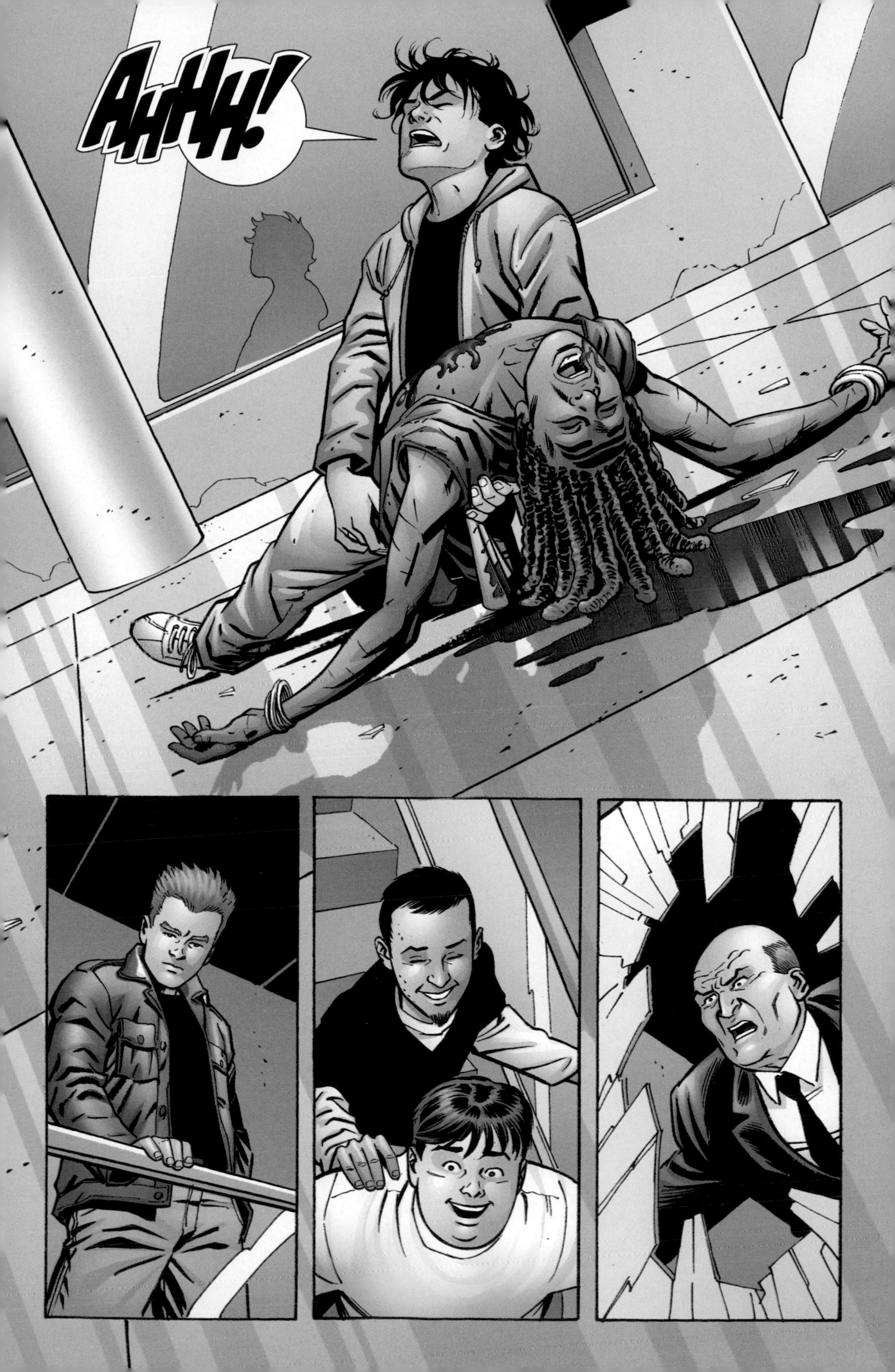
AHHH!

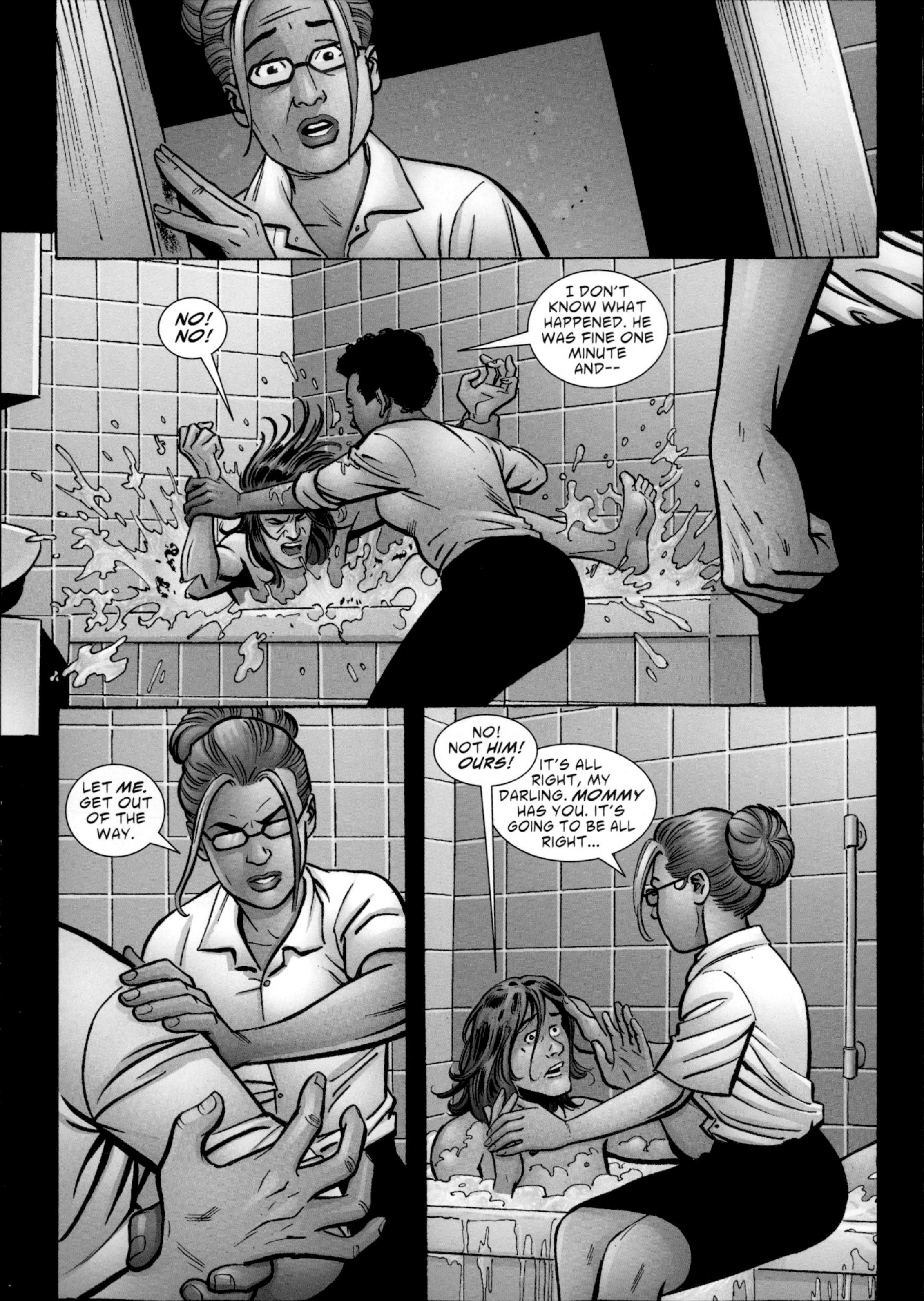
NO! NO!
I DON'T KNOW WHAT HAPPENED. HE WAS FINE ONE MINUTE AND--
LET ME. GET OUT OF THE WAY.
NO! NOT HIM! OURS!
IT'S ALL RIGHT, MY DARLING. MOMMY HAS YOU. IT'S GOING TO BE ALL RIGHT...

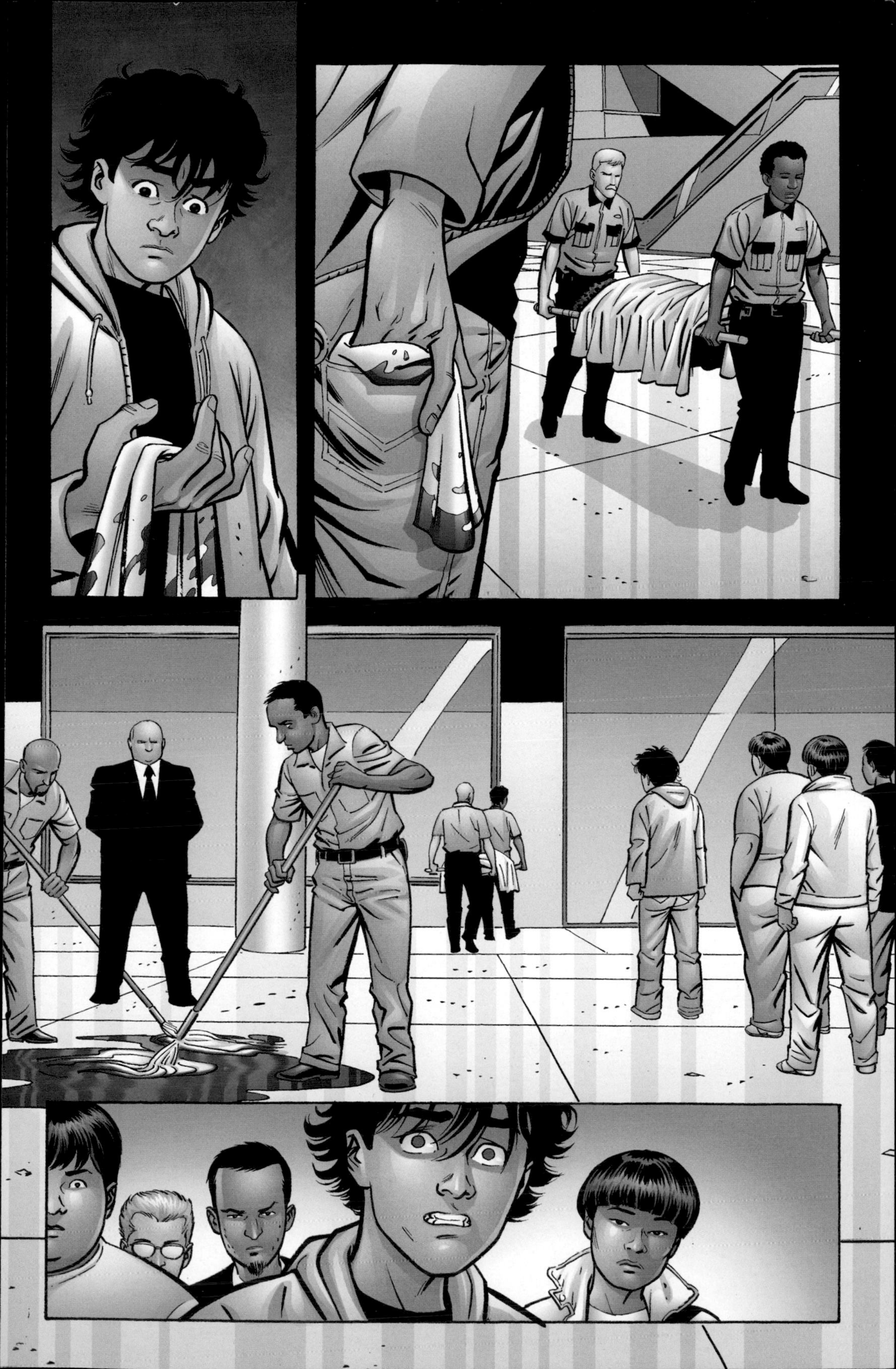

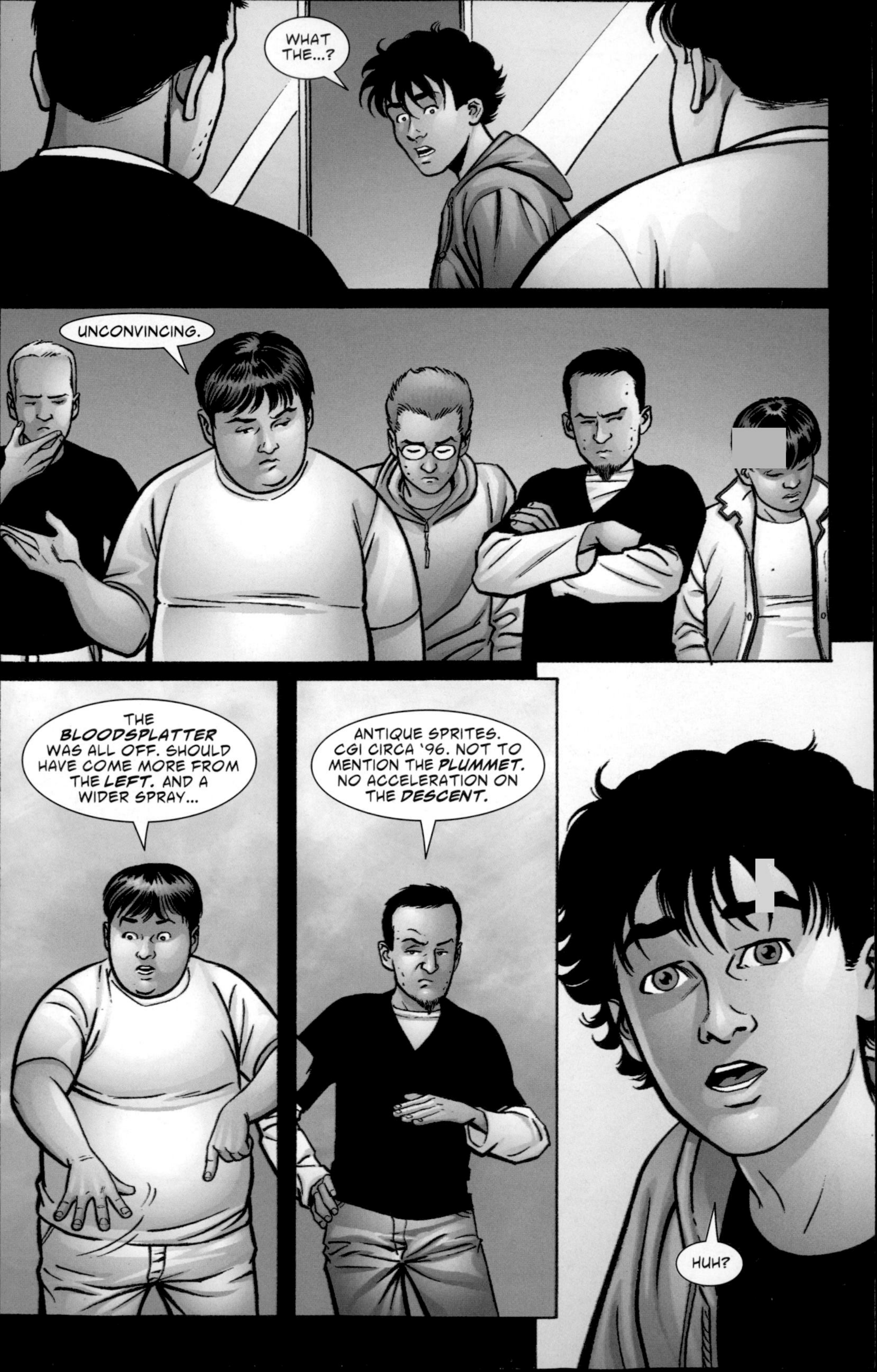
WHAT THE...?
UNCONVINCING.
THE BLOODSPLATTER WAS ALL OFF. SHOULD HAVE COME MORE FROM THE LEFT. AND A WIDER SPRAY...
ANTIQUE SPRITES. CGI CIRCA '96. NOT TO MENTION THE PLUMMET. NO ACCELERATION ON THE DESCENT.
HUH?

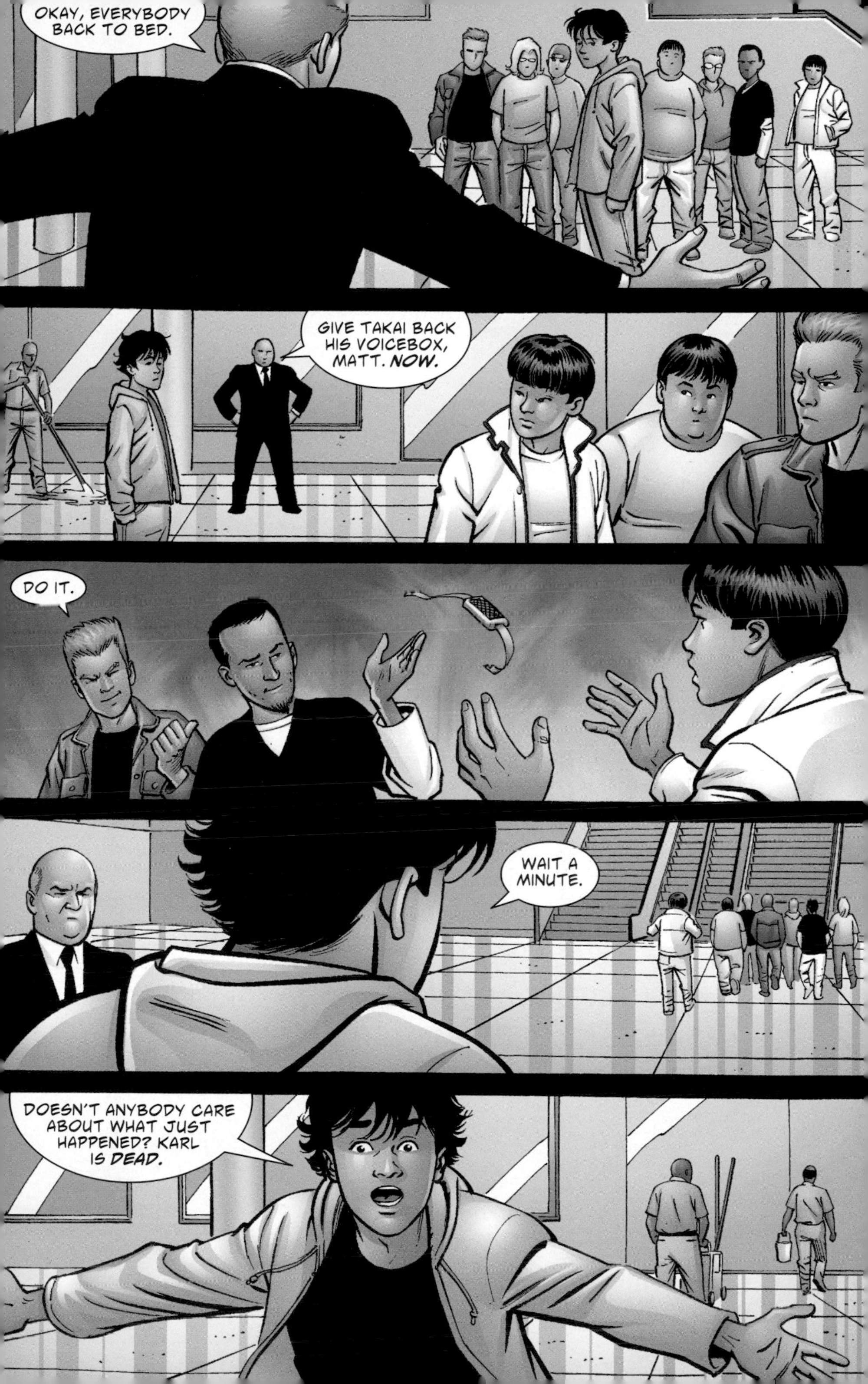
OKAY, EVERYBODY BACK TO BED.
GIVE TAKAI BACK HIS VOICEBOX, MATT. *NOW.*
DO IT.
WAIT A MINUTE.
DOESN'T ANYBODY CARE ABOUT WHAT JUST HAPPENED? KARL IS *DEAD*.

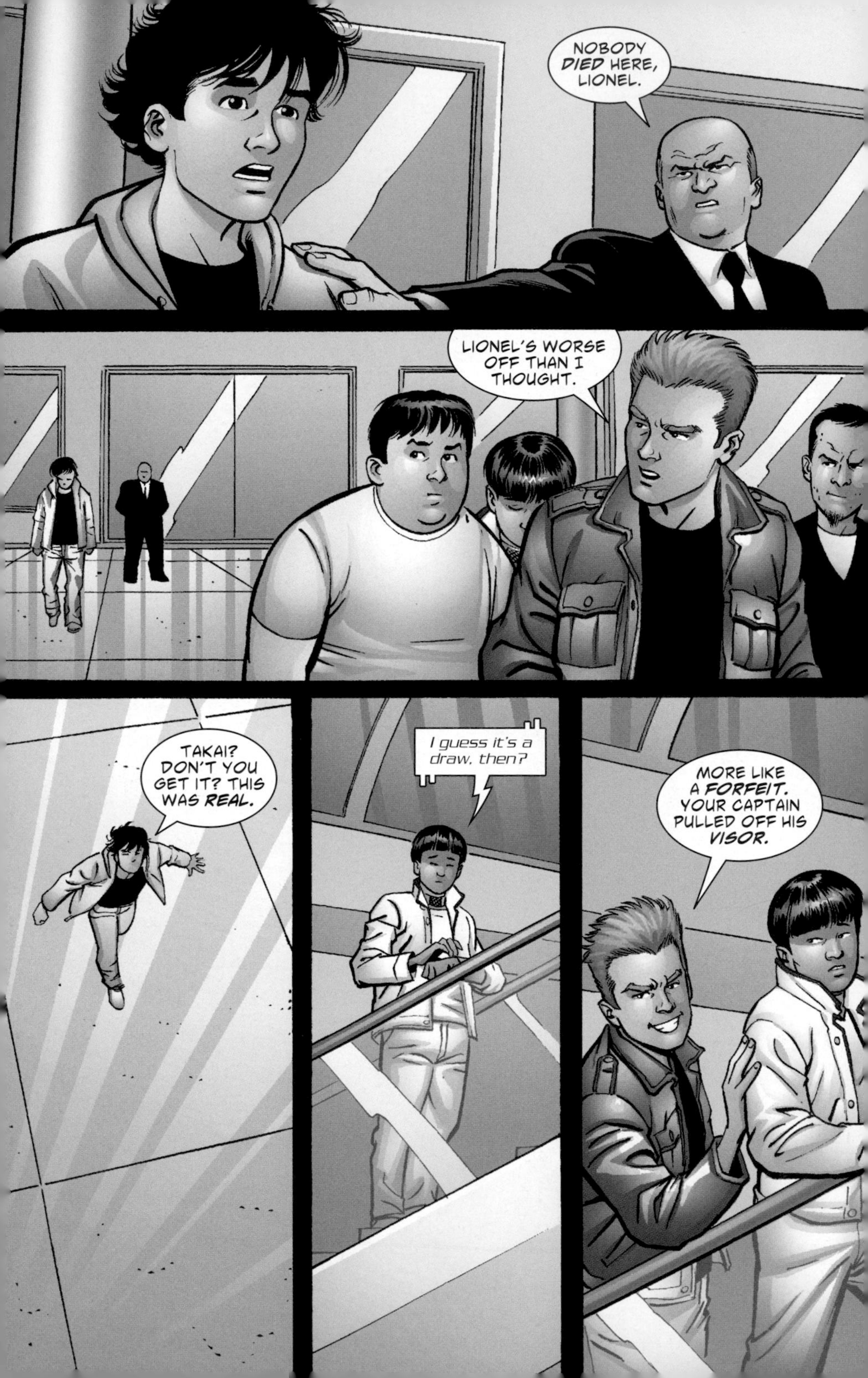
NOBODY DIED HERE, LIONEL.
LIONEL'S WORSE OFF THAN I THOUGHT.
TAKAI? DON'T YOU GET IT? THIS WAS REAL.
I guess it's a draw, then?
MORE LIKE A FORFEIT. YOUR CAPTAIN PULLED OFF HIS VISOR.

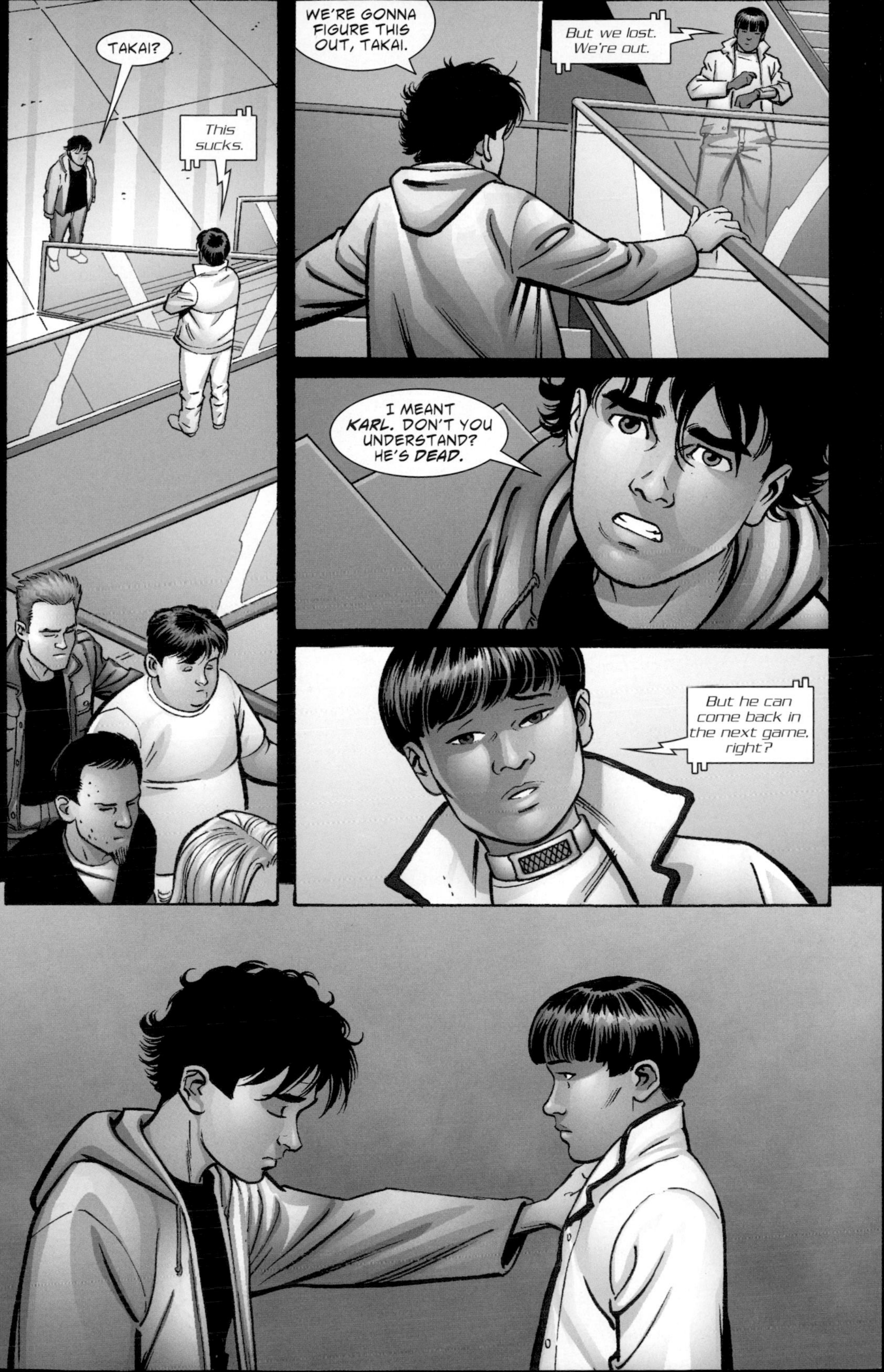
TAKAI?
This sucks.
WE'RE GONNA FIGURE THIS OUT, TAKAI.
But we lost. We're out.
I MEANT *KARL*. DON'T YOU UNDERSTAND? HE'S *DEAD*.
But he can come back in the next game, right?

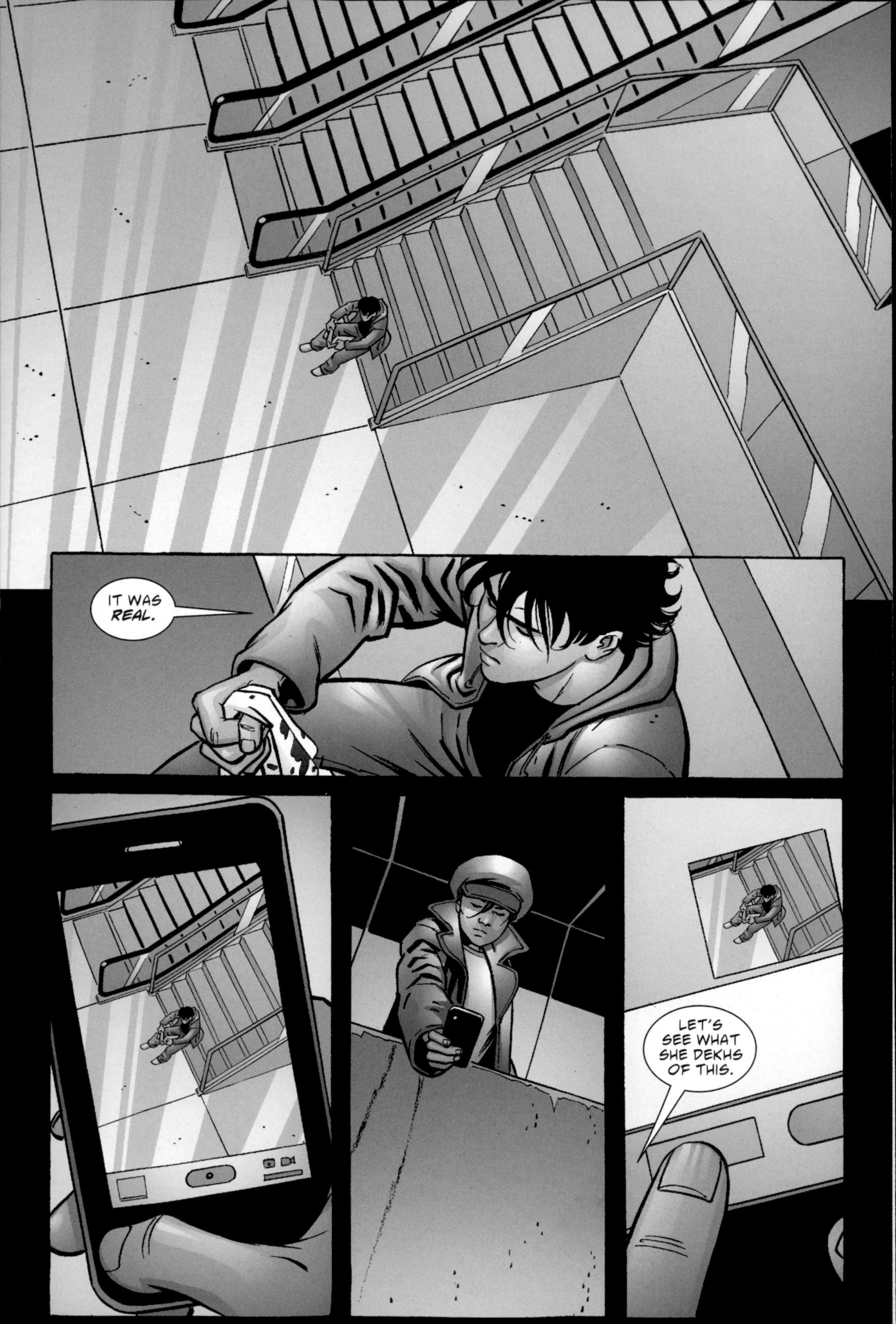
IT WAS REAL.
LET'S SEE WHAT SHE DEKHS OF THIS.

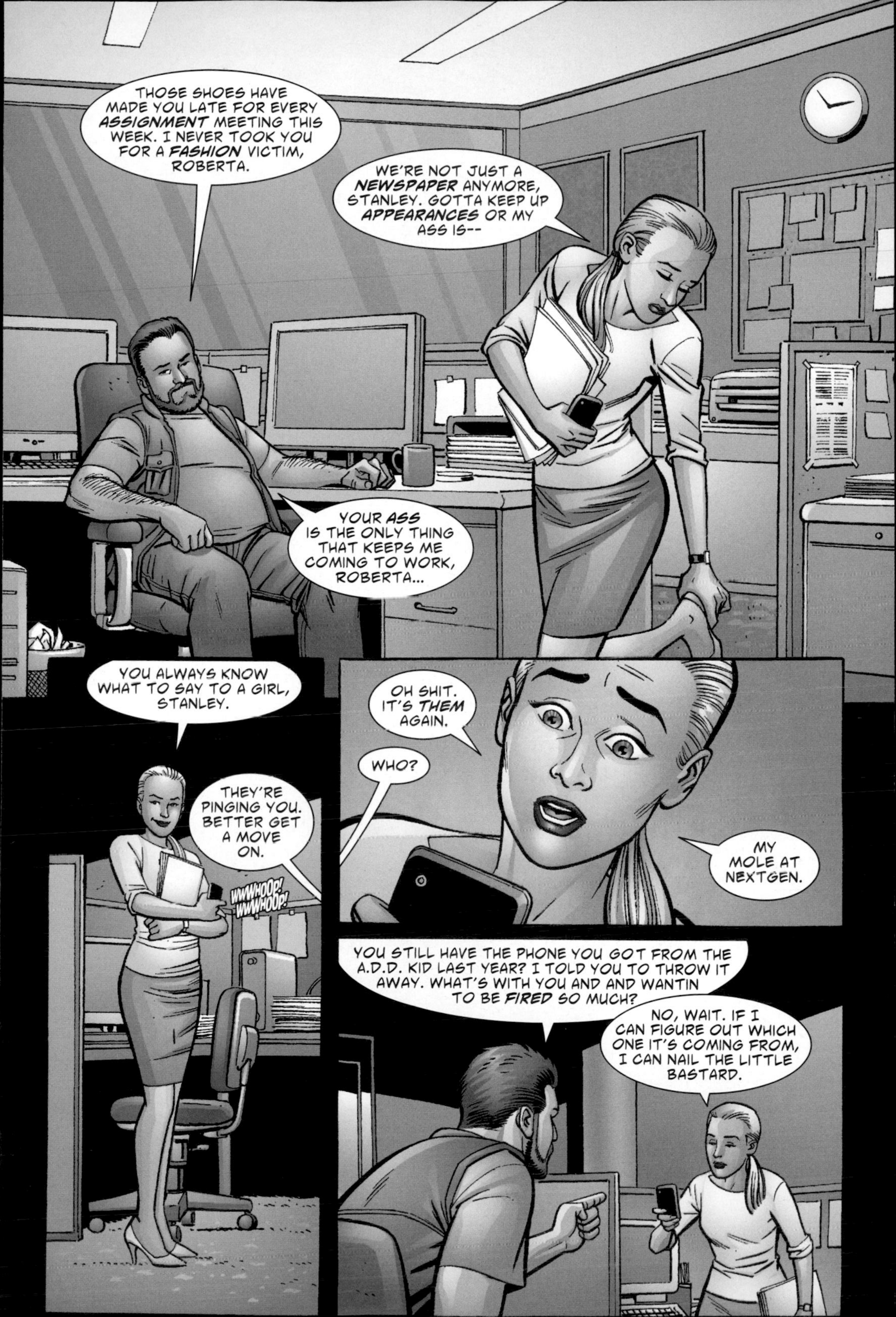
THOSE SHOES HAVE MADE YOU LATE FOR EVERY ASSIGNMENT MEETING THIS WEEK. I NEVER TOOK YOU FOR A FASHION VICTIM, ROBERTA.
WE'RE NOT JUST A NEWSPAPER ANYMORE, STANLEY. GOTTA KEEP UP APPEARANCES OR MY ASS IS--
YOUR ASS IS THE ONLY THING THAT KEEPS ME COMING TO WORK, ROBERTA...
YOU ALWAYS KNOW WHAT TO SAY TO A GIRL, STANLEY.
THEY'RE PINGING YOU. BETTER GET A MOVE ON.
WWWHOOP! WWWHOOP!
OH SHIT. IT'S THEM AGAIN.
WHO?
MY MOLE AT NEXTGEN.
YOU STILL HAVE THE PHONE YOU GOT FROM THE A.D.D. KID LAST YEAR? I TOLD YOU TO THROW IT AWAY. WHAT'S WITH YOU AND AND WANTIN TO BE FIRED SO MUCH?
NO, WAIT. IF I CAN FIGURE OUT WHICH ONE IT'S COMING FROM, I CAN NAIL THE LITTLE BASTARD.

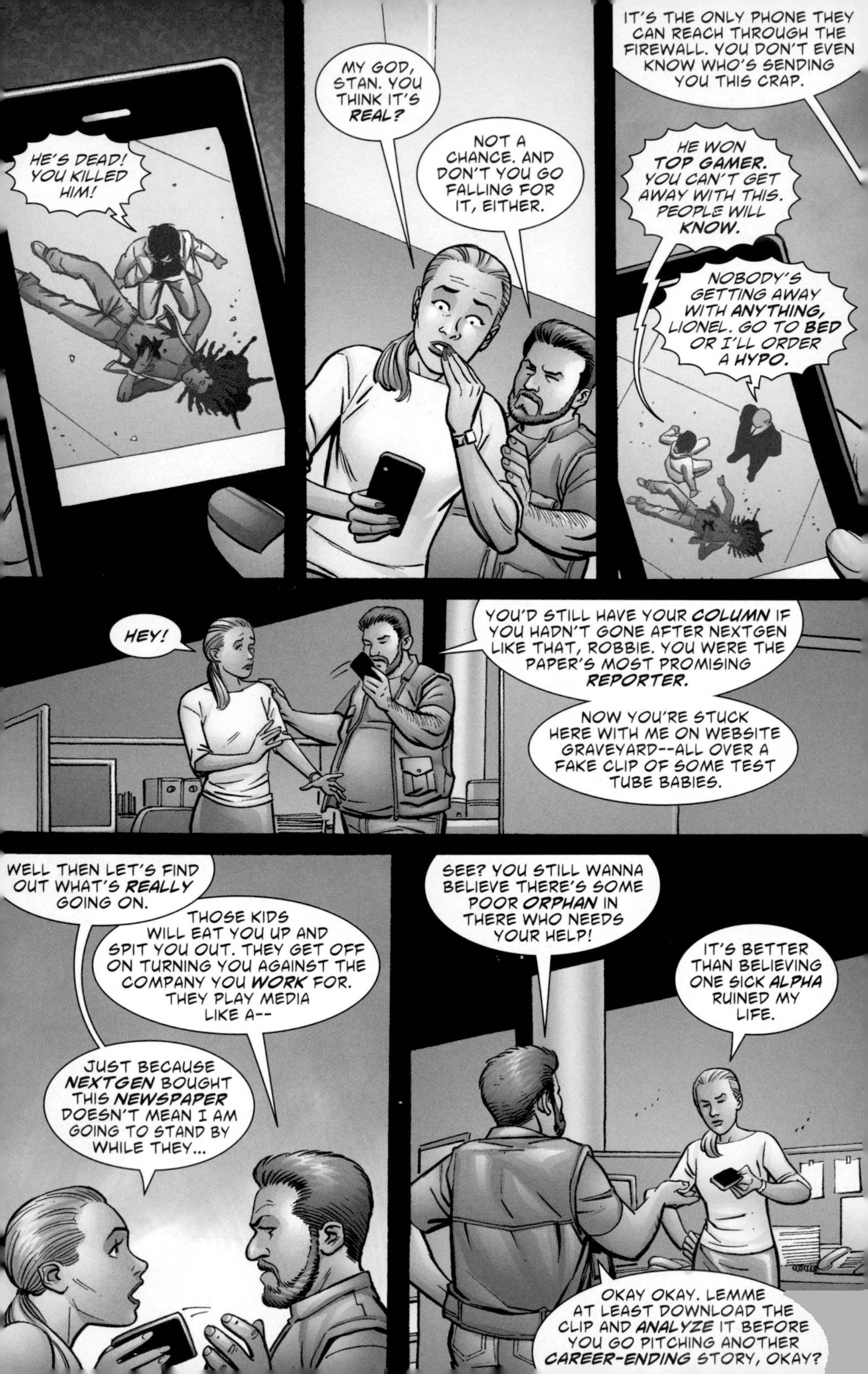
HE'S DEAD! YOU KILLED HIM!
MY GOD, STAN. YOU THINK IT'S REAL?
NOT A CHANCE. AND DON'T YOU GO FALLING FOR IT, EITHER.
IT'S THE ONLY PHONE THEY CAN REACH THROUGH THE FIREWALL. YOU DON'T EVEN KNOW WHO'S SENDING YOU THIS CRAP.
HE WON TOP GAMER. YOU CAN'T GET AWAY WITH THIS. PEOPLE WILL KNOW.
NOBODY'S GETTING AWAY WITH ANYTHING, LIONEL. GO TO BED OR I'LL ORDER A HYPO.
HEY!
YOU'D STILL HAVE YOUR COLUMN IF YOU HADN'T GONE AFTER NEXTGEN LIKE THAT, ROBBIE. YOU WERE THE PAPER'S MOST PROMISING REPORTER.
NOW YOU'RE STUCK HERE WITH ME ON WEBSITE GRAVEYARD--ALL OVER A FAKE CLIP OF SOME TEST TUBE BABIES.
WELL THEN LET'S FIND OUT WHAT'S REALLY GOING ON.
THOSE KIDS WILL EAT YOU UP AND SPIT YOU OUT. THEY GET OFF ON TURNING YOU AGAINST THE COMPANY YOU WORK FOR. THEY PLAY MEDIA LIKE A--
JUST BECAUSE NEXTGEN BOUGHT THIS NEWSPAPER DOESN'T MEAN I AM GOING TO STAND BY WHILE THEY...
SEE? YOU STILL WANNA BELIEVE THERE'S SOME POOR ORPHAN IN THERE WHO NEEDS YOUR HELP!
IT'S BETTER THAN BELIEVING ONE SICK ALPHA RUINED MY LIFE.
OKAY OKAY. LEMME AT LEAST DOWNLOAD THE CLIP AND ANALYZE IT BEFORE YOU GO PITCHING ANOTHER CAREER-ENDING STORY, OKAY?

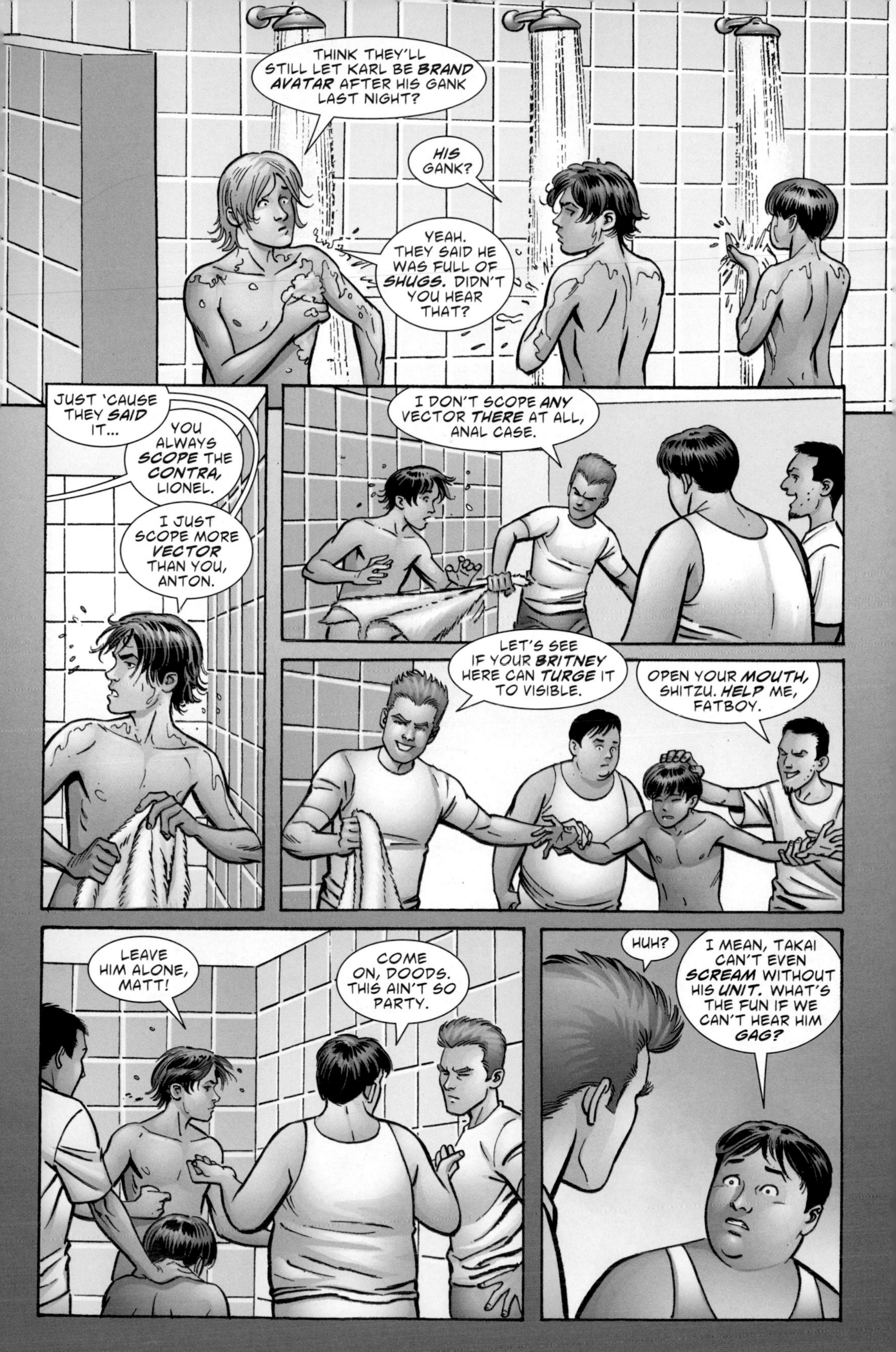
THINK THEY'LL STILL LET KARL BE BRAND AVATAR AFTER HIS GANK LAST NIGHT?
HIS GANK?
YEAH. THEY SAID HE WAS FULL OF SHUGS. DIDN'T YOU HEAR THAT?
JUST 'CAUSE THEY SAID IT...
YOU ALWAYS SCOPE THE CONTRA, LIONEL.
I JUST SCOPE MORE VECTOR THAN YOU, ANTON.
I DON'T SCOPE ANY VECTOR THERE AT ALL, ANAL CASE.
LET'S SEE IF YOUR BRITNEY HERE CAN TURGE IT TO VISIBLE.
OPEN YOUR MOUTH, SHITZU. HELP ME, FATBOY.
LEAVE HIM ALONE, MATT!
COME ON, DOODS. THIS AIN'T SO PARTY.
HUH?
I MEAN, TAKAI CAN'T EVEN SCREAM WITHOUT HIS UNIT. WHAT'S THE FUN IF WE CAN'T HEAR HIM GAG?

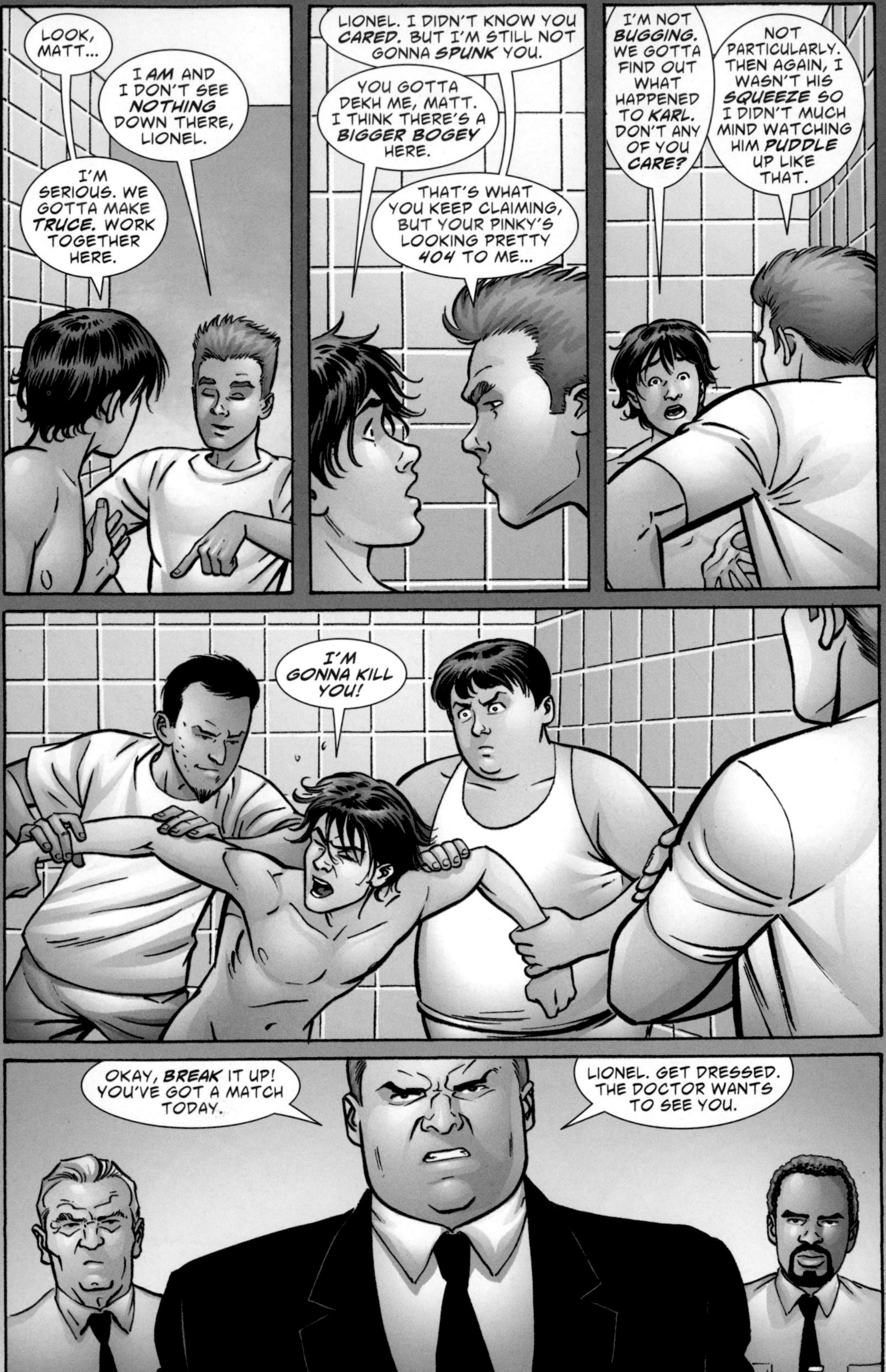
LOOK, MATT...
I AM AND I DON'T SEE NOTHING DOWN THERE, LIONEL.
I'M SERIOUS. WE GOTTA MAKE TRUCE. WORK TOGETHER HERE.
LIONEL. I DIDN'T KNOW YOU CARED. BUT I'M STILL NOT GONNA SPUNK YOU.
YOU GOTTA DEKH ME, MATT. I THINK THERE'S A BIGGER BOGEY HERE.
THAT'S WHAT YOU KEEP CLAIMING, BUT YOUR PINKY'S LOOKING PRETTY 404 TO ME...
I'M NOT BUGGING. WE GOTTA FIND OUT WHAT HAPPENED TO KARL. DON'T ANY OF YOU CARE?
NOT PARTICULARLY. THEN AGAIN, I WASN'T HIS SQUEEZE SO I DIDN'T MUCH MIND WATCHING HIM PUDDLE UP LIKE THAT.
I'M GONNA KILL YOU!
OKAY, BREAK IT UP! YOU'VE GOT A MATCH TODAY.
LIONEL. GET DRESSED. THE DOCTOR WANTS TO SEE YOU.

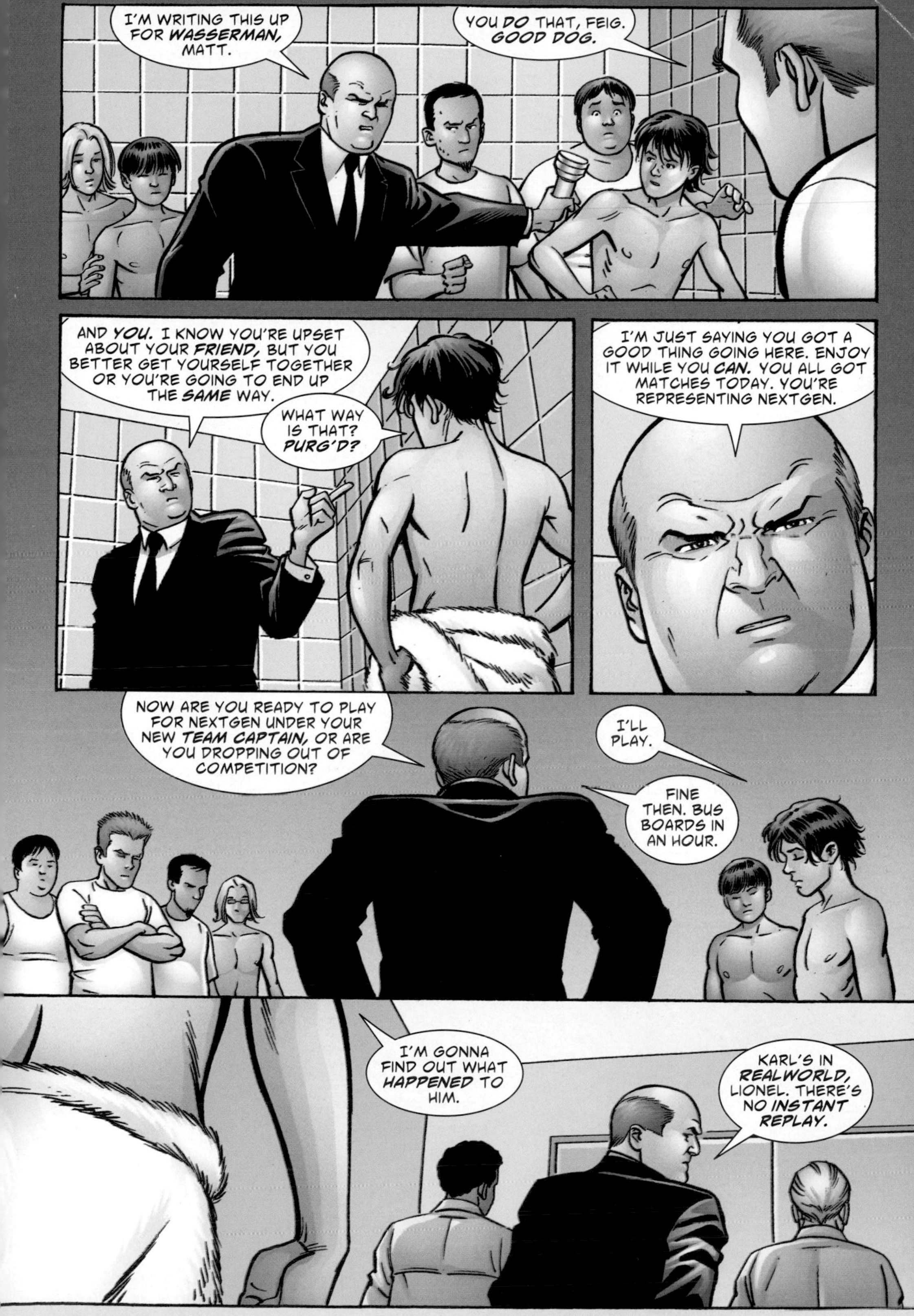
I'M WRITING THIS UP FOR WASSERMAN, MATT.
YOU DO THAT, FEIG. GOOD DOG.
AND YOU. I KNOW YOU'RE UPSET ABOUT YOUR FRIEND, BUT YOU BETTER GET YOURSELF TOGETHER OR YOU'RE GOING TO END UP THE SAME WAY.
WHAT WAY IS THAT? PURG'D?
I'M JUST SAYING YOU GOT A GOOD THING GOING HERE. ENJOY IT WHILE YOU CAN. YOU ALL GOT MATCHES TODAY. YOU'RE REPRESENTING NEXTGEN.
NOW ARE YOU READY TO PLAY FOR NEXTGEN UNDER YOUR NEW TEAM CAPTAIN, OR ARE YOU DROPPING OUT OF COMPETITION?
I'LL PLAY.
FINE THEN. BUS BOARDS IN AN HOUR.
I'M GONNA FIND OUT WHAT HAPPENED TO HIM.
KARL'S IN REALWORLD, LIONEL. THERE'S NO INSTANT REPLAY.

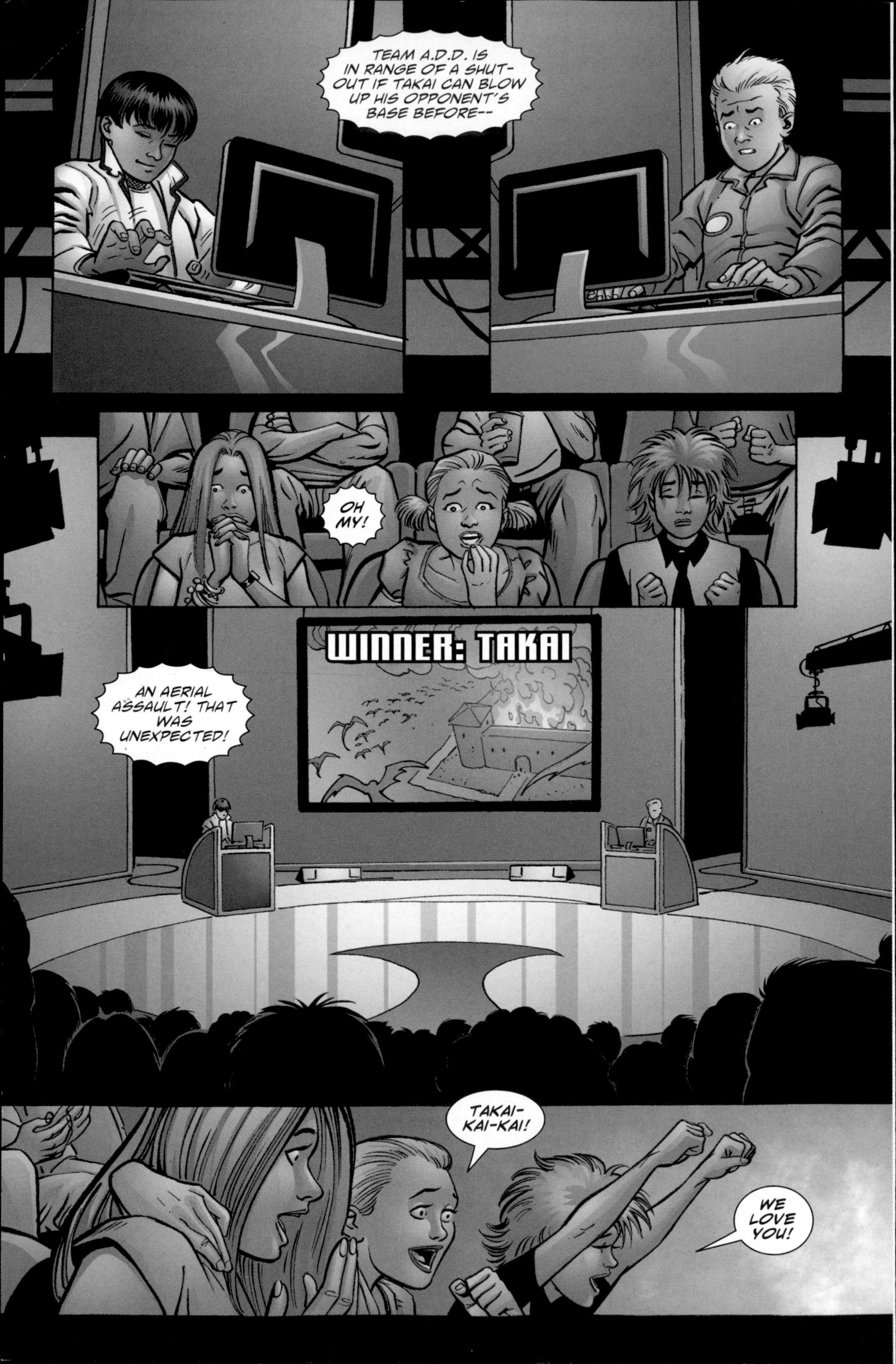
TEAM A.D.D. IS IN RANGE OF A SHUT-OUT IF TAKAI CAN BLOW UP HIS OPPONENT'S BASE BEFORE--
OH MY!
WINNER: TAKAI
AN AERIAL ASSAULT! THAT WAS UNEXPECTED!
TAKAI-KAI-KAI!
WE LOVE YOU!

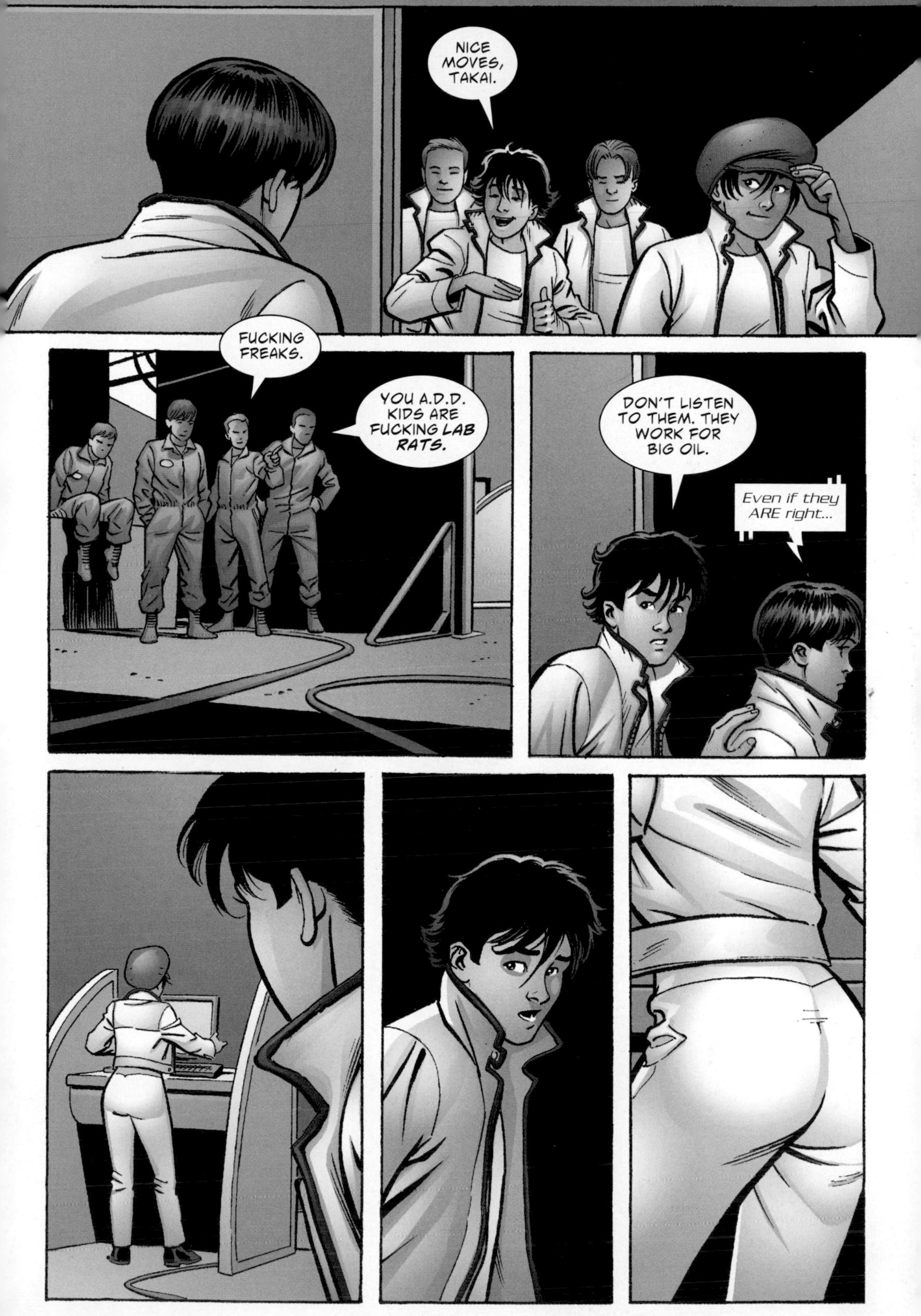
NICE MOVES, TAKAI.
FUCKING FREAKS.
YOU A.D.D. KIDS ARE FUCKING LAB RATS.
DON'T LISTEN TO THEM. THEY WORK FOR BIG OIL.
Even if they ARE right...

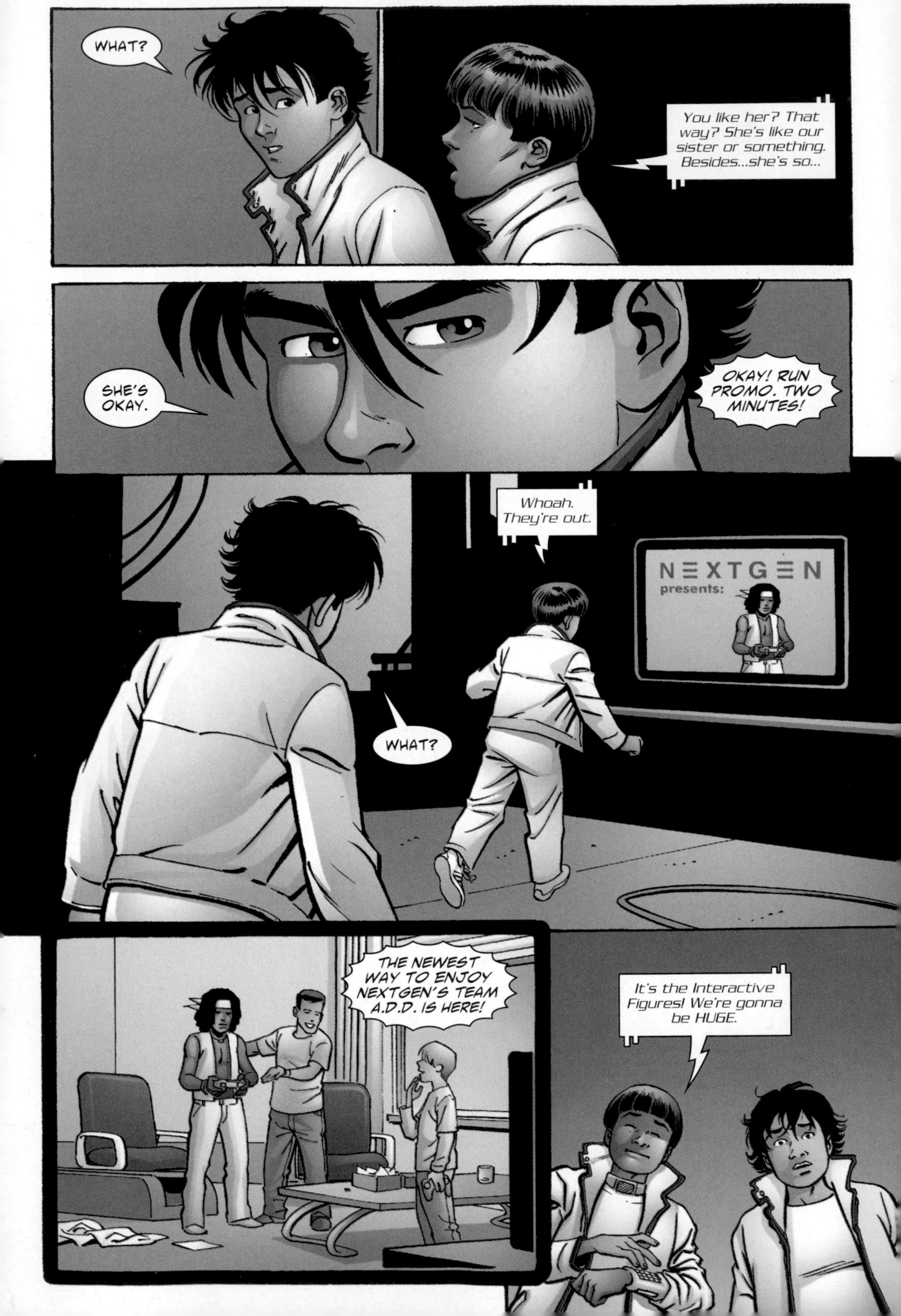
WHAT?
You like her? That way? She's like our sister or something. Besides...she's so...
SHE'S OKAY.
OKAY! RUN PROMO. TWO MINUTES!
Whoah. They're out.
NEXTGEN
presents:
WHAT?
THE NEWEST WAY TO ENJOY NEXTGEN'S TEAM A.D.D. IS HERE!
It's the Interactive Figures! We're gonna be HUGE.

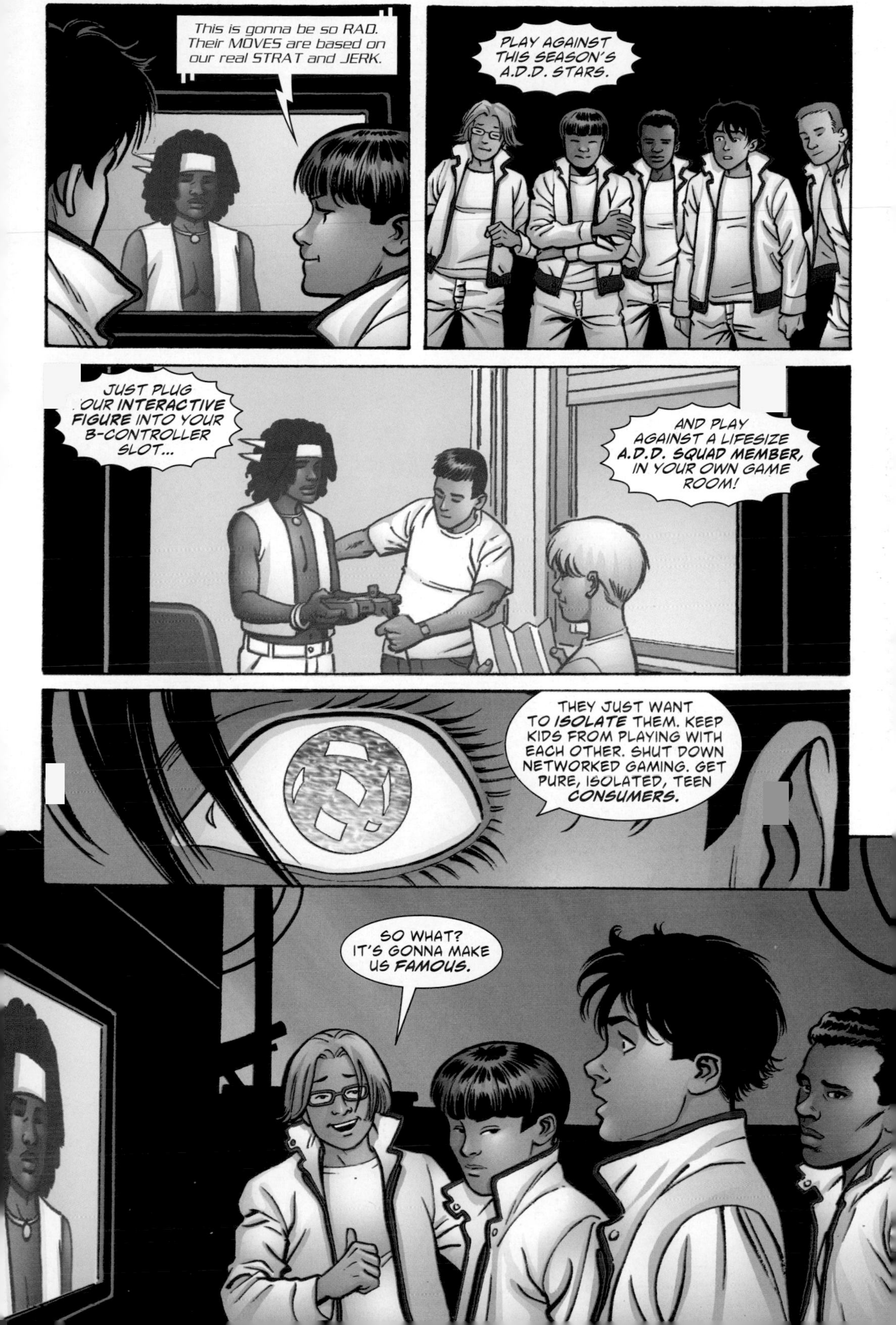
This is gonna be so RAD. Their MOVES are based on our real STRAT and JERK.
PLAY AGAINST THIS SEASON'S A.D.D. STARS.
JUST PLUG YOUR INTERACTIVE FIGURE INTO YOUR B-CONTROLLER SLOT...
AND PLAY AGAINST A LIFESIZE A.D.D. SQUAD MEMBER, IN YOUR OWN GAME ROOM!
THEY JUST WANT TO ISOLATE THEM. KEEP KIDS FROM PLAYING WITH EACH OTHER. SHUT DOWN NETWORKED GAMING. GET PURE, ISOLATED, TEEN CONSUMERS.
SO WHAT? IT'S GONNA MAKE US FAMOUS.

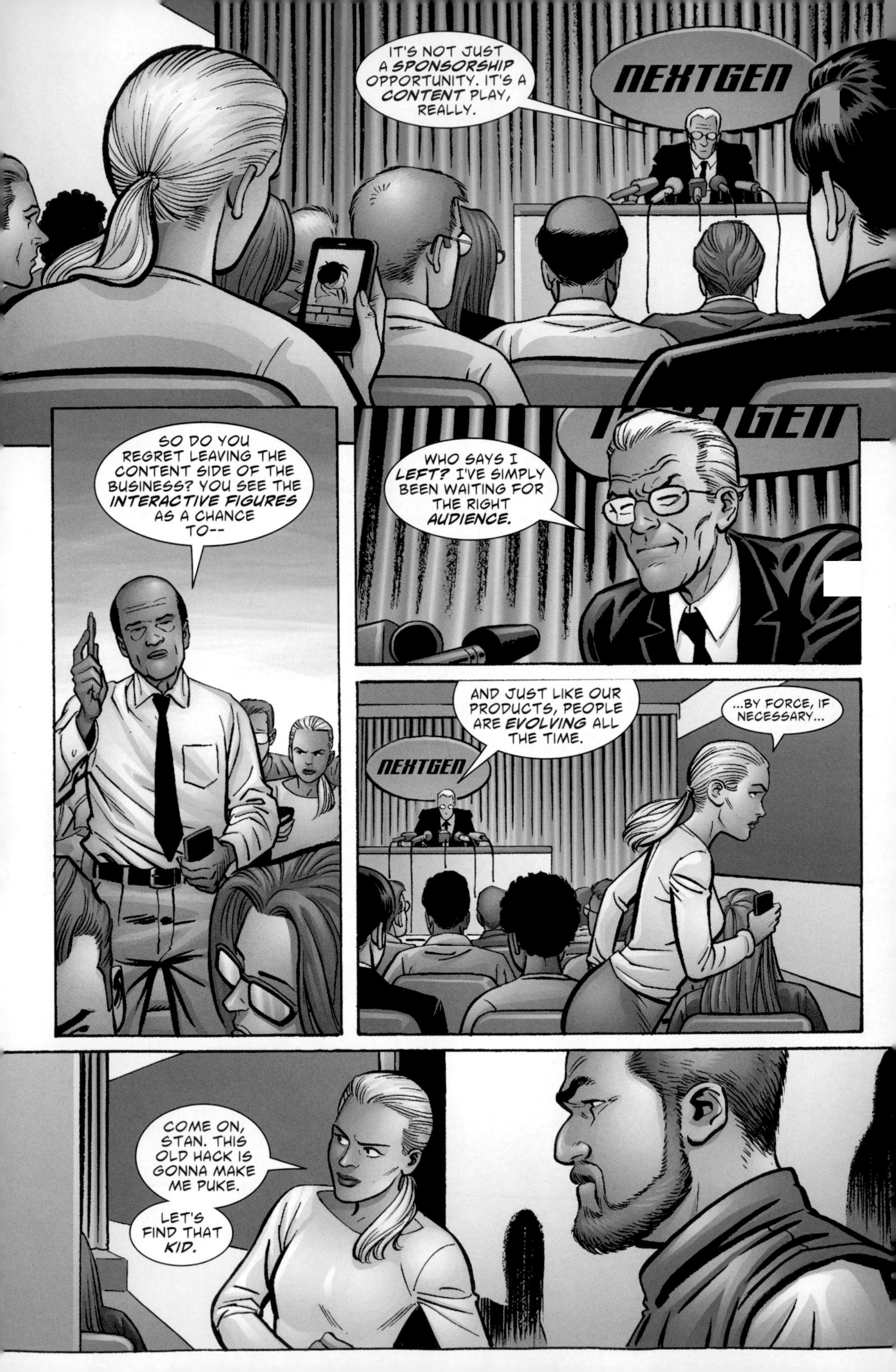
IT'S NOT JUST A SPONSORSHIP OPPORTUNITY. IT'S A CONTENT PLAY, REALLY.
NEXTGEN
SO DO YOU REGRET LEAVING THE CONTENT SIDE OF THE BUSINESS? YOU SEE THE INTERACTIVE FIGURES AS A CHANCE TO--
WHO SAYS I LEFT? I'VE SIMPLY BEEN WAITING FOR THE RIGHT AUDIENCE.
AND JUST LIKE OUR PRODUCTS, PEOPLE ARE EVOLVING ALL THE TIME.
NEXTGEN
...BY FORCE, IF NECESSARY...
COME ON, STAN. THIS OLD HACK IS GONNA MAKE ME PUKE.
LET'S FIND THAT KID.

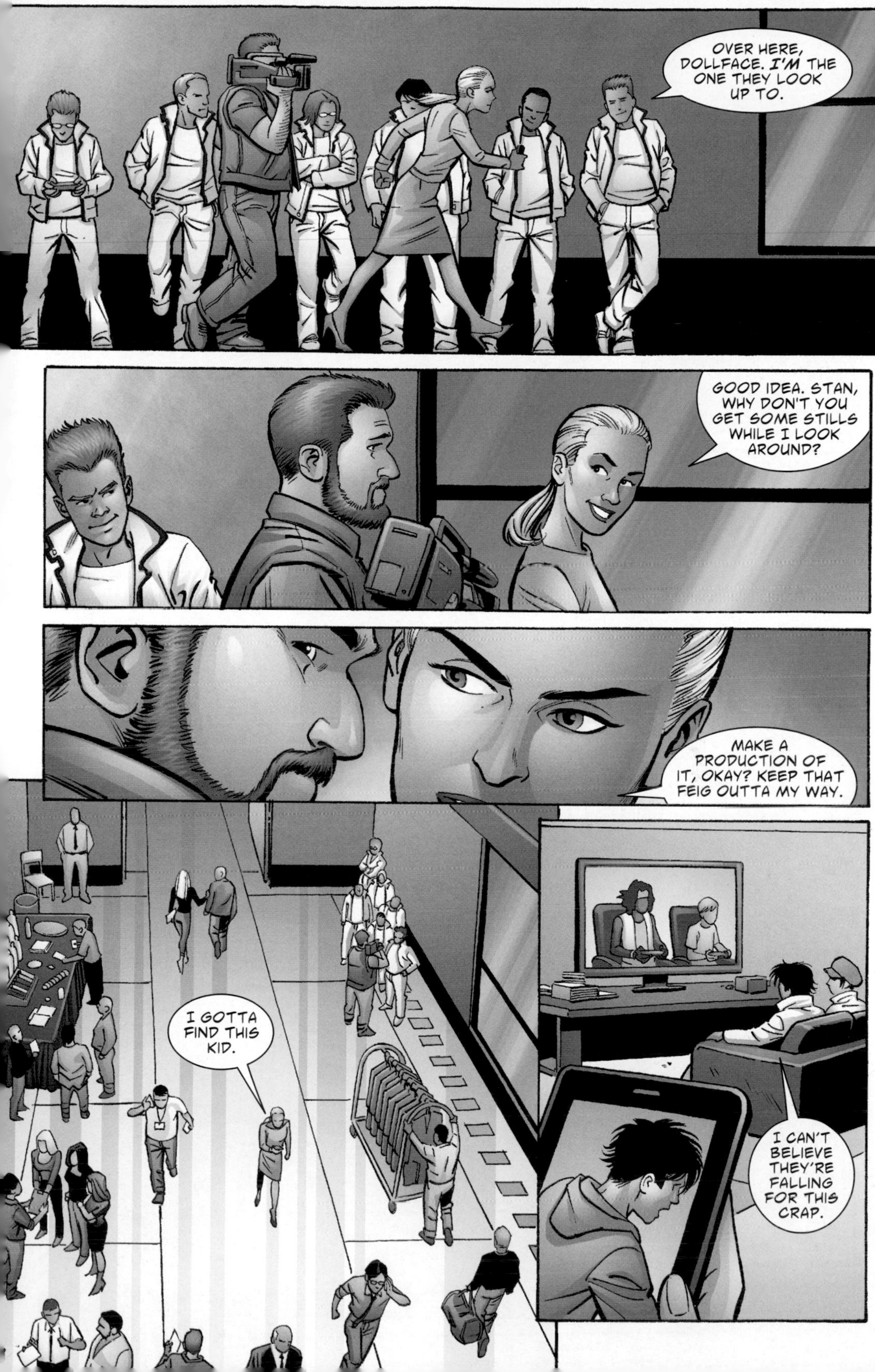
OVER HERE, DOLLFACE. I'M THE ONE THEY LOOK UP TO.
GOOD IDEA. STAN, WHY DON'T YOU GET SOME STILLS WHILE I LOOK AROUND?
MAKE A PRODUCTION OF IT, OKAY? KEEP THAT FEIG OUTTA MY WAY.
I GOTTA FIND THIS KID.
I CAN'T BELIEVE THEY'RE FALLING FOR THIS CRAP.

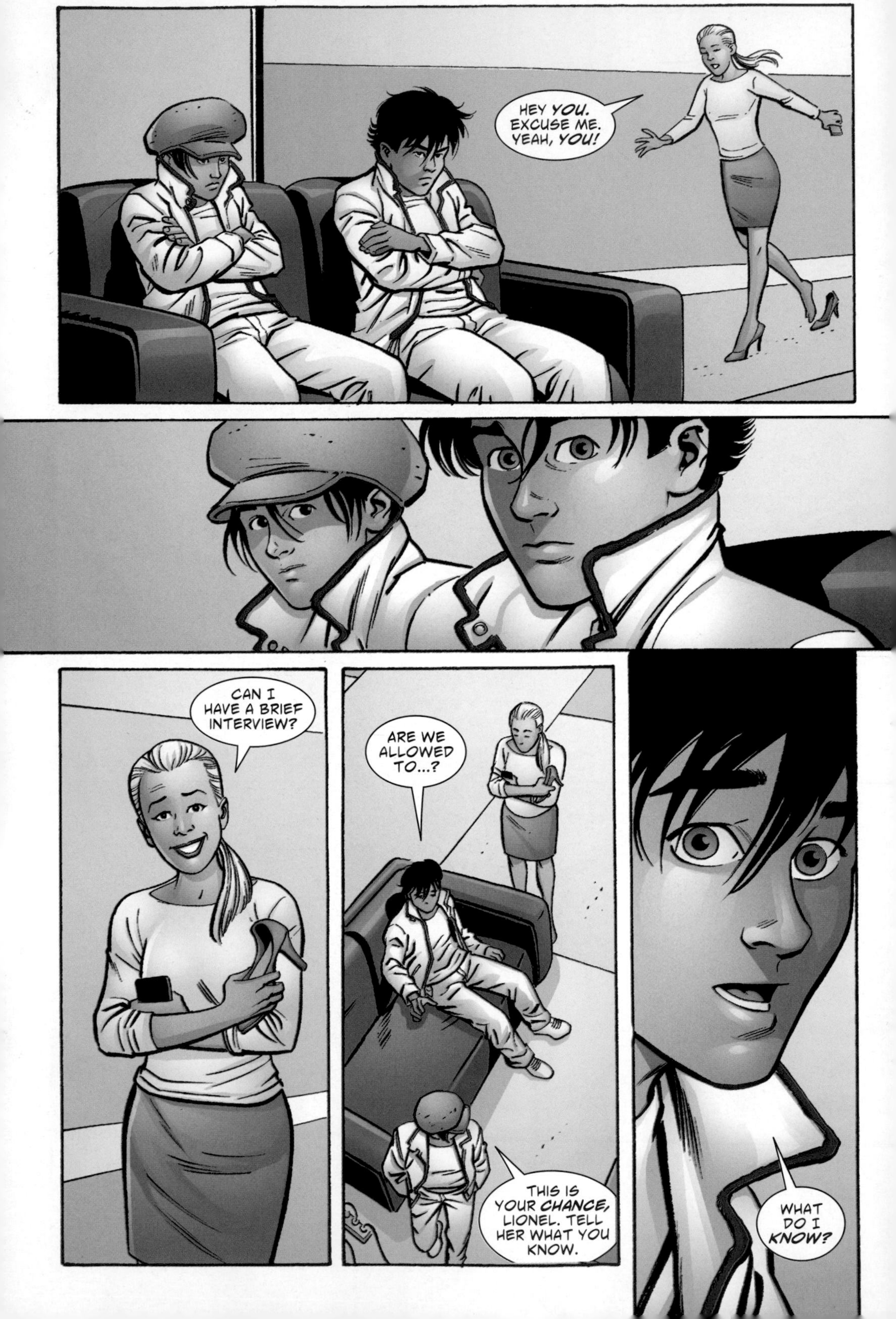
HEY YOU. EXCUSE ME. YEAH, YOU!
CAN I HAVE A BRIEF INTERVIEW?
ARE WE ALLOWED TO...?
THIS IS YOUR CHANCE, LIONEL. TELL HER WHAT YOU KNOW.
WHAT DO I KNOW?

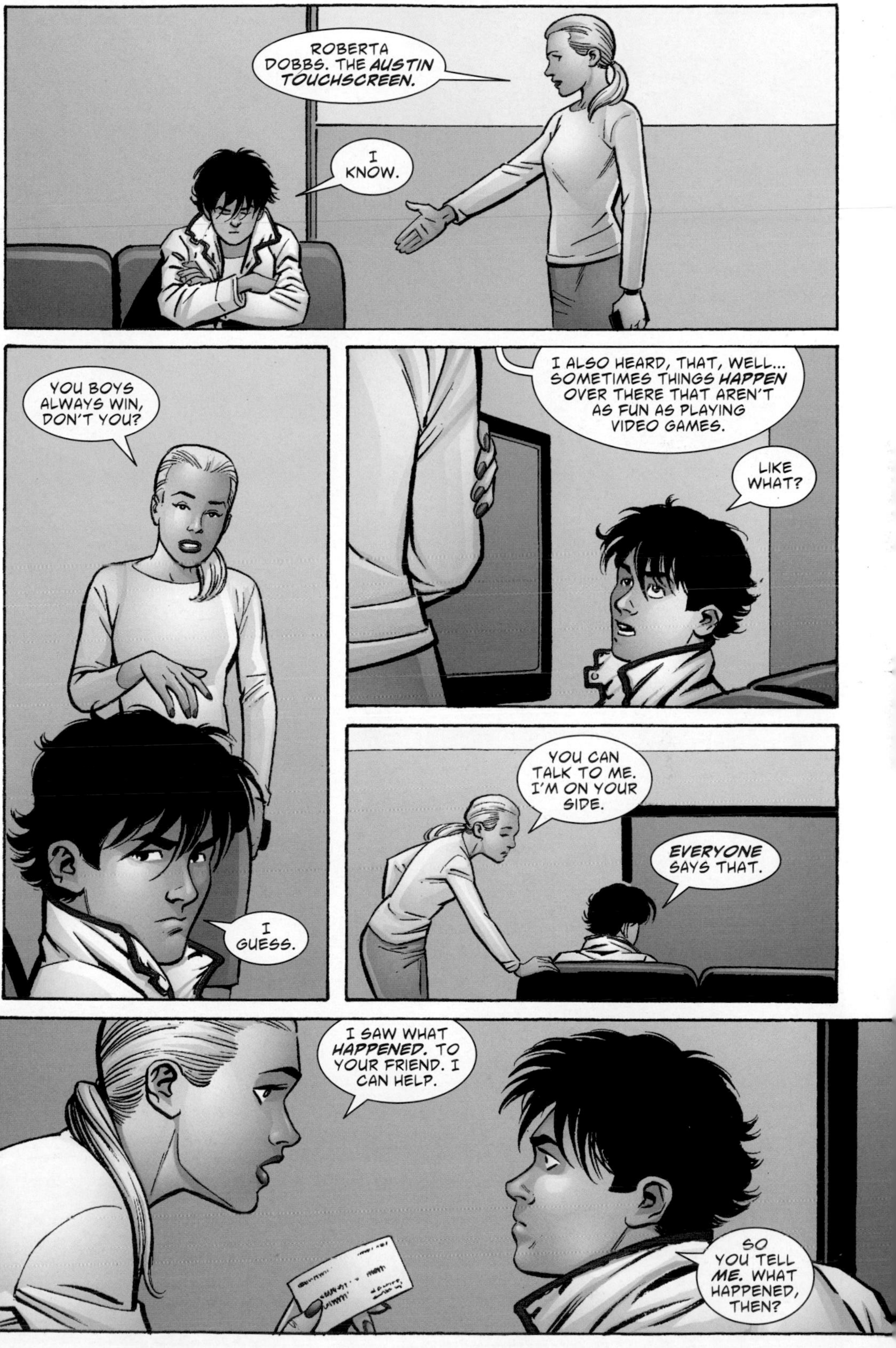
ROBERTA DOBBS. THE AUSTIN TOUCHSCREEN.
I KNOW.
YOU BOYS ALWAYS WIN, DON'T YOU?
I GUESS.
I ALSO HEARD, THAT, WELL... SOMETIMES THINGS HAPPEN OVER THERE THAT AREN'T AS FUN AS PLAYING VIDEO GAMES.
LIKE WHAT?
YOU CAN TALK TO ME. I'M ON YOUR SIDE.
EVERYONE SAYS THAT.
I SAW WHAT HAPPENED. TO YOUR FRIEND. I CAN HELP.
SO YOU TELL ME. WHAT HAPPENED, THEN?

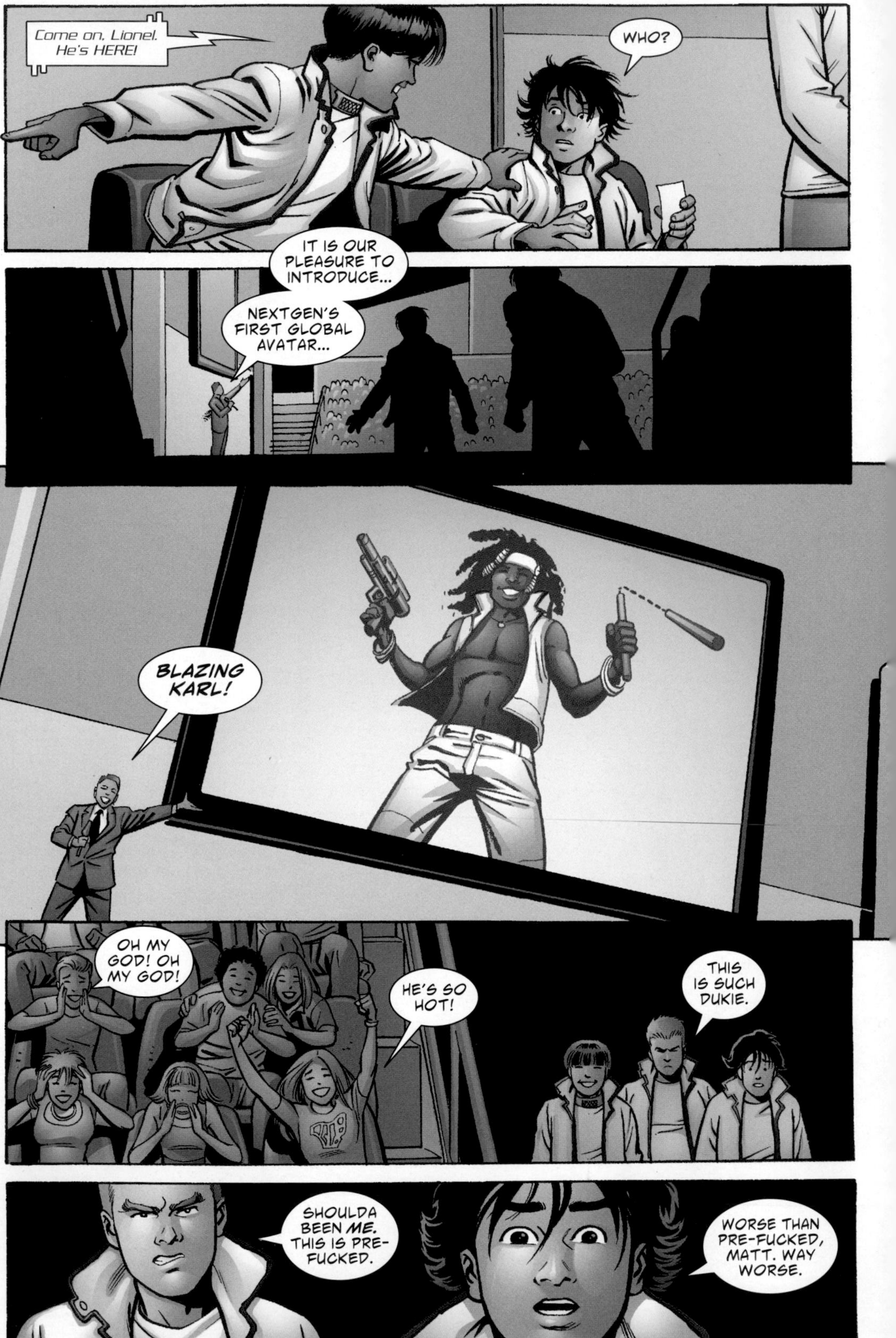
Come on, Lionel. He's HERE!
WHO?
IT IS OUR PLEASURE TO INTRODUCE...
NEXTGEN'S FIRST GLOBAL AVATAR...
BLAZING KARL!
OH MY GOD! OH MY GOD!
HE'S SO HOT!
THIS IS SUCH DUKIE.
SHOULDA BEEN ME. THIS IS PRE-FUCKED.
WORSE THAN PRE-FUCKED, MATT. WAY WORSE.

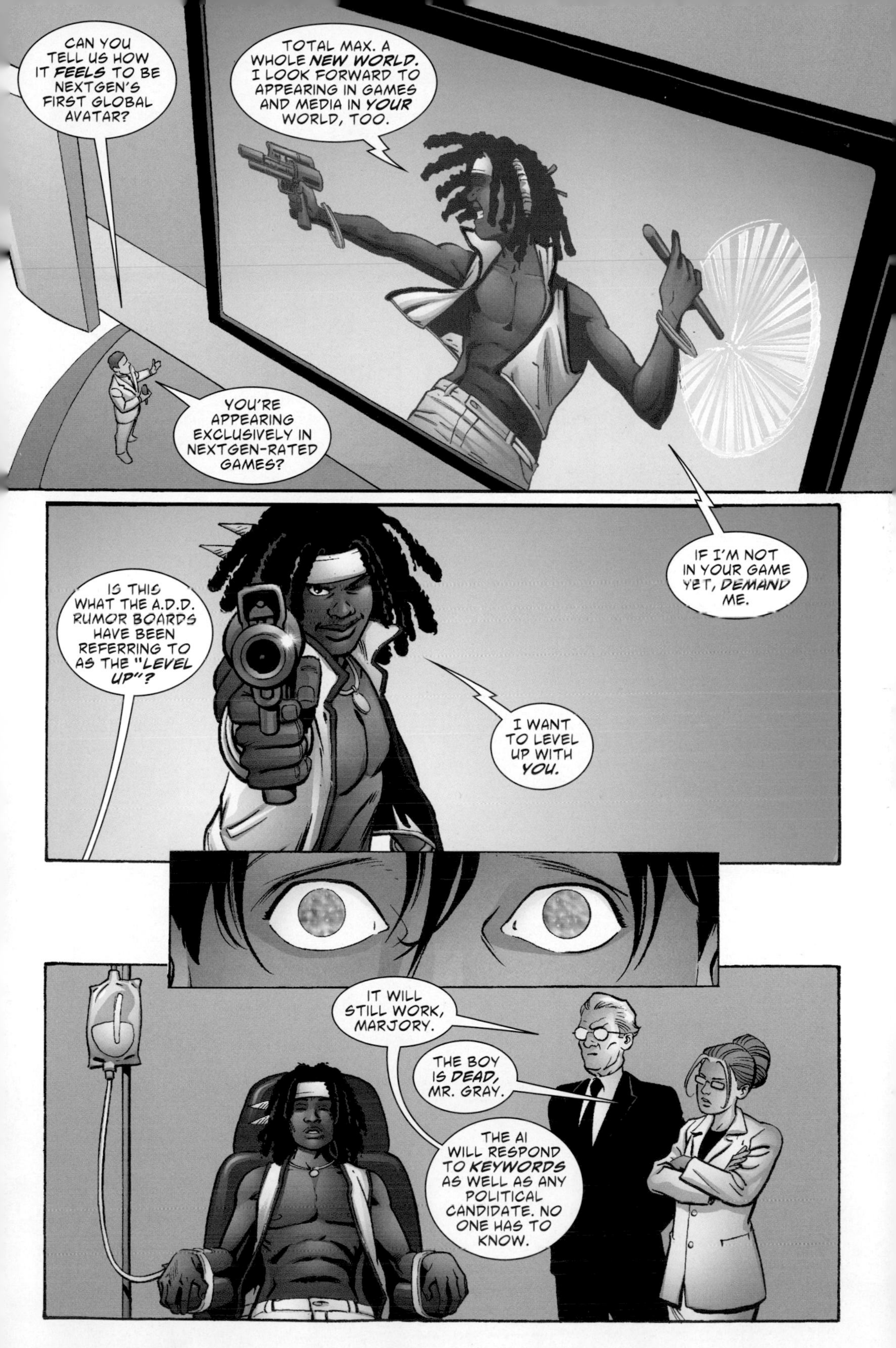

CAN YOU TELL US HOW IT FEELS TO BE NEXTGEN'S FIRST GLOBAL AVATAR?
TOTAL MAX. A WHOLE NEW WORLD. I LOOK FORWARD TO APPEARING IN GAMES AND MEDIA IN YOUR WORLD, TOO.
YOU'RE APPEARING EXCLUSIVELY IN NEXTGEN-RATED GAMES?
IF I'M NOT IN YOUR GAME YET, DEMAND ME.
IS THIS WHAT THE A.D.D. RUMOR BOARDS HAVE BEEN REFERRING TO AS THE "LEVEL UP"?
I WANT TO LEVEL UP WITH YOU.
IT WILL STILL WORK, MARJORY.
THE BOY IS DEAD, MR. GRAY.
THE AI WILL RESPOND TO KEYWORDS AS WELL AS ANY POLITICAL CANDIDATE. NO ONE HAS TO KNOW.

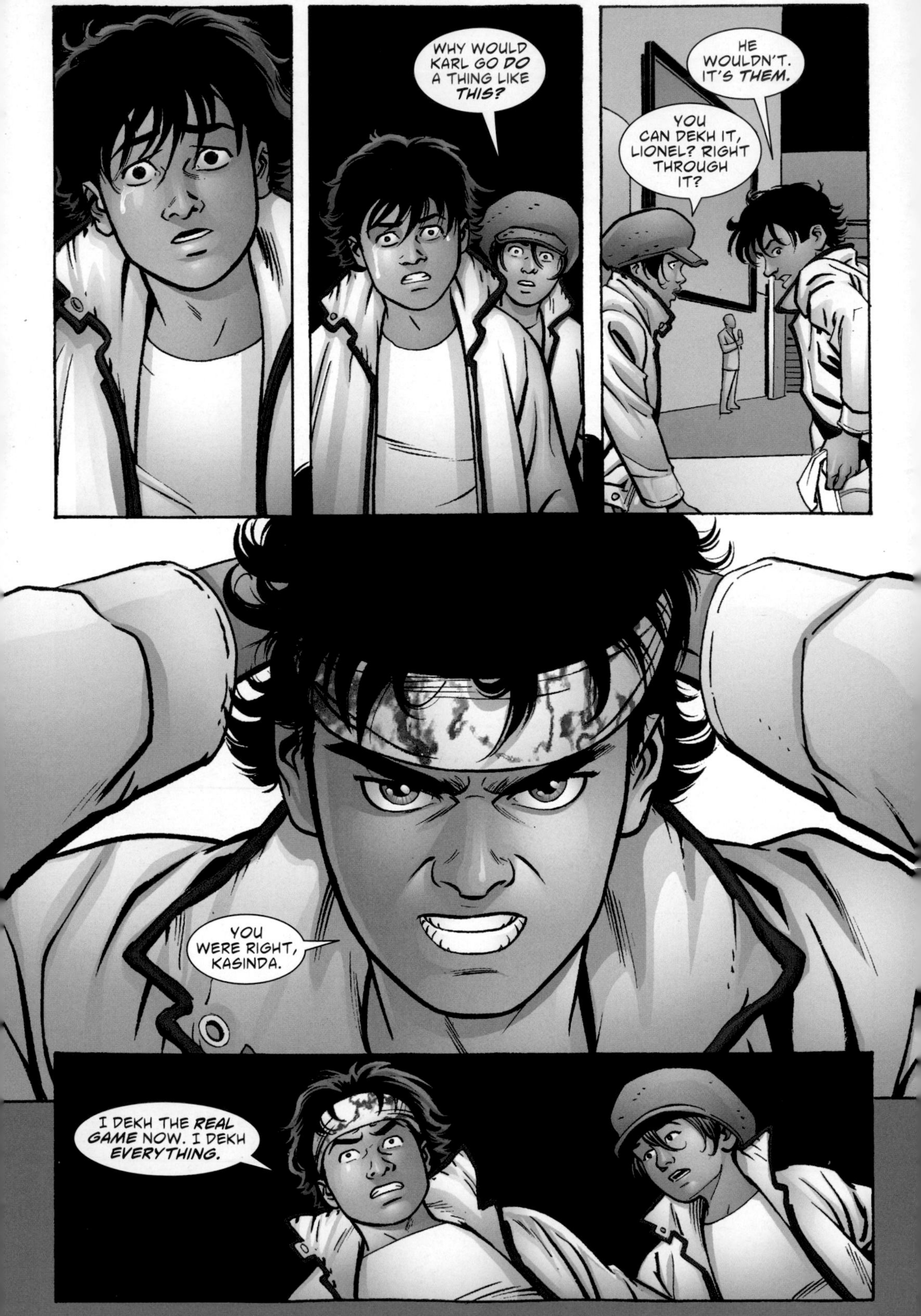
WHY WOULD KARL GO DO A THING LIKE THIS?
HE WOULDN'T. IT'S THEM.
YOU CAN DEKH IT, LIONEL? RIGHT THROUGH IT?
YOU WERE RIGHT, KASINDA.
I DEKH THE REAL GAME NOW. I DEKH EVERYTHING.

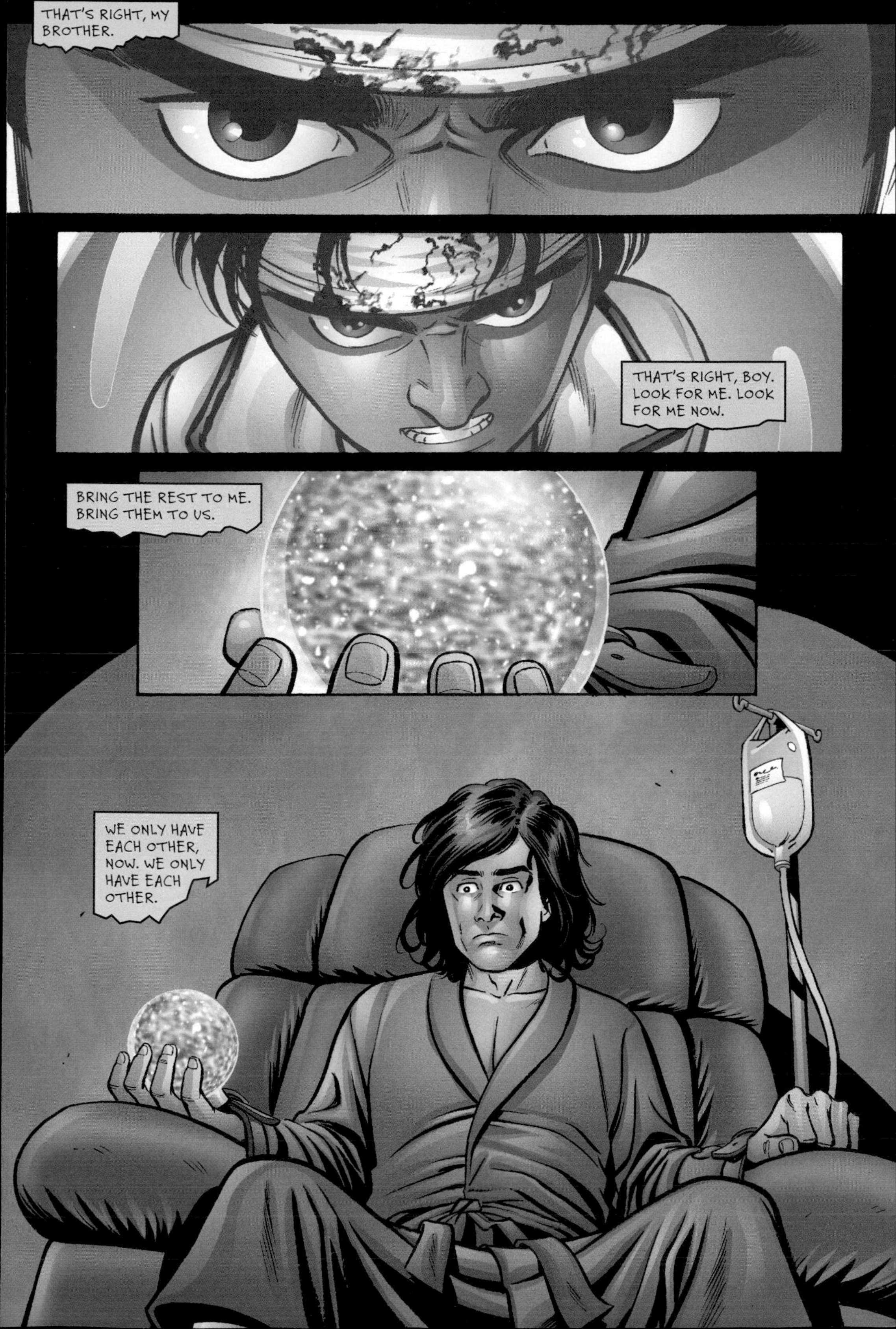
THAT'S RIGHT, MY BROTHER.
THAT'S RIGHT, BOY. LOOK FOR ME. LOOK FOR ME NOW.
BRING THE REST TO ME. BRING THEM TO US.
WE ONLY HAVE EACH OTHER, NOW. WE ONLY HAVE EACH OTHER.

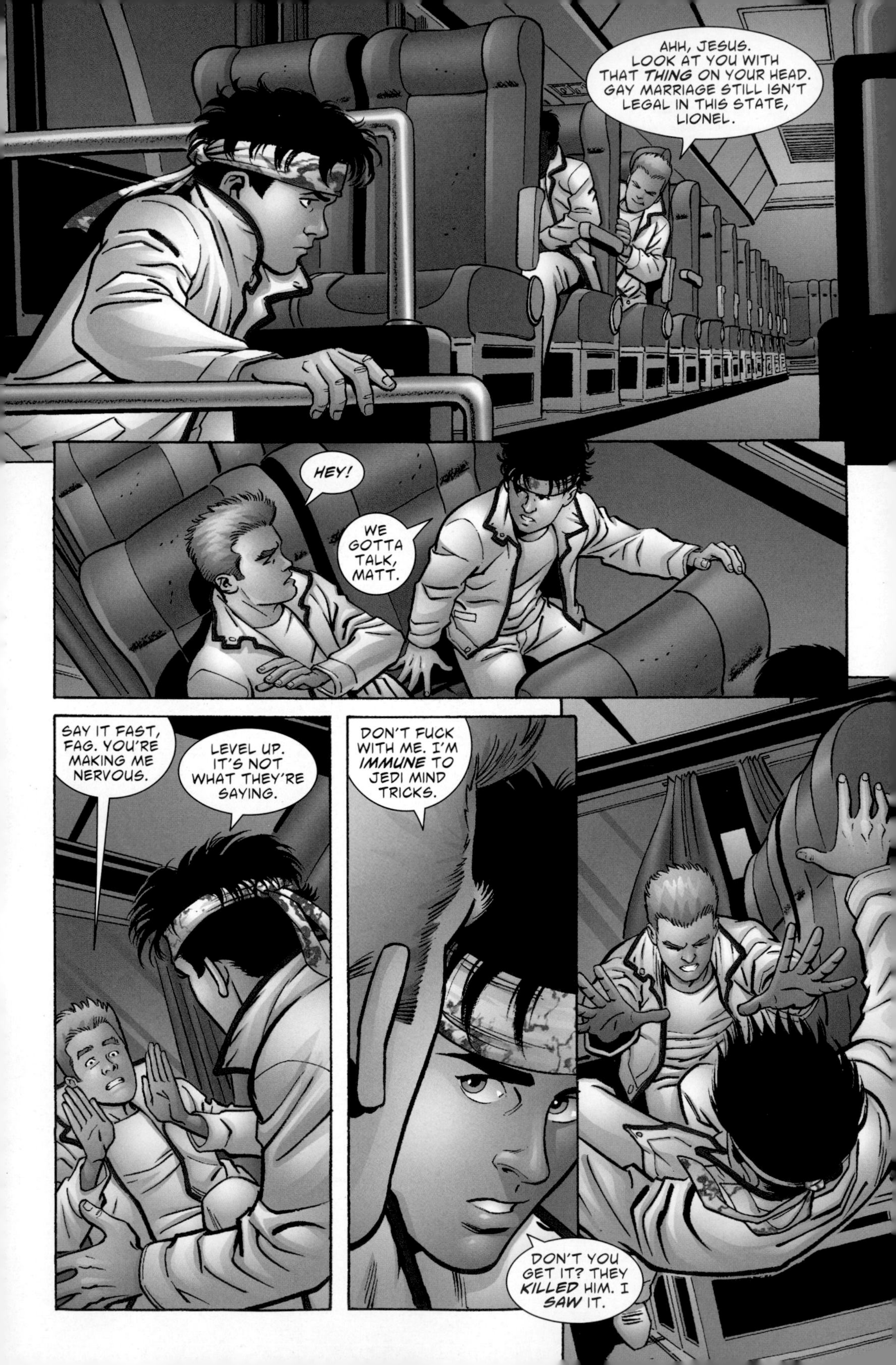
AHH, JESUS. LOOK AT YOU WITH THAT THING ON YOUR HEAD. GAY MARRIAGE STILL ISN'T LEGAL IN THIS STATE, LIONEL.
HEY!
WE GOTTA TALK, MATT.
SAY IT FAST, FAG. YOU'RE MAKING ME NERVOUS.
LEVEL UP. IT'S NOT WHAT THEY'RE SAYING.
DON'T FUCK WITH ME. I'M IMMUNE TO JEDI MIND TRICKS.
DON'T YOU GET IT? THEY KILLED HIM. I SAW IT.

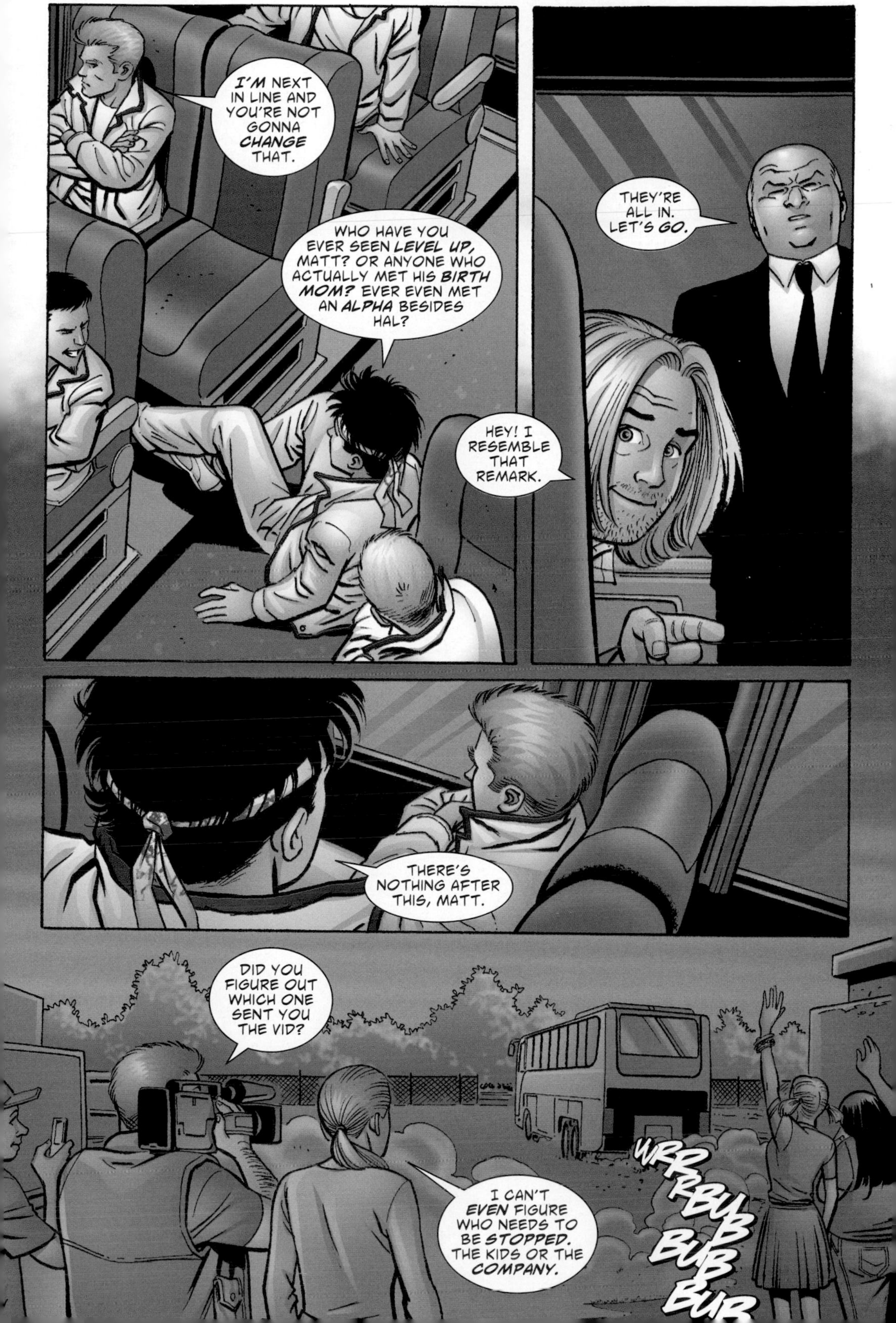
I'M NEXT IN LINE AND YOU'RE NOT GONNA CHANGE THAT.
WHO HAVE YOU EVER SEEN LEVEL UP, MATT? OR ANYONE WHO ACTUALLY MET HIS BIRTH MOM? EVER EVEN MET AN ALPHA BESIDES HAL?
THEY'RE ALL IN. LET'S GO.
HEY! I RESEMBLE THAT REMARK.
THERE'S NOTHING AFTER THIS, MATT.
DID YOU FIGURE OUT WHICH ONE SENT YOU THE VID?
I CAN'T EVEN FIGURE WHO NEEDS TO BE STOPPED. THE KIDS OR THE COMPANY.
WRRBUB BUB BUB

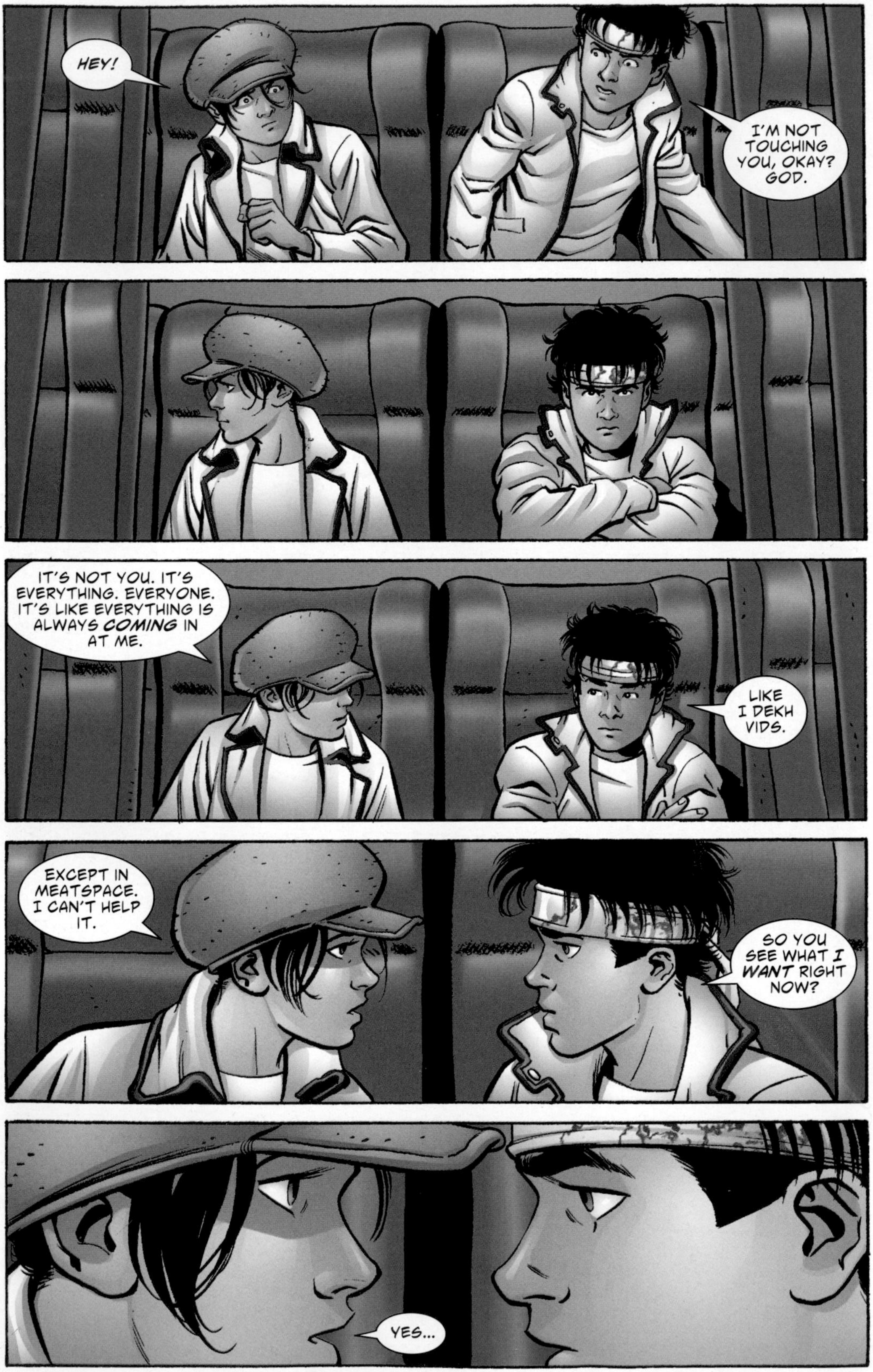
HEY!
I'M NOT TOUCHING YOU, OKAY? GOD.
IT'S NOT YOU. IT'S EVERYTHING. EVERYONE. IT'S LIKE EVERYTHING IS ALWAYS COMING IN AT ME.
LIKE I DEKH VIDS.
EXCEPT IN MEATSPACE. I CAN'T HELP IT.
SO YOU SEE WHAT I WANT RIGHT NOW?
YES...

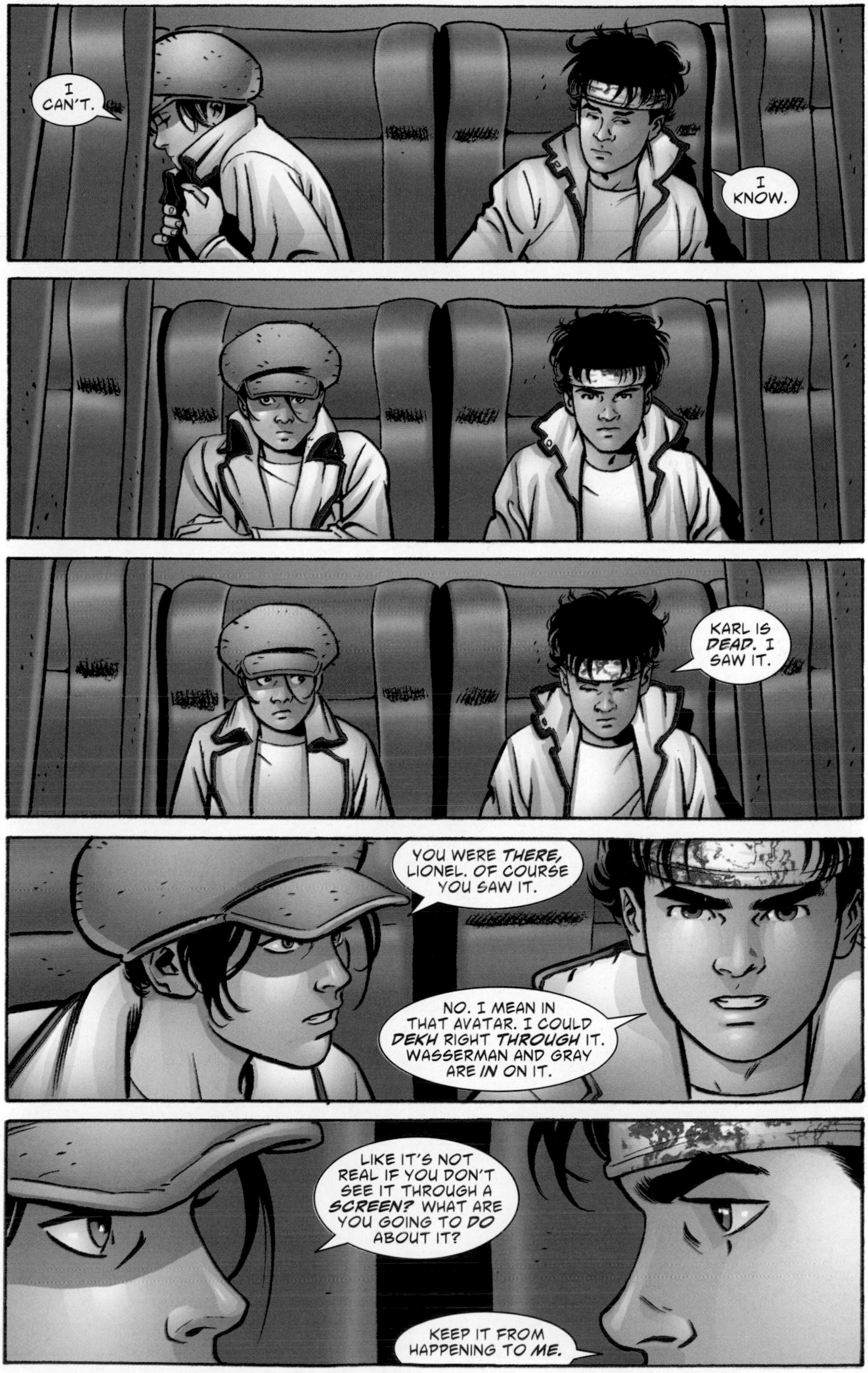
I CAN'T.
I KNOW.
KARL IS DEAD. I SAW IT.
YOU WERE THERE, LIONEL. OF COURSE YOU SAW IT.
NO. I MEAN IN THAT AVATAR. I COULD DEKH RIGHT THROUGH IT. WASSERMAN AND GRAY ARE IN ON IT.
LIKE IT'S NOT REAL IF YOU DON'T SEE IT THROUGH A SCREEN? WHAT ARE YOU GOING TO DO ABOUT IT?
KEEP IT FROM HAPPENING TO ME.

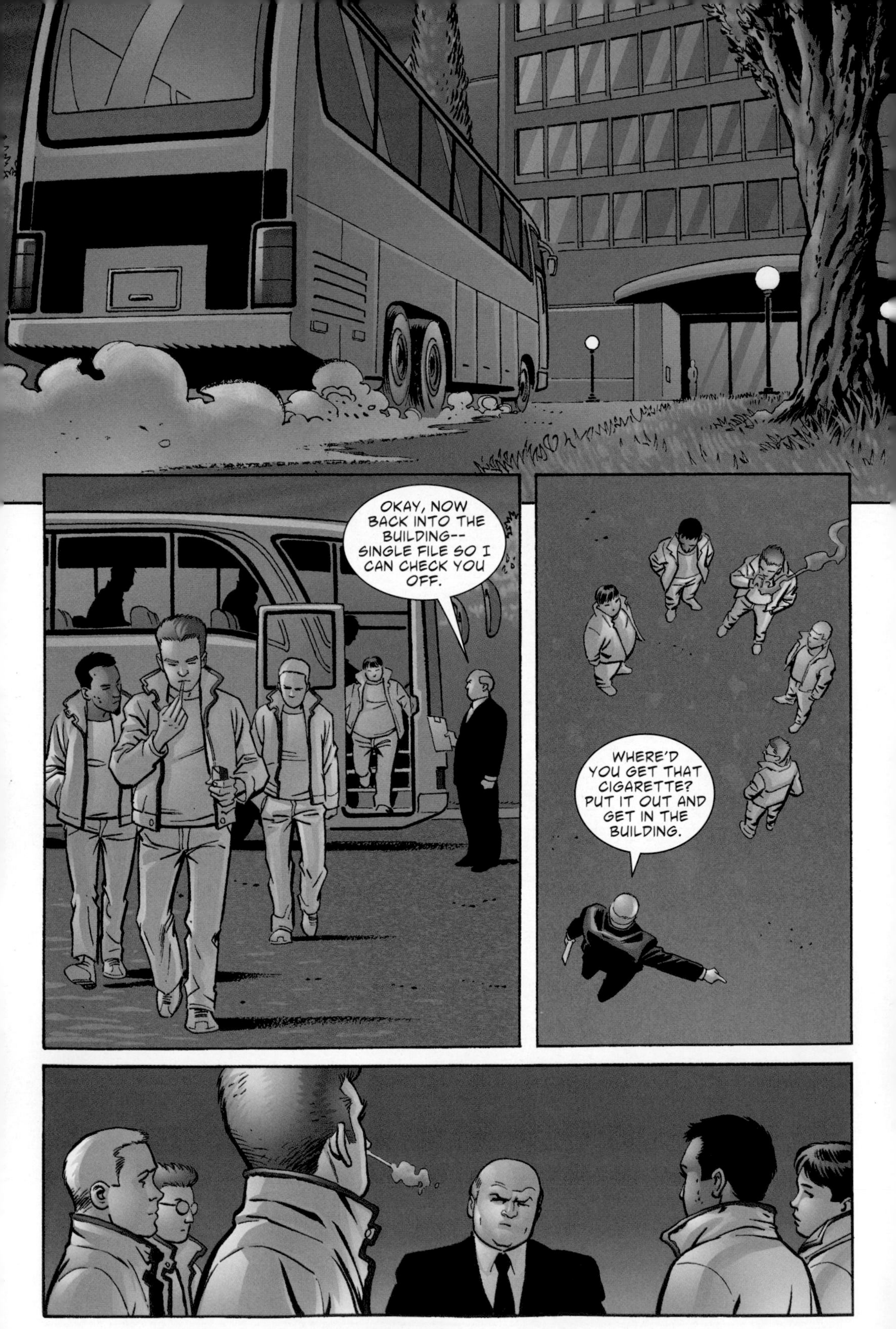
OKAY, NOW BACK INTO THE BUILDING-- SINGLE FILE SO I CAN CHECK YOU OFF.
WHERE'D YOU GET THAT CIGARETTE? PUT IT OUT AND GET IN THE BUILDING.

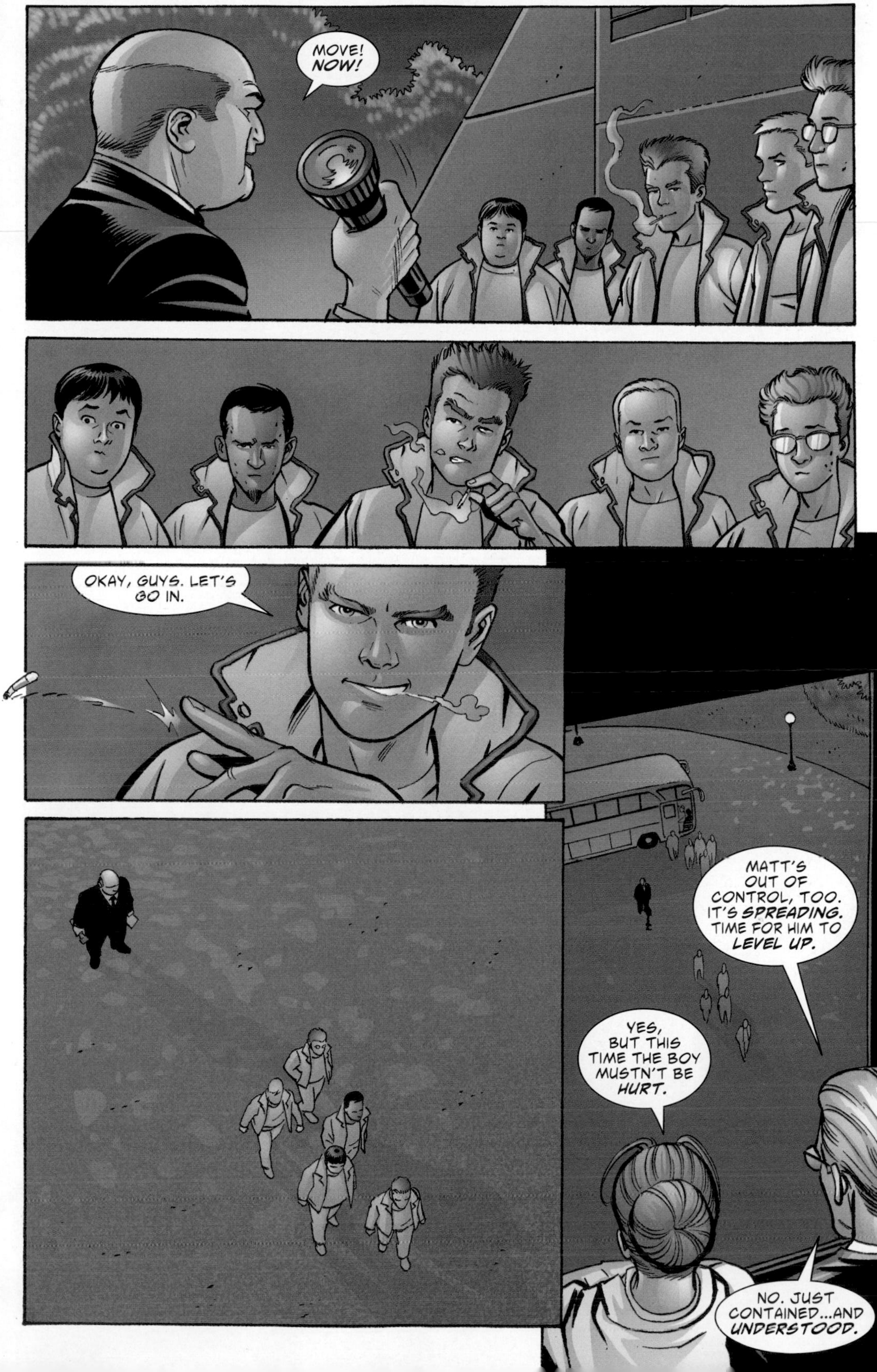
MOVE! NOW!
OKAY, GUYS. LET'S GO IN.
MATT'S OUT OF CONTROL, TOO. IT'S SPREADING. TIME FOR HIM TO LEVEL UP.
YES, BUT THIS TIME THE BOY MUSTN'T BE HURT.
NO. JUST CONTAINED...AND UNDERSTOOD.

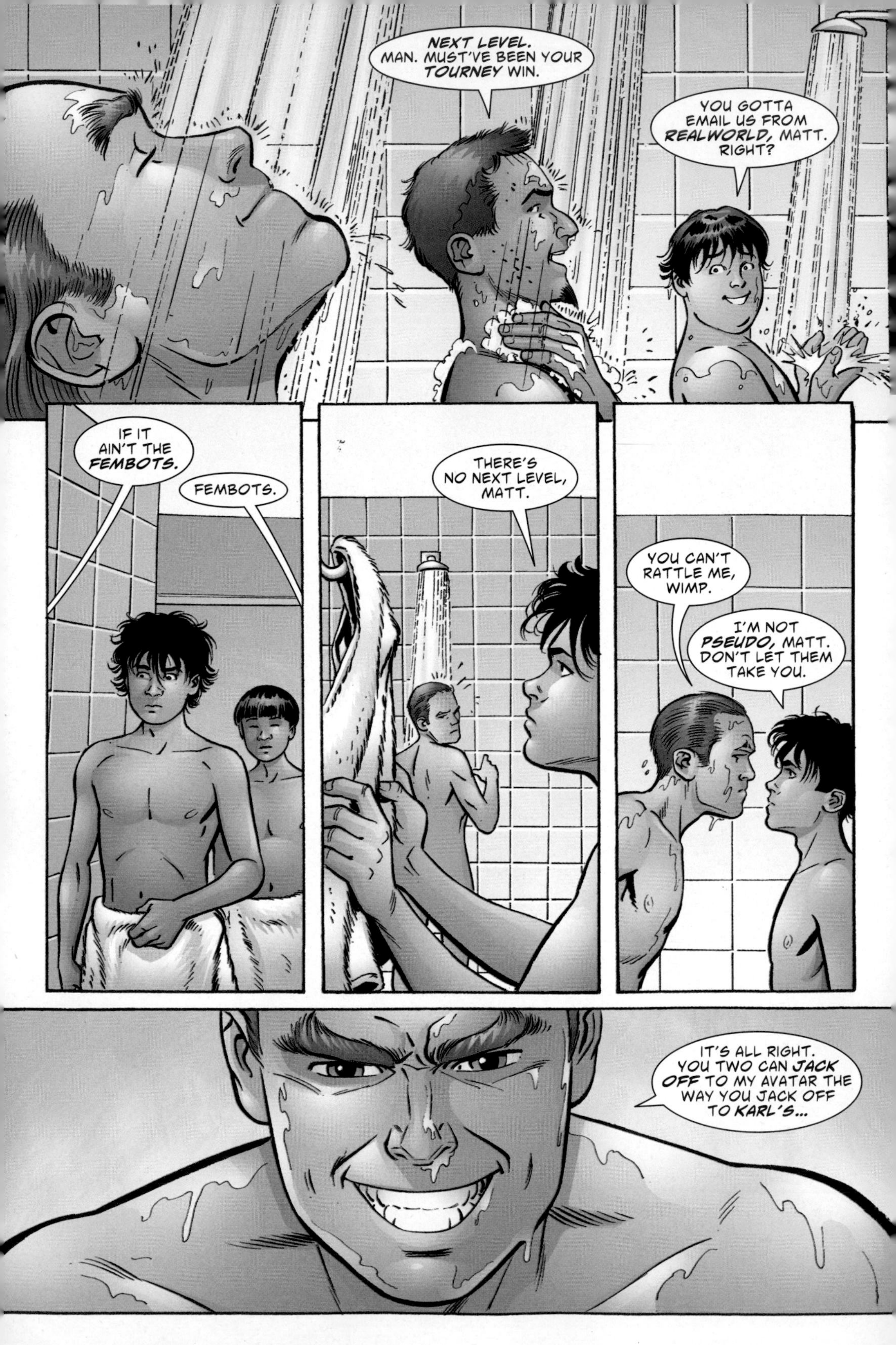
NEXT LEVEL. MAN. MUST'VE BEEN YOUR TOURNEY WIN.
YOU GOTTA EMAIL US FROM REALWORLD, MATT. RIGHT?
IF IT AIN'T THE FEMBOTS.
FEMBOTS.
THERE'S NO NEXT LEVEL, MATT.
YOU CAN'T RATTLE ME, WIMP.
I'M NOT PSEUDO, MATT. DON'T LET THEM TAKE YOU.
IT'S ALL RIGHT. YOU TWO CAN JACK OFF TO MY AVATAR THE WAY YOU JACK OFF TO KARL'S...

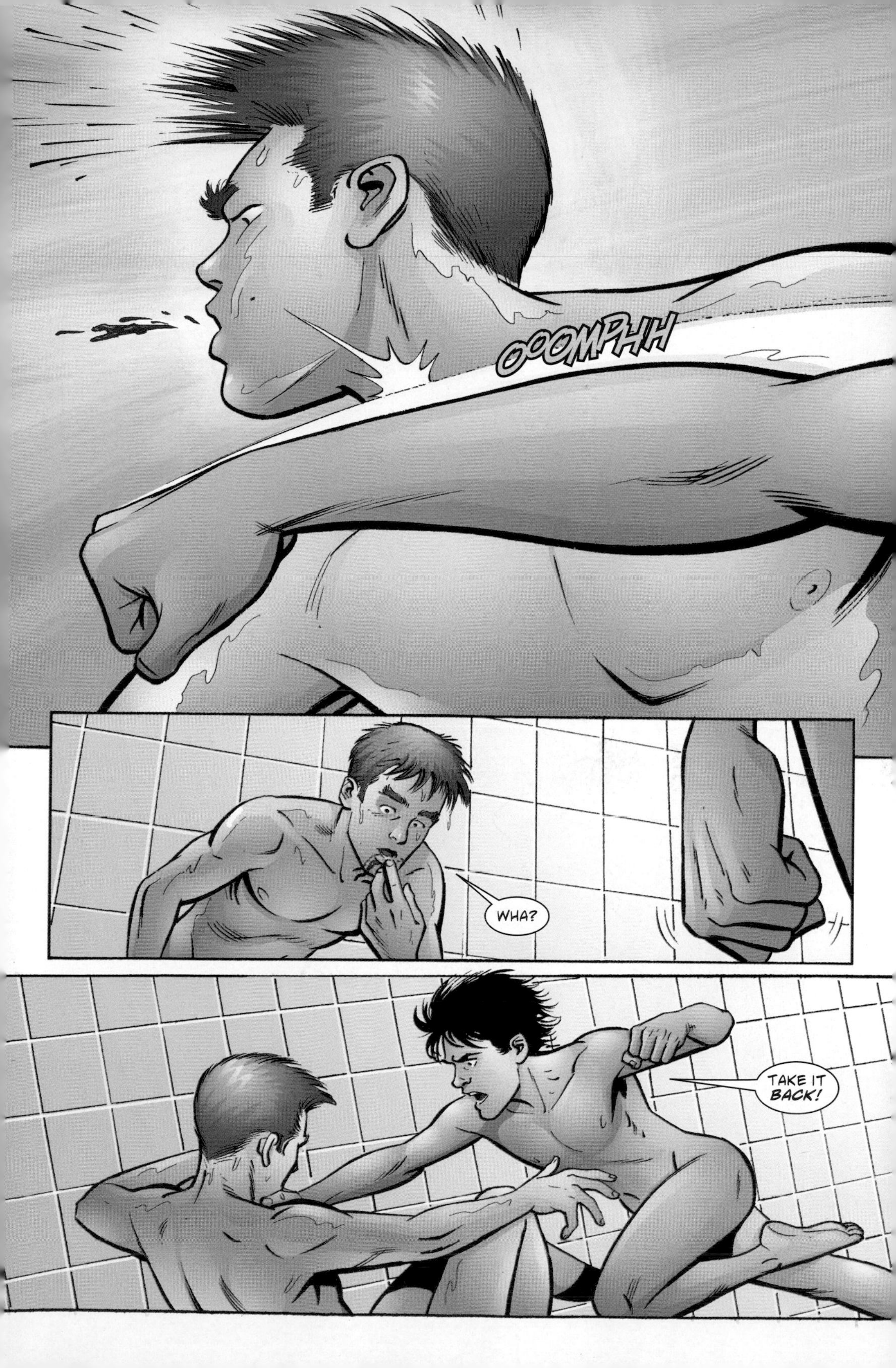
OOOMPHH
WHA?
TAKE IT BACK!

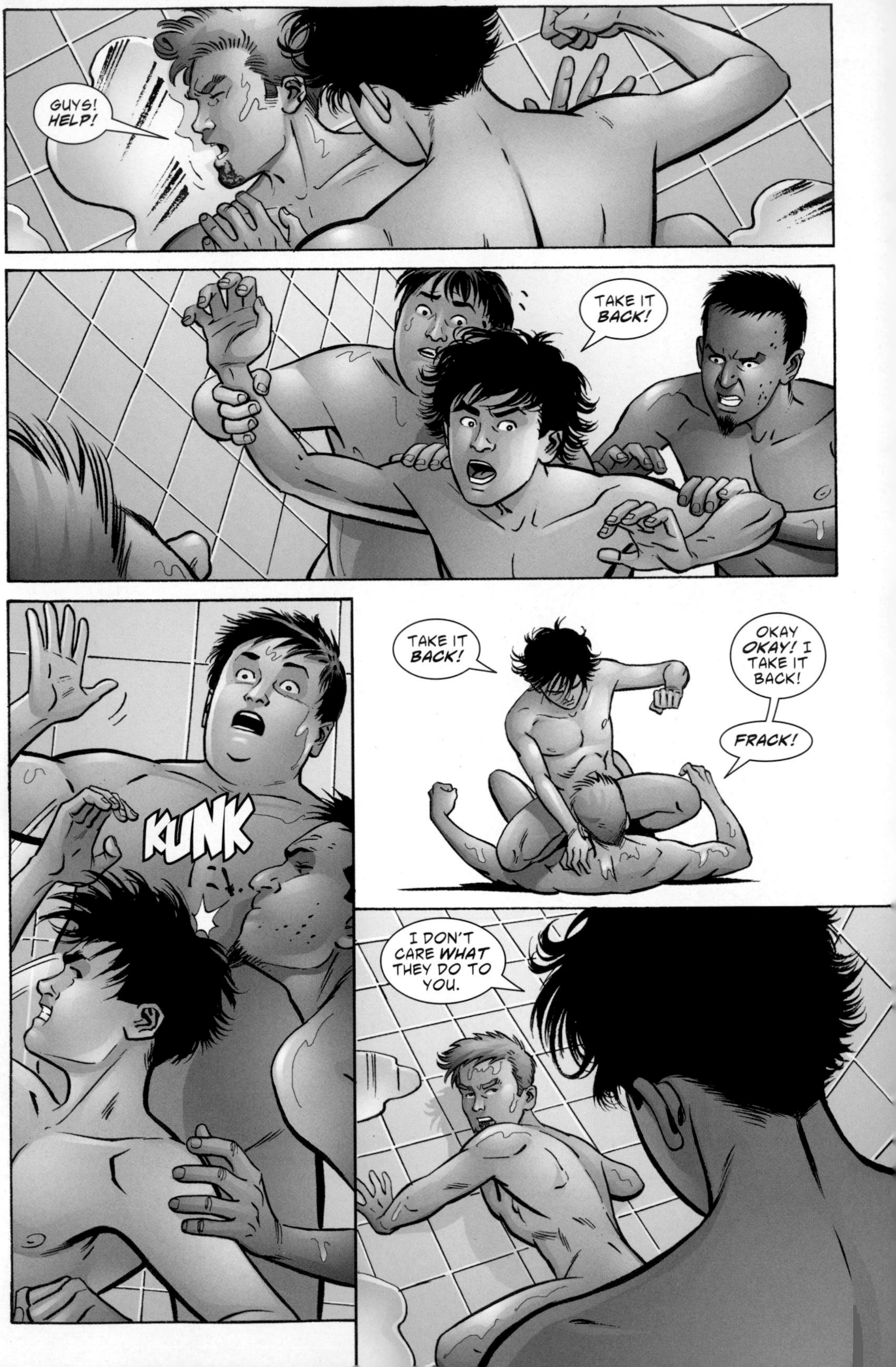
GUYS! HELP!
TAKE IT BACK!
KUNK
TAKE IT BACK!
OKAY OKAY! I TAKE IT BACK!
FRACK!
I DON'T CARE WHAT THEY DO TO YOU.

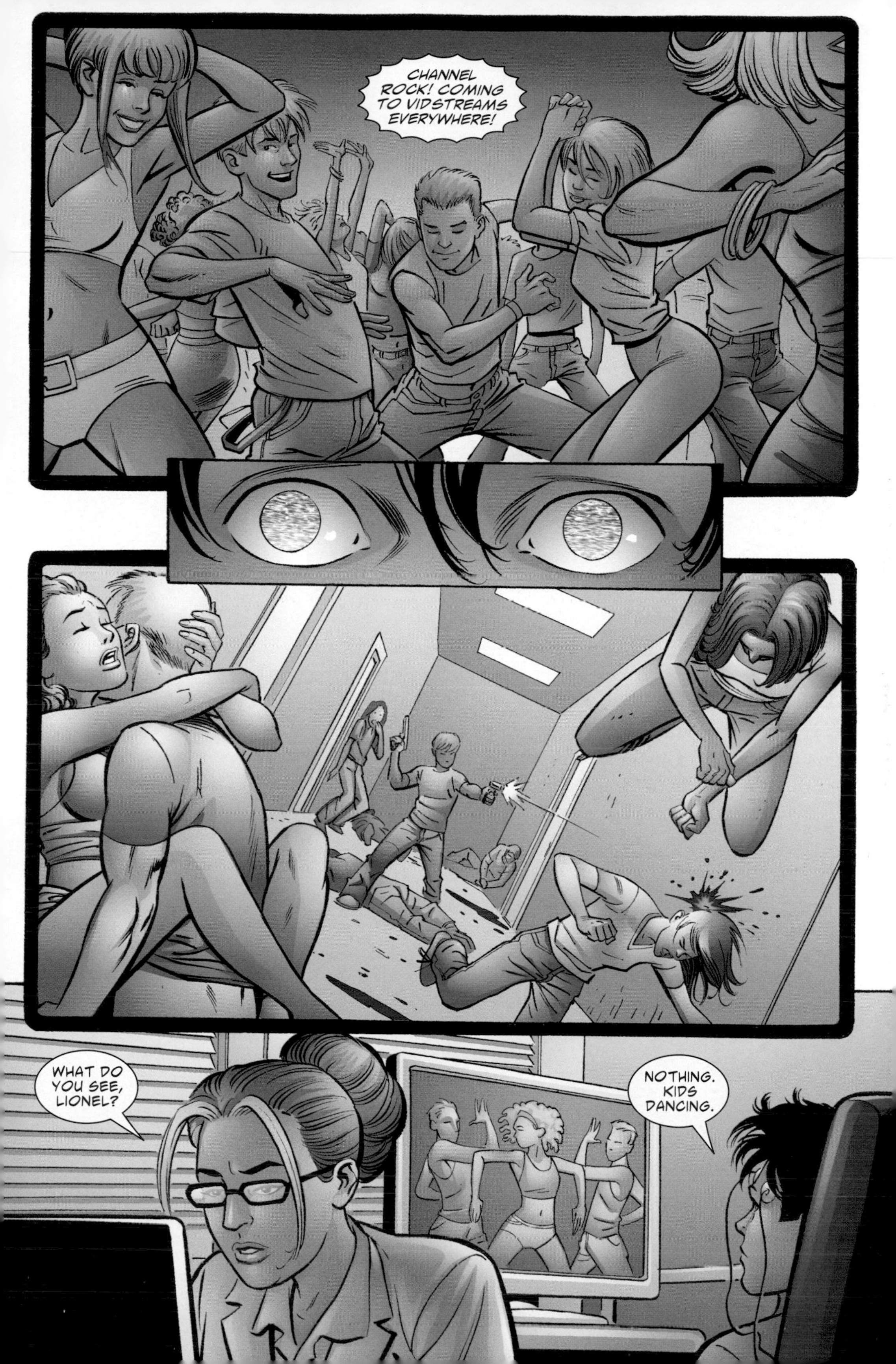

CHANNEL ROCK! COMING TO VIDSTREAMS EVERYWHERE!
WHAT DO YOU SEE, LIONEL?
NOTHING. KIDS DANCING.

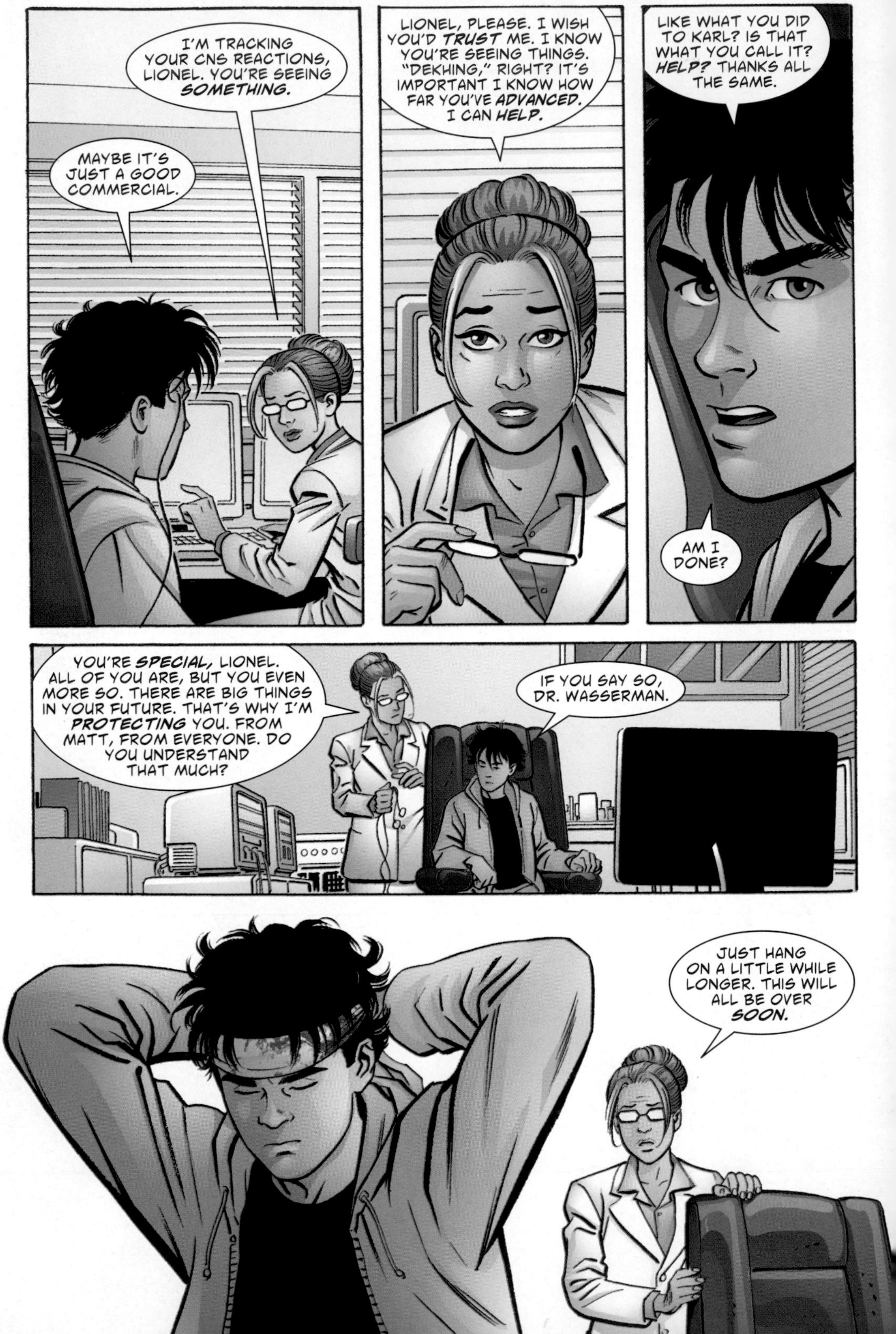

I'M TRACKING YOUR CNS REACTIONS, LIONEL. YOU'RE SEEING *SOMETHING.*
MAYBE IT'S JUST A GOOD COMMERCIAL.
LIONEL, PLEASE. I WISH YOU'D *TRUST* ME. I KNOW YOU'RE SEEING THINGS. "DEKHING," RIGHT? IT'S IMPORTANT I KNOW HOW FAR YOU'VE *ADVANCED.* I CAN *HELP.*
LIKE WHAT YOU DID TO KARL? IS THAT WHAT YOU CALL IT? *HELP?* THANKS ALL THE SAME.
AM I DONE?
YOU'RE *SPECIAL,* LIONEL. ALL OF YOU ARE, BUT YOU EVEN MORE SO. THERE ARE BIG THINGS IN YOUR FUTURE. THAT'S WHY I'M *PROTECTING* YOU. FROM MATT, FROM EVERYONE. DO YOU UNDERSTAND THAT MUCH?
IF YOU SAY SO, DR. WASSERMAN.
JUST HANG ON A LITTLE WHILE LONGER. THIS WILL ALL BE OVER *SOON.*

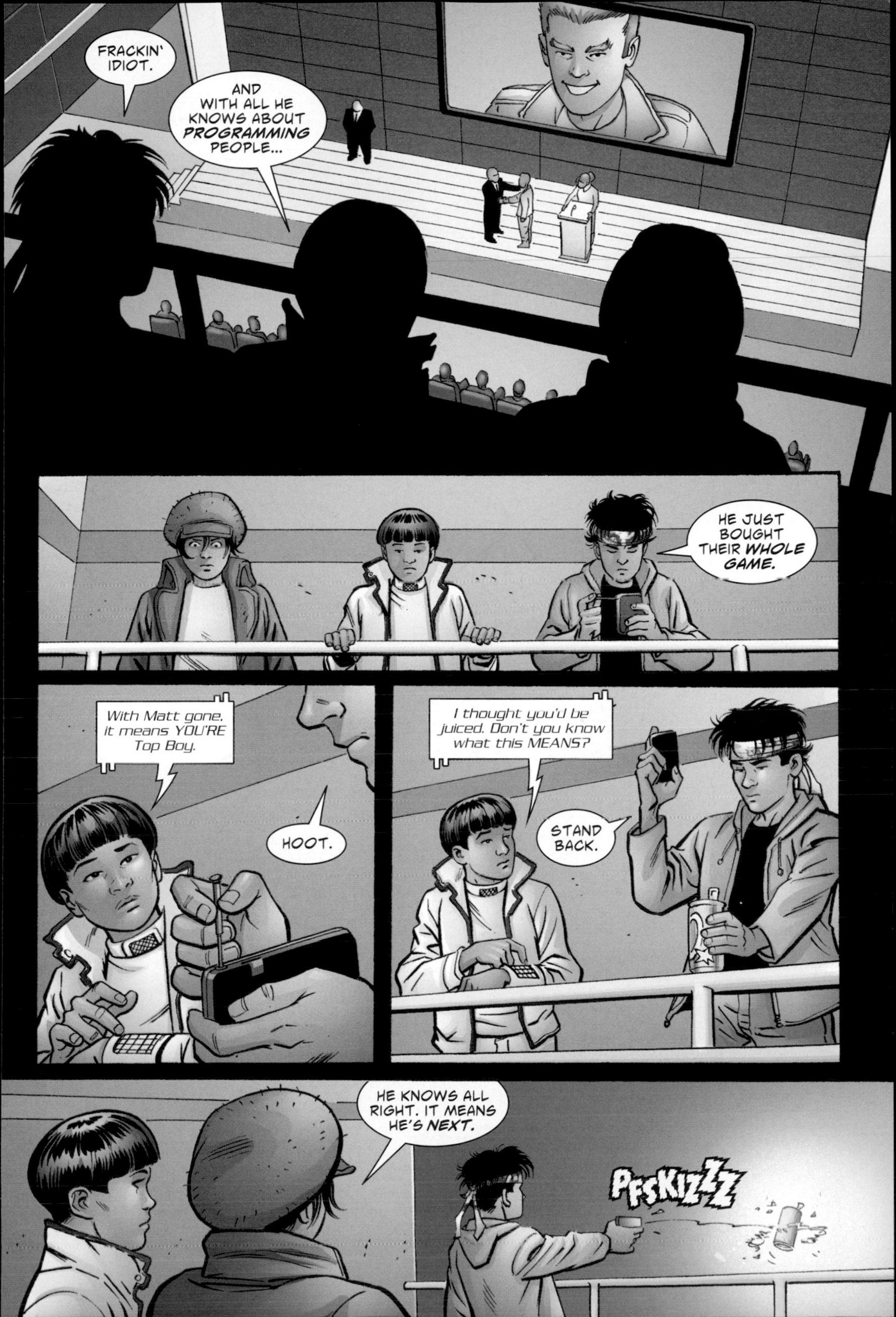
FRACKIN' IDIOT.
AND WITH ALL HE KNOWS ABOUT PROGRAMMING PEOPLE...
HE JUST BOUGHT THEIR WHOLE GAME.
With Matt gone, it means YOU'RE Top Boy.
HOOT.
I thought you'd be juiced. Don't you know what this MEANS?
STAND BACK.
HE KNOWS ALL RIGHT. IT MEANS HE'S NEXT.
PFSKIZZZ

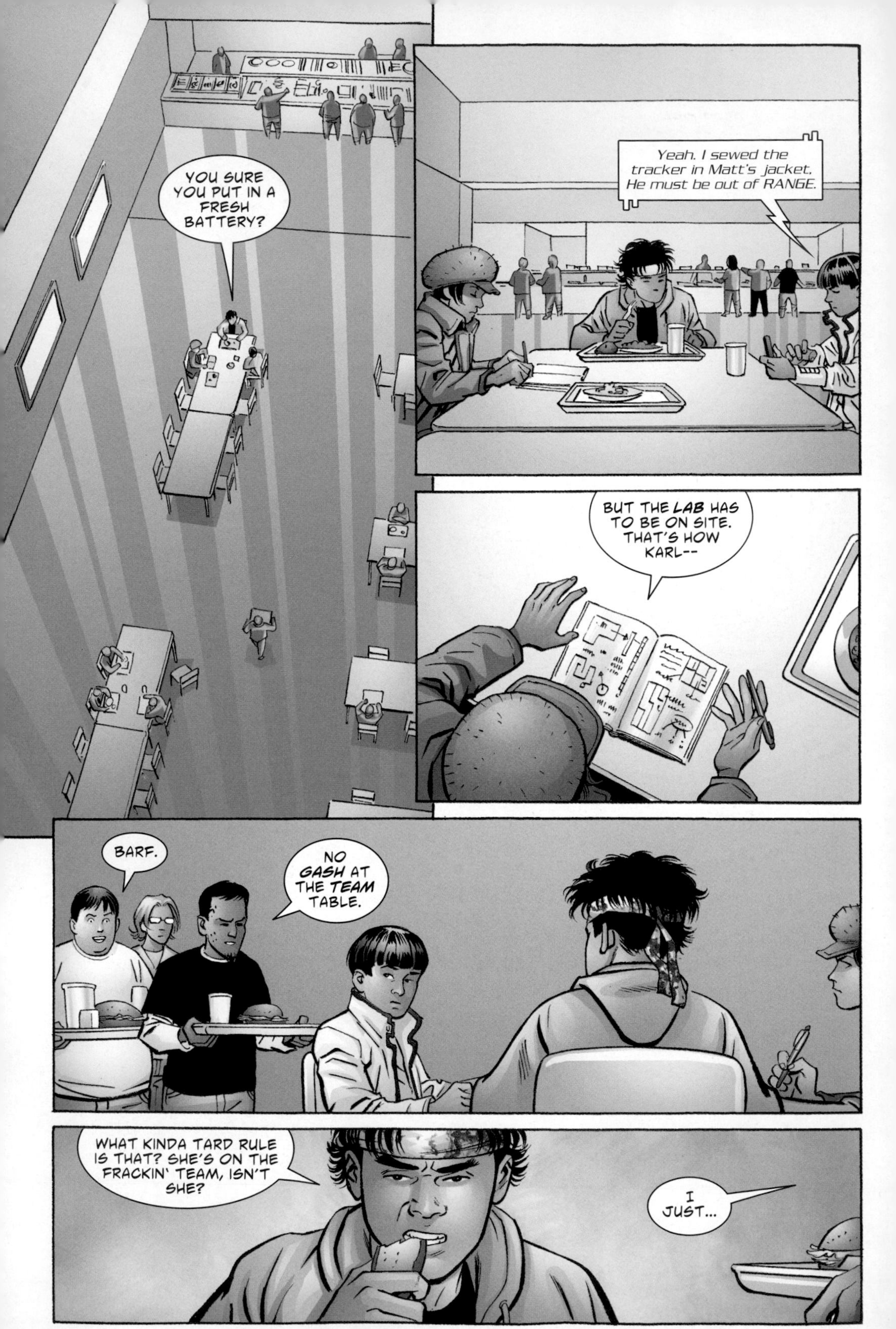
YOU SURE YOU PUT IN A FRESH BATTERY?
Yeah. I sewed the tracker in Matt's jacket. He must be out of RANGE.
BUT THE LAB HAS TO BE ON SITE. THAT'S HOW KARL--
BARF.
NO GASH AT THE TEAM TABLE.
WHAT KINDA TARD RULE IS THAT? SHE'S ON THE FRACKIN' TEAM, ISN'T SHE?
I JUST...

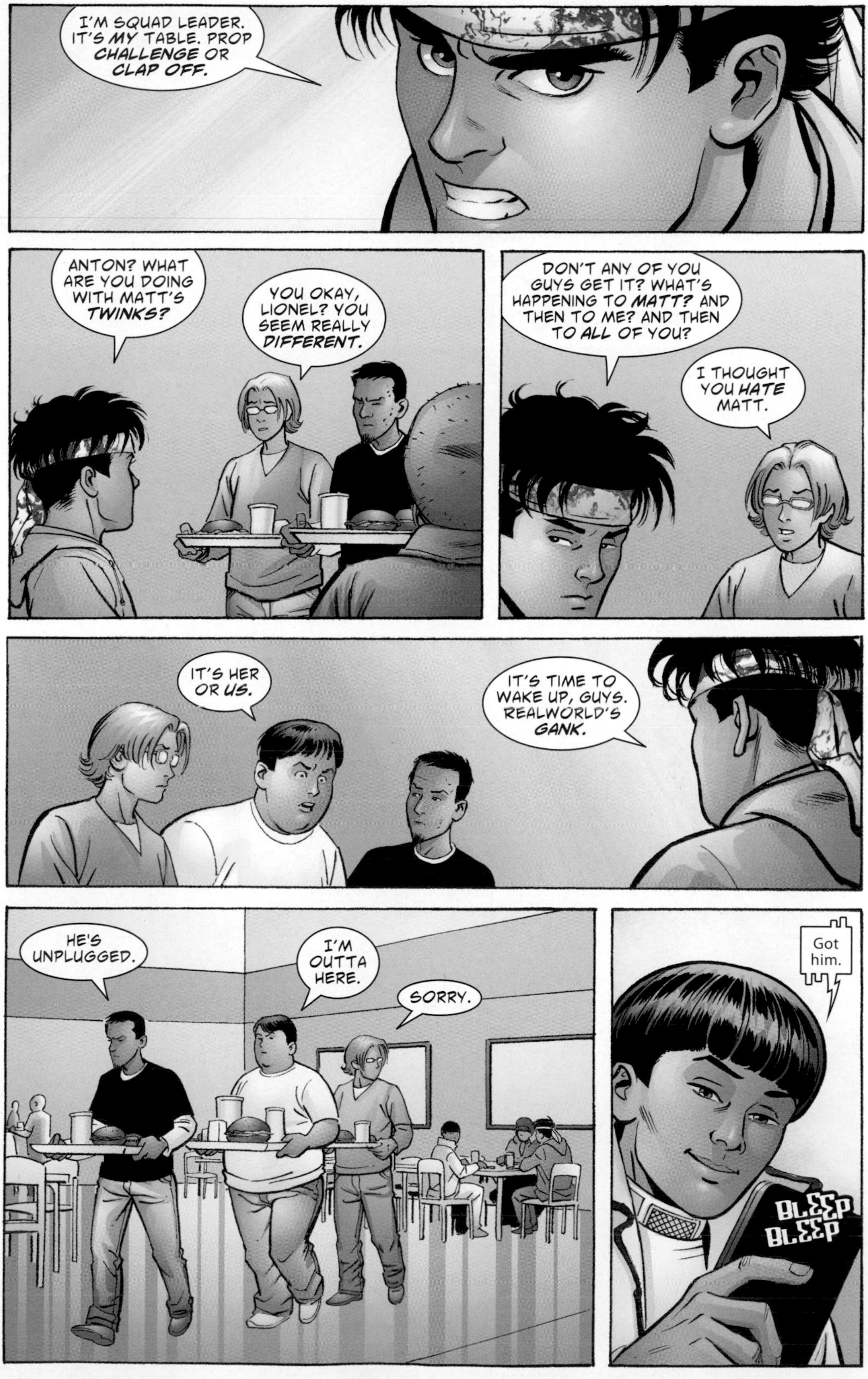
I'M SQUAD LEADER. IT'S MY TABLE. PROP CHALLENGE OR CLAP OFF.
ANTON? WHAT ARE YOU DOING WITH MATT'S TWINKS?
YOU OKAY, LIONEL? YOU SEEM REALLY DIFFERENT.
DON'T ANY OF YOU GUYS GET IT? WHAT'S HAPPENING TO MATT? AND THEN TO ME? AND THEN TO ALL OF YOU?
I THOUGHT YOU HATE MATT.
IT'S HER OR US.
IT'S TIME TO WAKE UP, GUYS. REALWORLD'S GANK.
HE'S UNPLUGGED.
I'M OUTTA HERE.
SORRY.
Got him.
BLEEP BLEEP

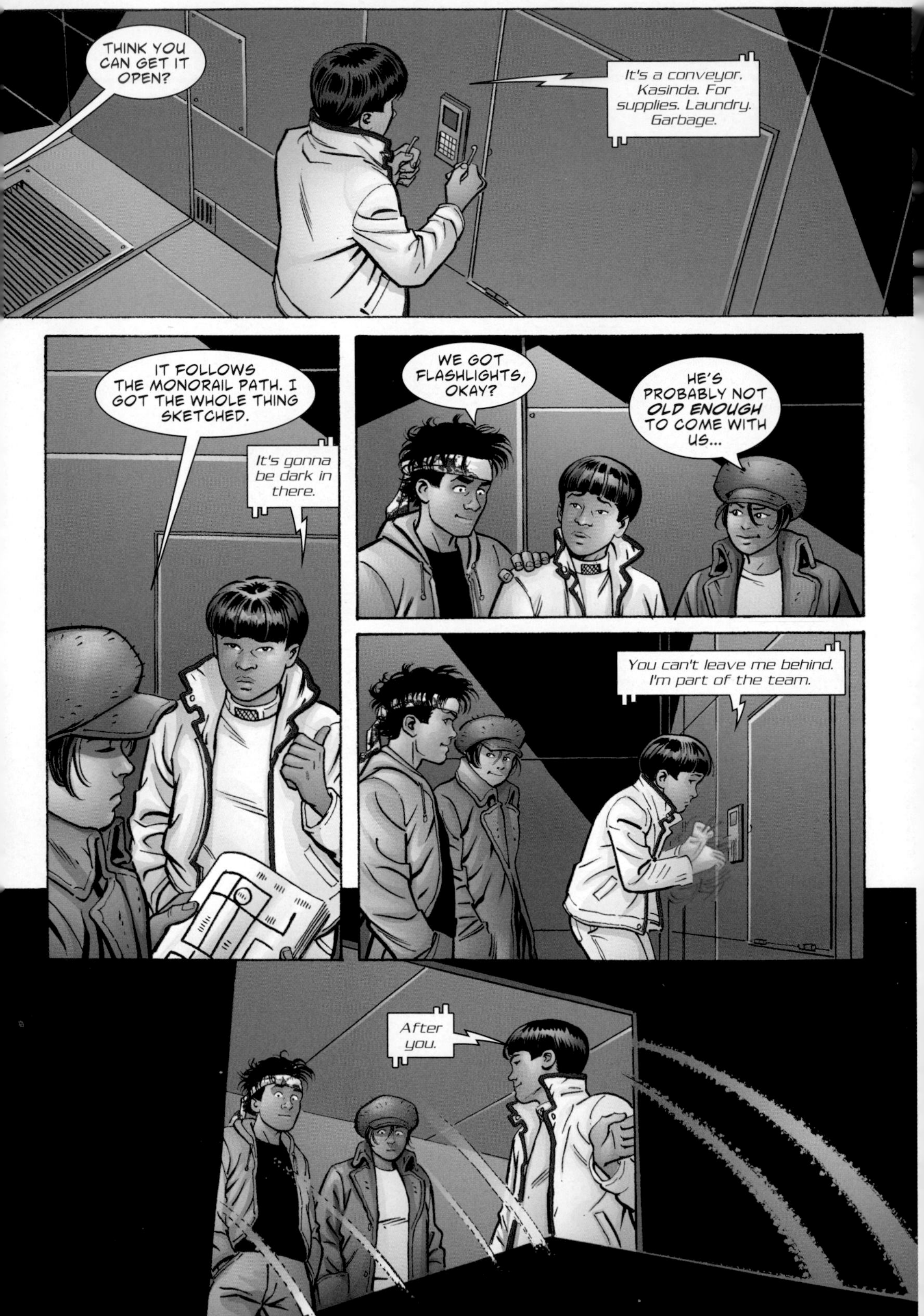
THINK YOU CAN GET IT OPEN?
It's a conveyor, Kasinda. For supplies. Laundry. Garbage.
IT FOLLOWS THE MONORAIL PATH. I GOT THE WHOLE THING SKETCHED.
It's gonna be dark in there.
WE GOT FLASHLIGHTS, OKAY?
HE'S PROBABLY NOT OLD ENOUGH TO COME WITH US...
You can't leave me behind. I'm part of the team.
After you.

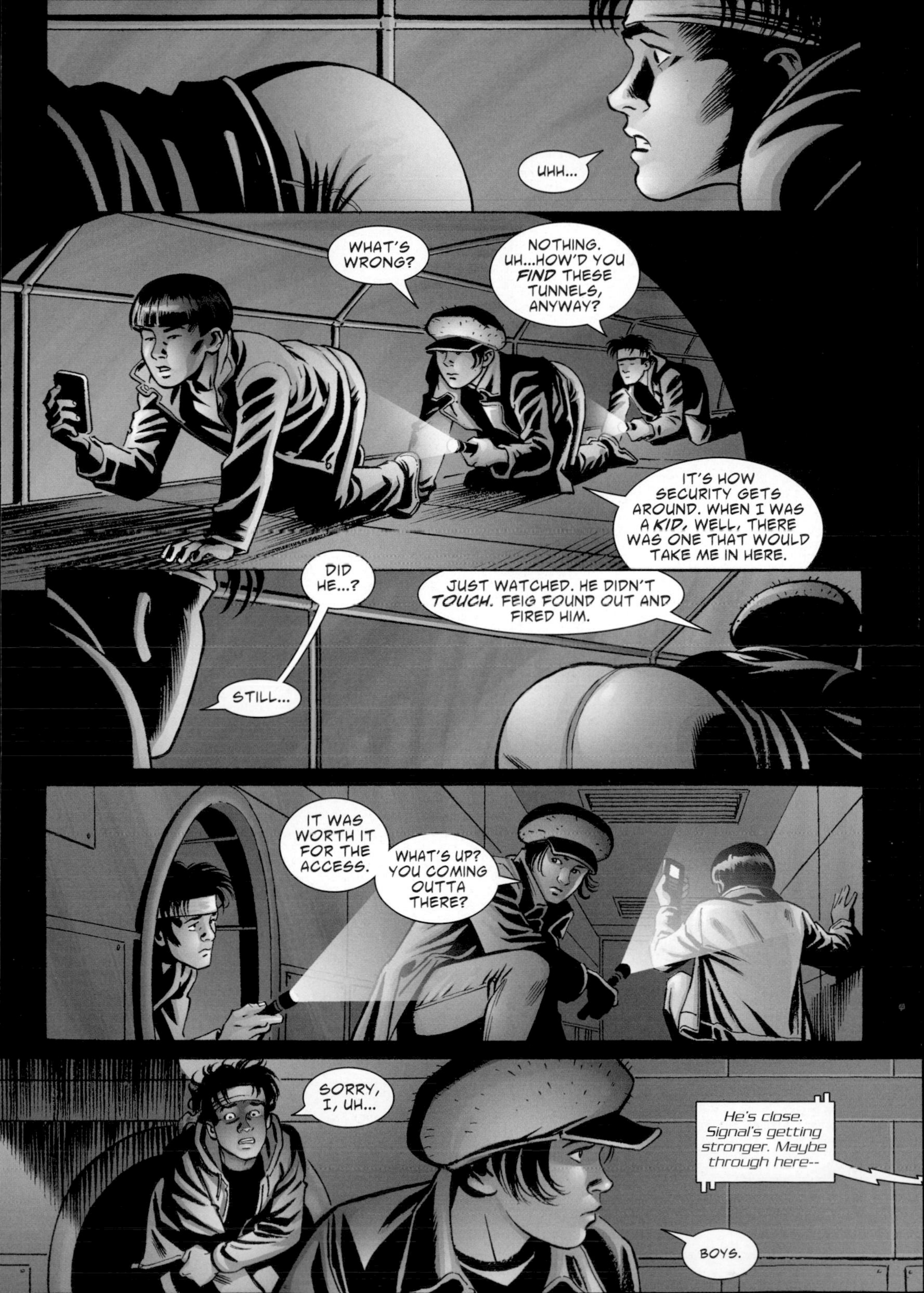
UHH...
WHAT'S WRONG?
NOTHING. UH...HOW'D YOU FIND THESE TUNNELS, ANYWAY?
IT'S HOW SECURITY GETS AROUND. WHEN I WAS A KID, WELL, THERE WAS ONE THAT WOULD TAKE ME IN HERE.
DID HE...?
JUST WATCHED. HE DIDN'T TOUCH. FEIG FOUND OUT AND FIRED HIM.
STILL...
IT WAS WORTH IT FOR THE ACCESS.
WHAT'S UP? YOU COMING OUTTA THERE?
SORRY, I, UH...
He's close. Signal's getting stronger. Maybe through here--
BOYS.

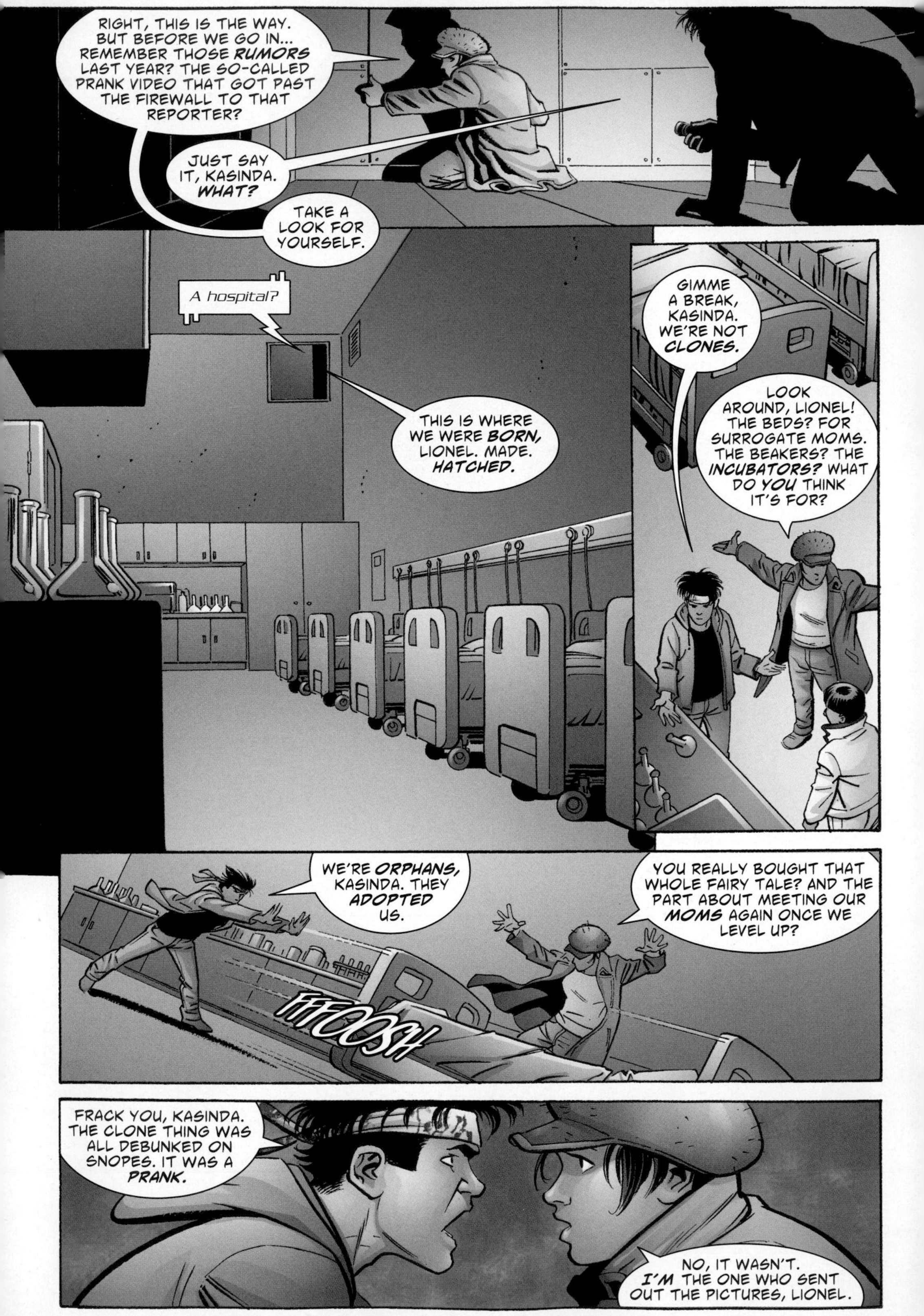
RIGHT, THIS IS THE WAY. BUT BEFORE WE GO IN... REMEMBER THOSE *RUMORS* LAST YEAR? THE SO-CALLED PRANK VIDEO THAT GOT PAST THE FIREWALL TO THAT REPORTER?
JUST SAY IT, KASINDA. *WHAT?*
TAKE A LOOK FOR YOURSELF.
A hospital?
THIS IS WHERE WE WERE *BORN,* LIONEL. MADE. *HATCHED.*
GIMME A BREAK, KASINDA. WE'RE NOT *CLONES.*
LOOK AROUND, LIONEL! THE BEDS? FOR SURROGATE MOMS. THE BEAKERS? THE *INCUBATORS?* WHAT DO *YOU* THINK IT'S FOR?
WE'RE *ORPHANS,* KASINDA. THEY *ADOPTED* US.
YOU REALLY BOUGHT THAT WHOLE FAIRY TALE? AND THE PART ABOUT MEETING OUR *MOMS* AGAIN ONCE WE LEVEL UP?
FFFOOSH
FRACK YOU, KASINDA. THE CLONE THING WAS ALL DEBUNKED ON SNOPES. IT WAS A *PRANK.*
NO, IT WASN'T. *I'M* THE ONE WHO SENT OUT THE PICTURES, LIONEL.

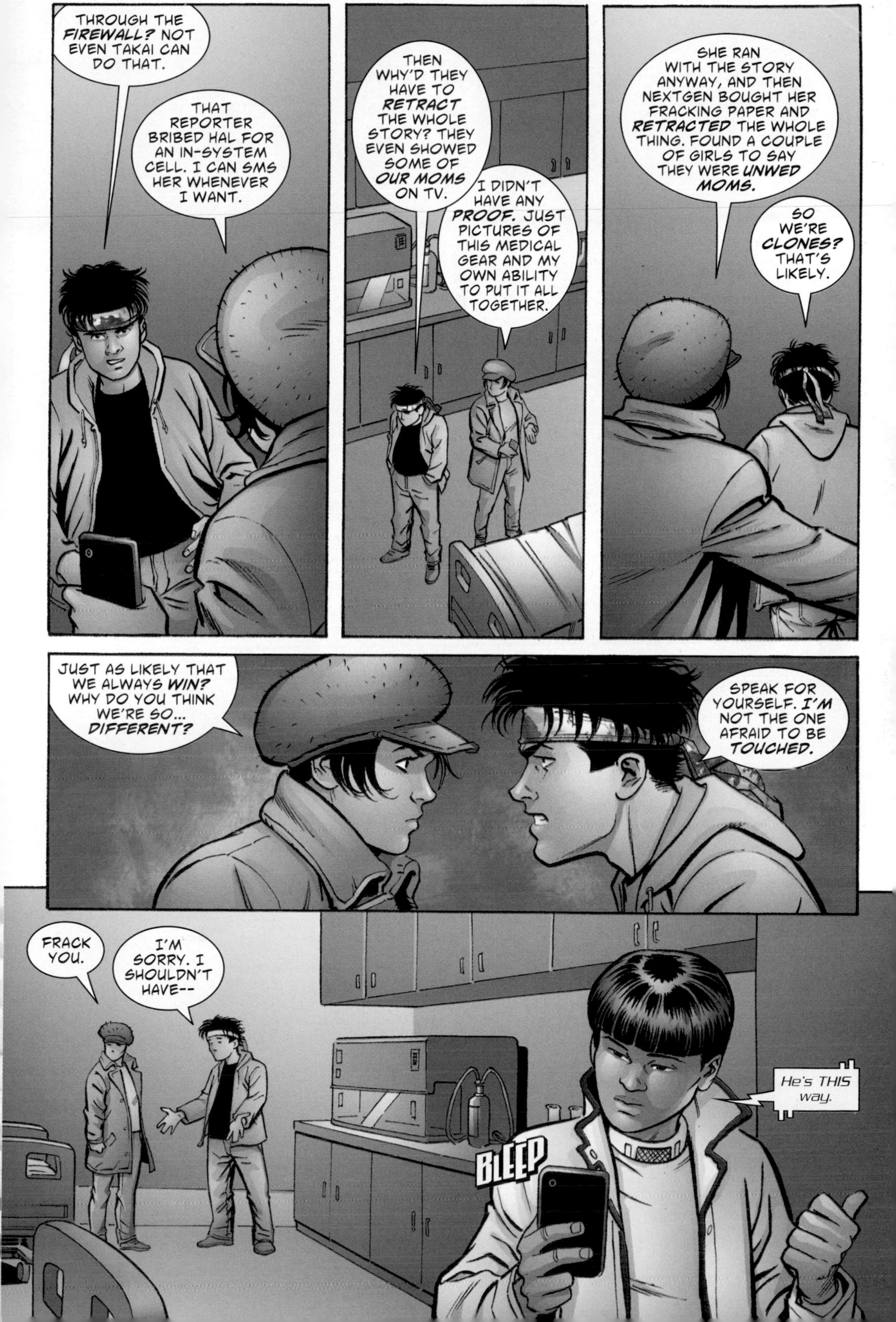
THROUGH THE FIREWALL? NOT EVEN TAKAI CAN DO THAT.
THAT REPORTER BRIBED HAL FOR AN IN-SYSTEM CELL. I CAN SMS HER WHENEVER I WANT.
THEN WHY'D THEY HAVE TO RETRACT THE WHOLE STORY? THEY EVEN SHOWED SOME OF OUR MOMS ON TV.
I DIDN'T HAVE ANY PROOF. JUST PICTURES OF THIS MEDICAL GEAR AND MY OWN ABILITY TO PUT IT ALL TOGETHER.
SHE RAN WITH THE STORY ANYWAY, AND THEN NEXTGEN BOUGHT HER FRACKING PAPER AND RETRACTED THE WHOLE THING. FOUND A COUPLE OF GIRLS TO SAY THEY WERE UNWED MOMS.
SO WE'RE CLONES? THAT'S LIKELY.
JUST AS LIKELY THAT WE ALWAYS WIN? WHY DO YOU THINK WE'RE SO... DIFFERENT?
SPEAK FOR YOURSELF. I'M NOT THE ONE AFRAID TO BE TOUCHED.
FRACK YOU.
I'M SORRY. I SHOULDN'T HAVE--
He's THIS way.
BLEEP

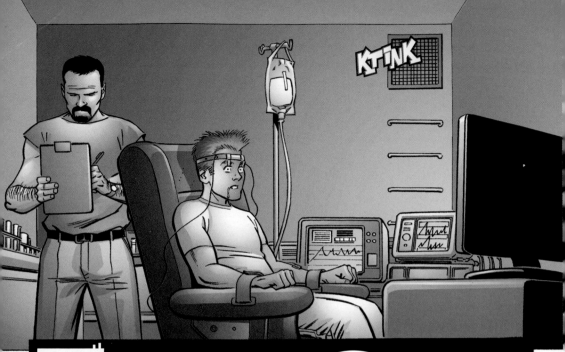

Is he playing a vid?

NOT EXACTLY, TAKAI.

WE GOTTA GET THIS OUT. I'M SIMSING ROBERTA.

Urine, gross. Let's go.

WE CAN'T *LEAVE* HIM HERE.

THE ATTENDANT IS GOING. THIS IS OUR CHANCE.

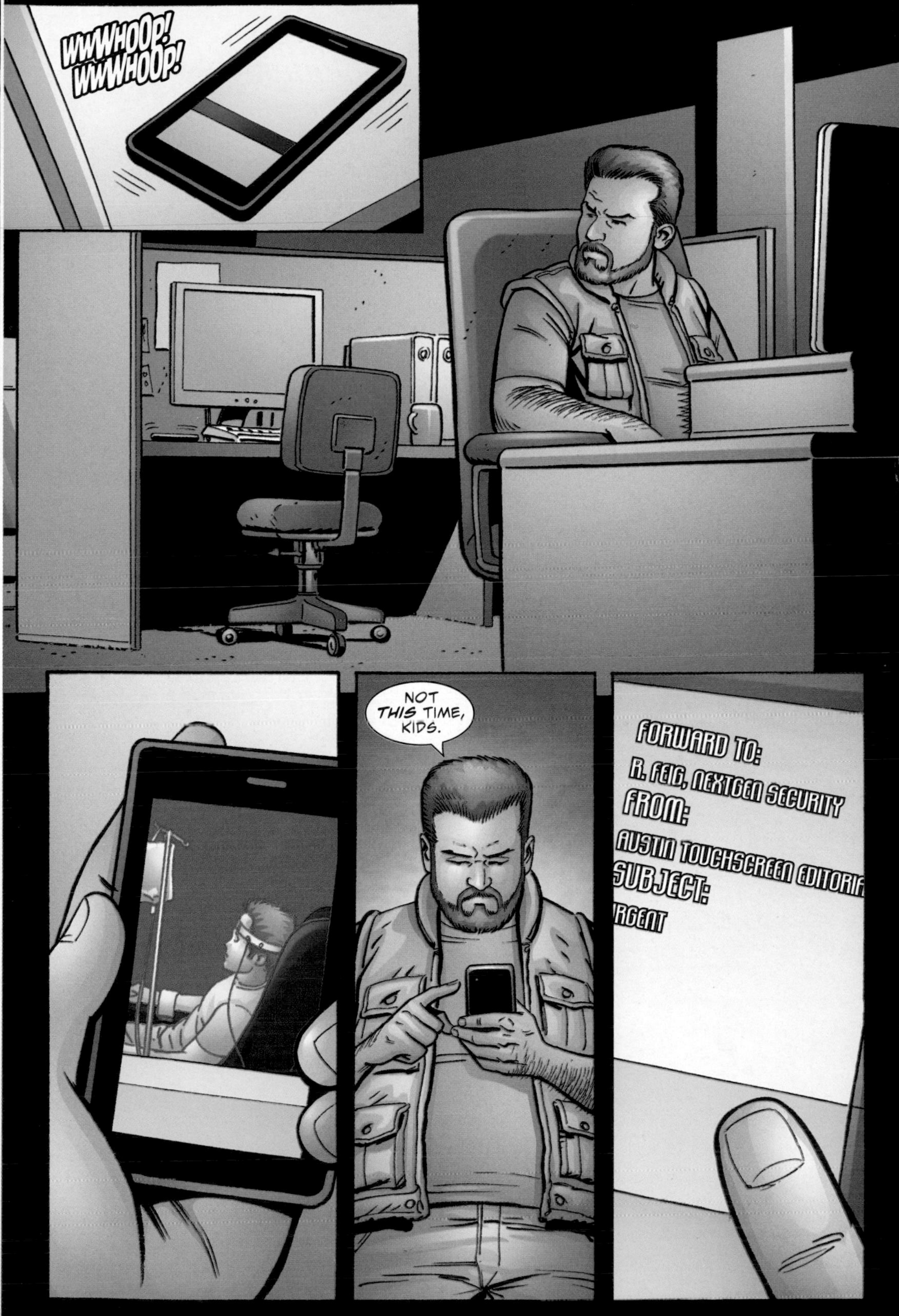
WWWHOOP! WWWHOOP!
NOT *THIS* TIME, KIDS.
FORWARD TO:
R. FEIG, NEXTGEN SECURITY
FROM:
AUSTIN TOUCHSCREEN EDITORIA
SUBJECT:
RGENT

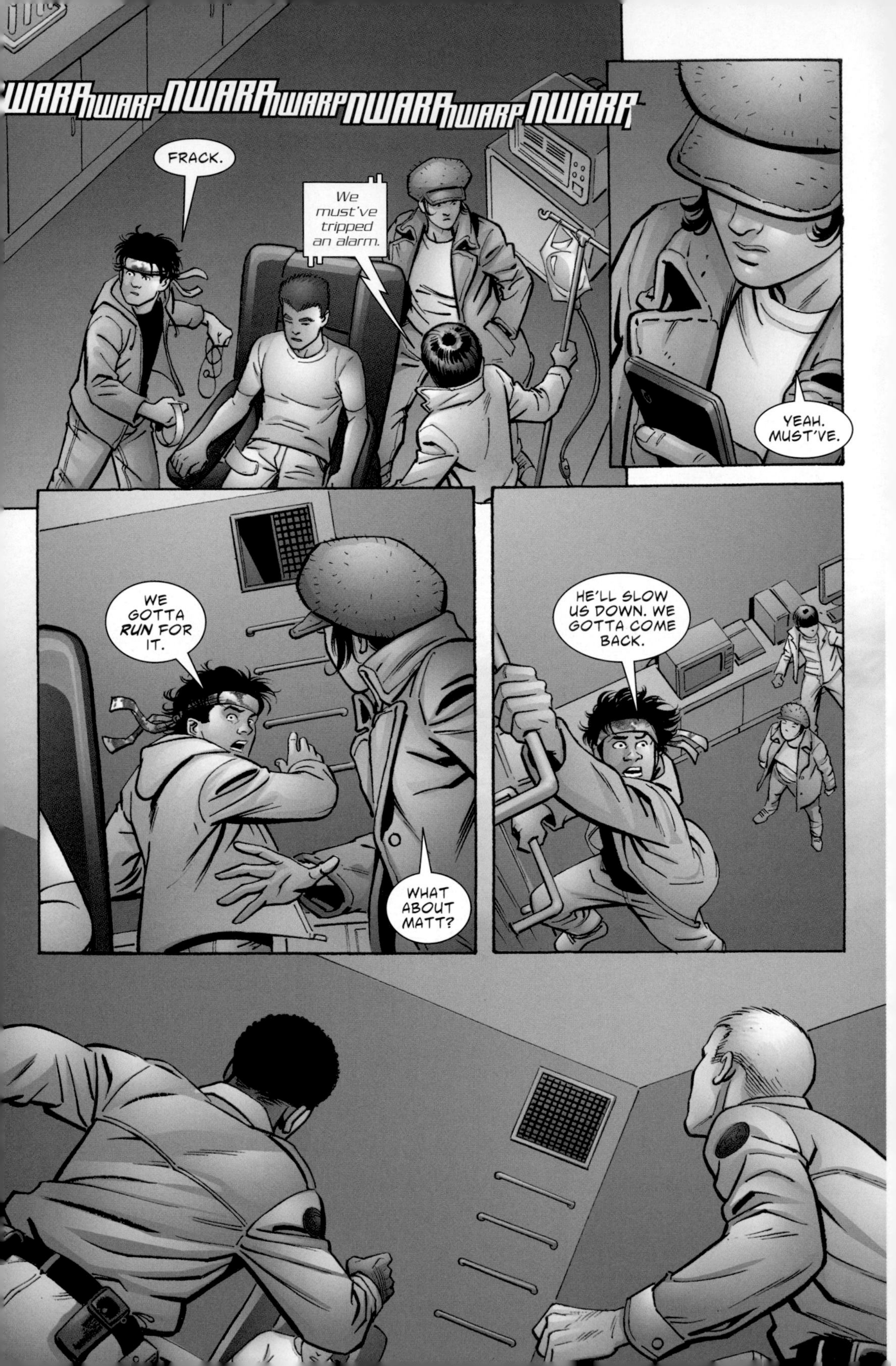
WARR NWARP NWARR NWARP NWARR NWARP NWARR
FRACK.
We must've tripped an alarm.
YEAH. MUST'VE.
WE GOTTA RUN FOR IT.
WHAT ABOUT MATT?
HE'LL SLOW US DOWN. WE GOTTA COME BACK.

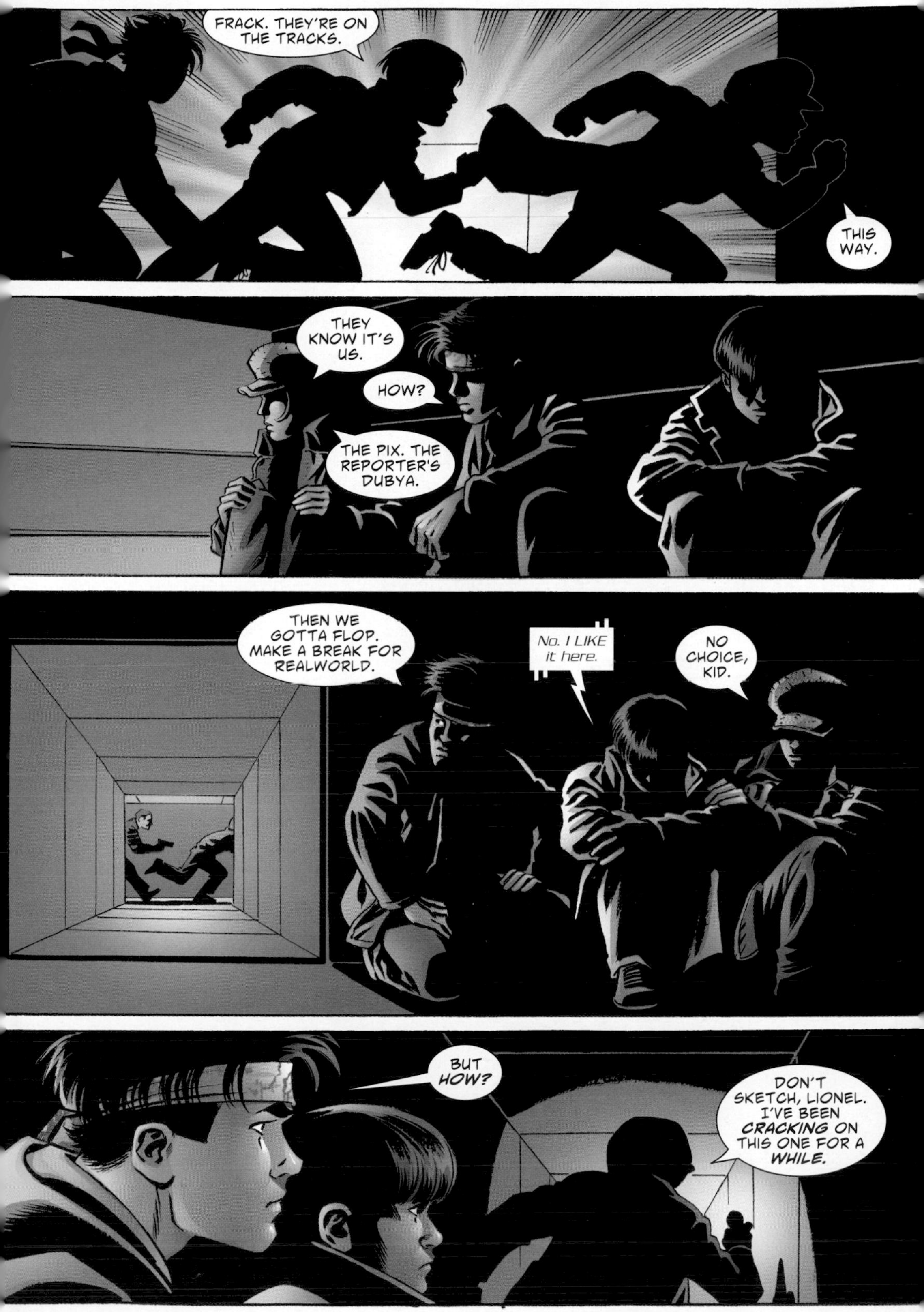
FRACK. THEY'RE ON THE TRACKS.
THIS WAY.
THEY KNOW IT'S US.
HOW?
THE PIX. THE REPORTER'S DUBYA.
THEN WE GOTTA FLOP. MAKE A BREAK FOR REALWORLD.
No. I LIKE it here.
NO CHOICE, KID.
BUT HOW?
DON'T SKETCH, LIONEL. I'VE BEEN CRACKING ON THIS ONE FOR A WHILE.

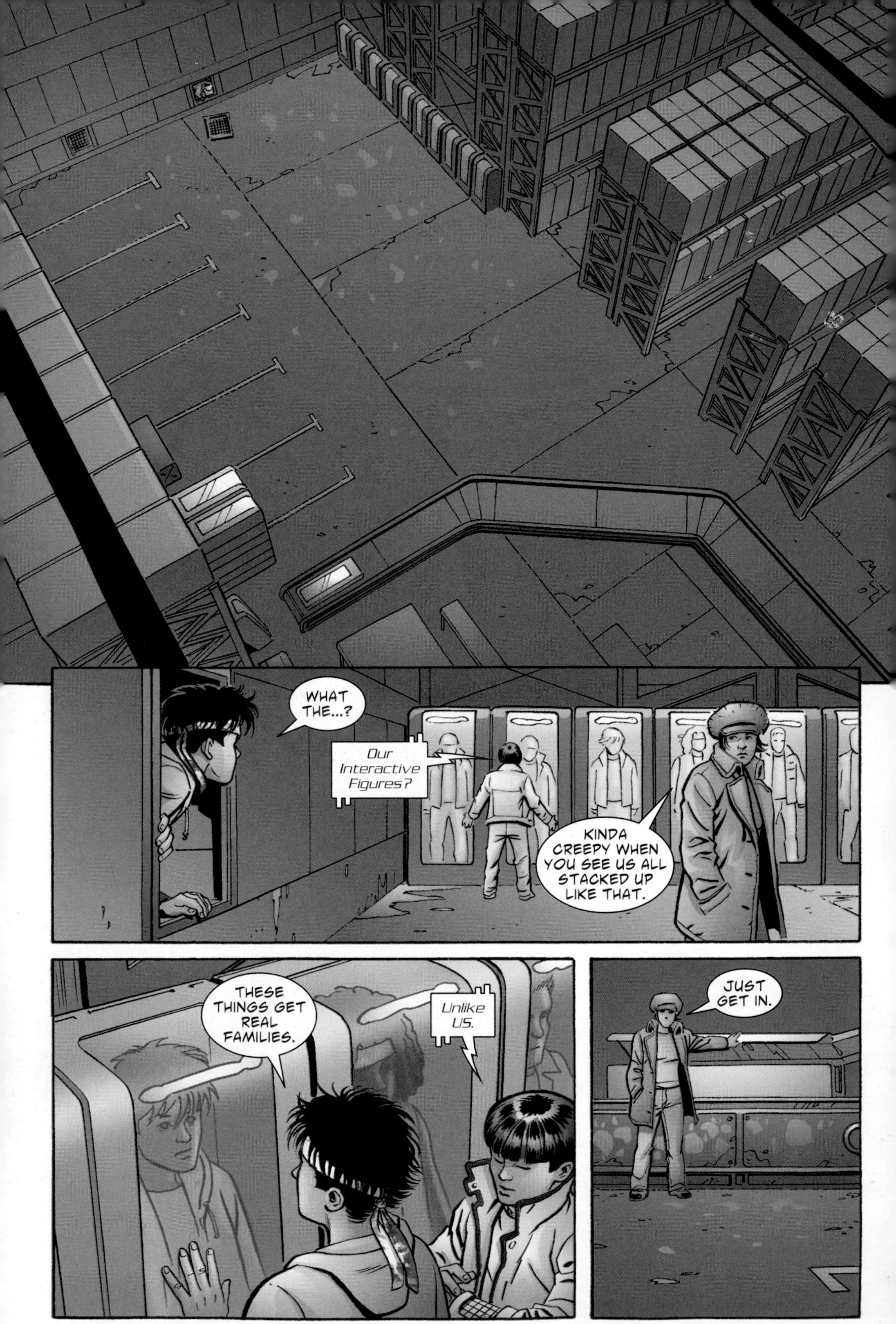
WHAT THE...?
Our Interactive Figures?
KINDA CREEPY WHEN YOU SEE US ALL STACKED UP LIKE THAT.
THESE THINGS GET REAL FAMILIES.
Unlike US.
JUST GET IN.

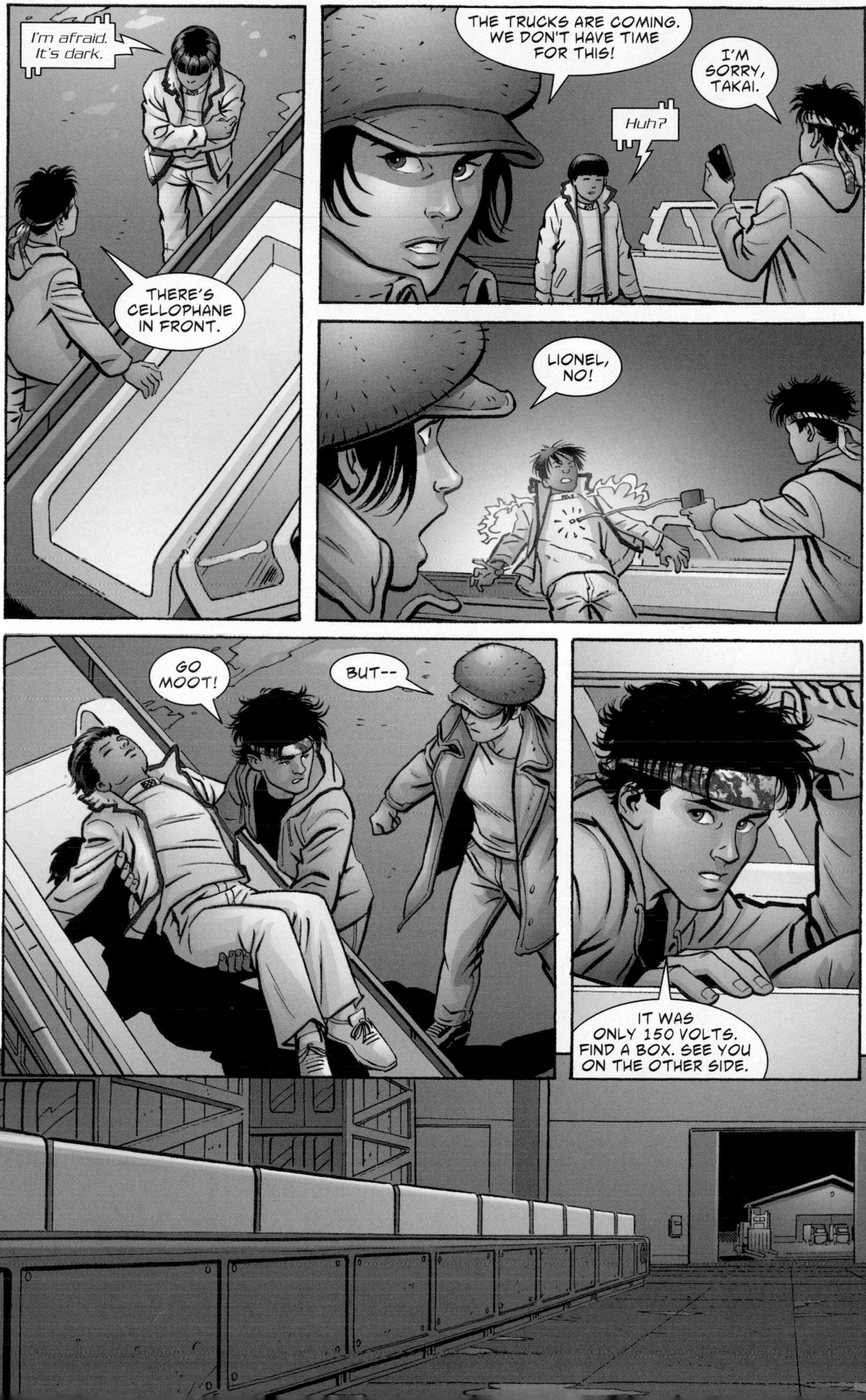

I'm afraid.
It's dark.
THERE'S CELLOPHANE IN FRONT.
THE TRUCKS ARE COMING. WE DON'T HAVE TIME FOR THIS!
Huh?
I'M SORRY, TAKAI.
LIONEL, NO!
GO MOOT!
BUT--
IT WAS ONLY 150 VOLTS. FIND A BOX. SEE YOU ON THE OTHER SIDE.

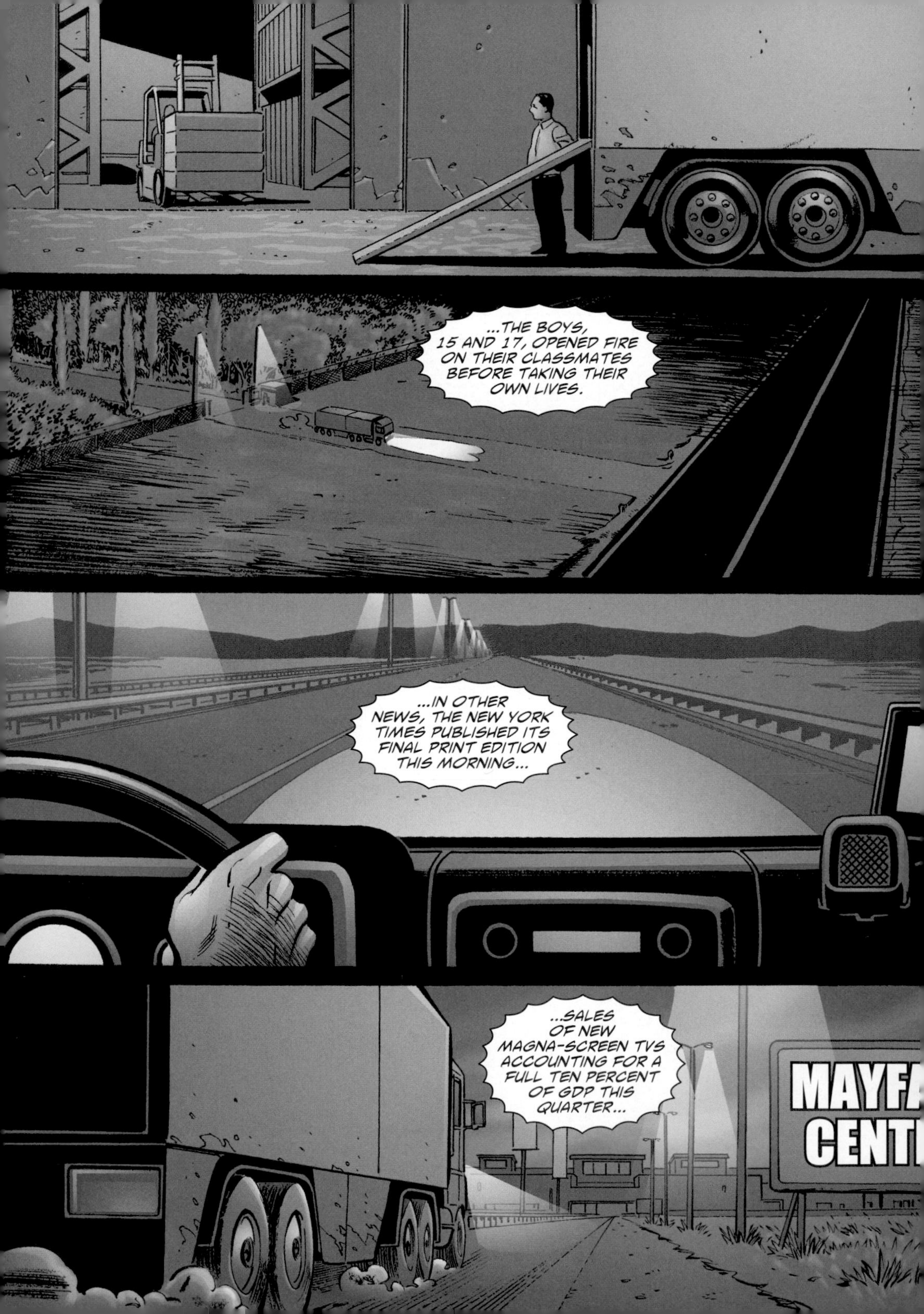
...THE BOYS, 15 AND 17, OPENED FIRE ON THEIR CLASSMATES BEFORE TAKING THEIR OWN LIVES.
...IN OTHER NEWS, THE NEW YORK TIMES PUBLISHED ITS FINAL PRINT EDITION THIS MORNING...
...SALES OF NEW MAGNA-SCREEN TVS ACCOUNTING FOR A FULL TEN PERCENT OF GDP THIS QUARTER...
MAYFA
CENT

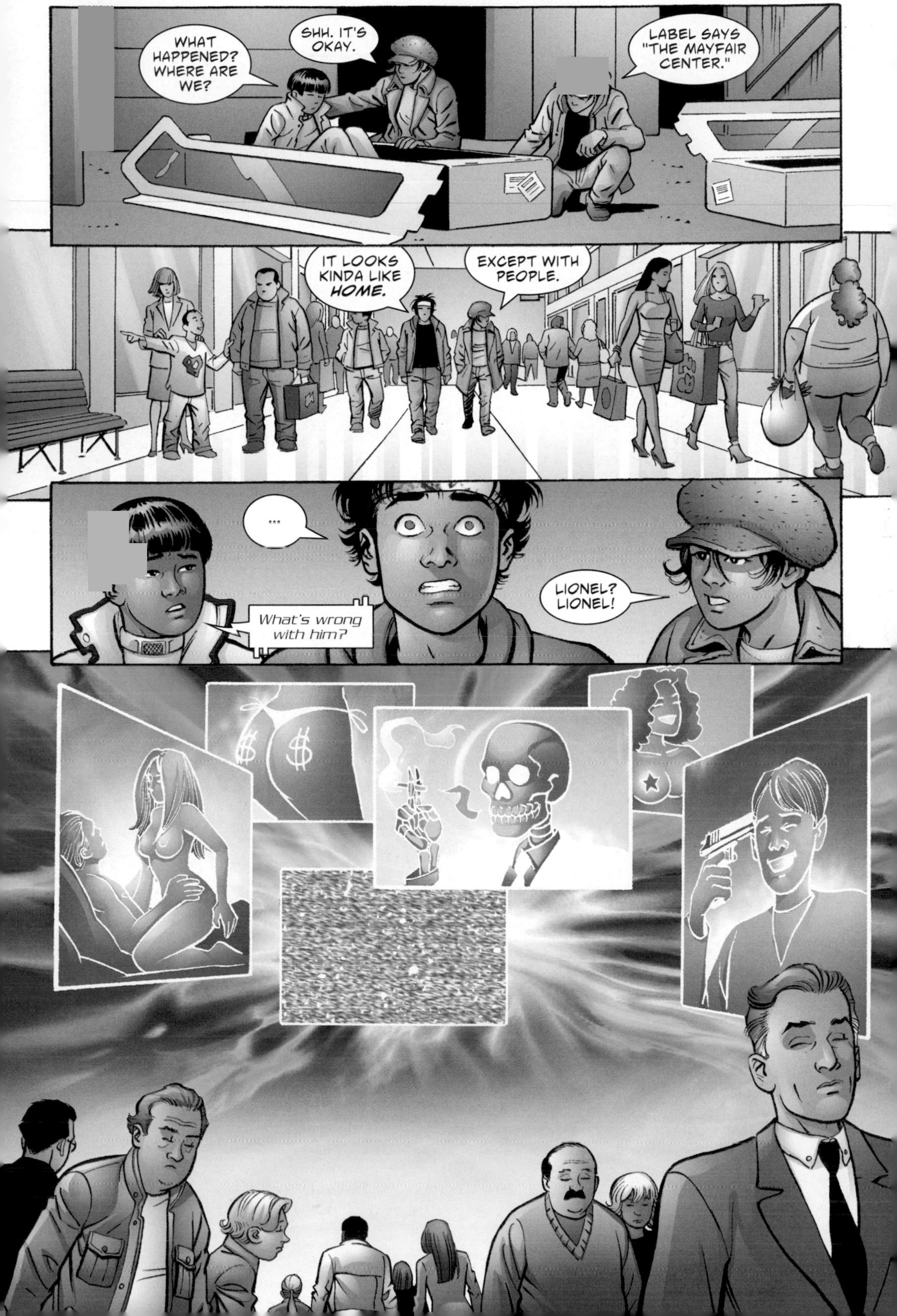
WHAT HAPPENED? WHERE ARE WE?
SHH. IT'S OKAY.
LABEL SAYS "THE MAYFAIR CENTER."
IT LOOKS KINDA LIKE *HOME.*
EXCEPT WITH PEOPLE.
...
What's wrong with him?
LIONEL? LIONEL!

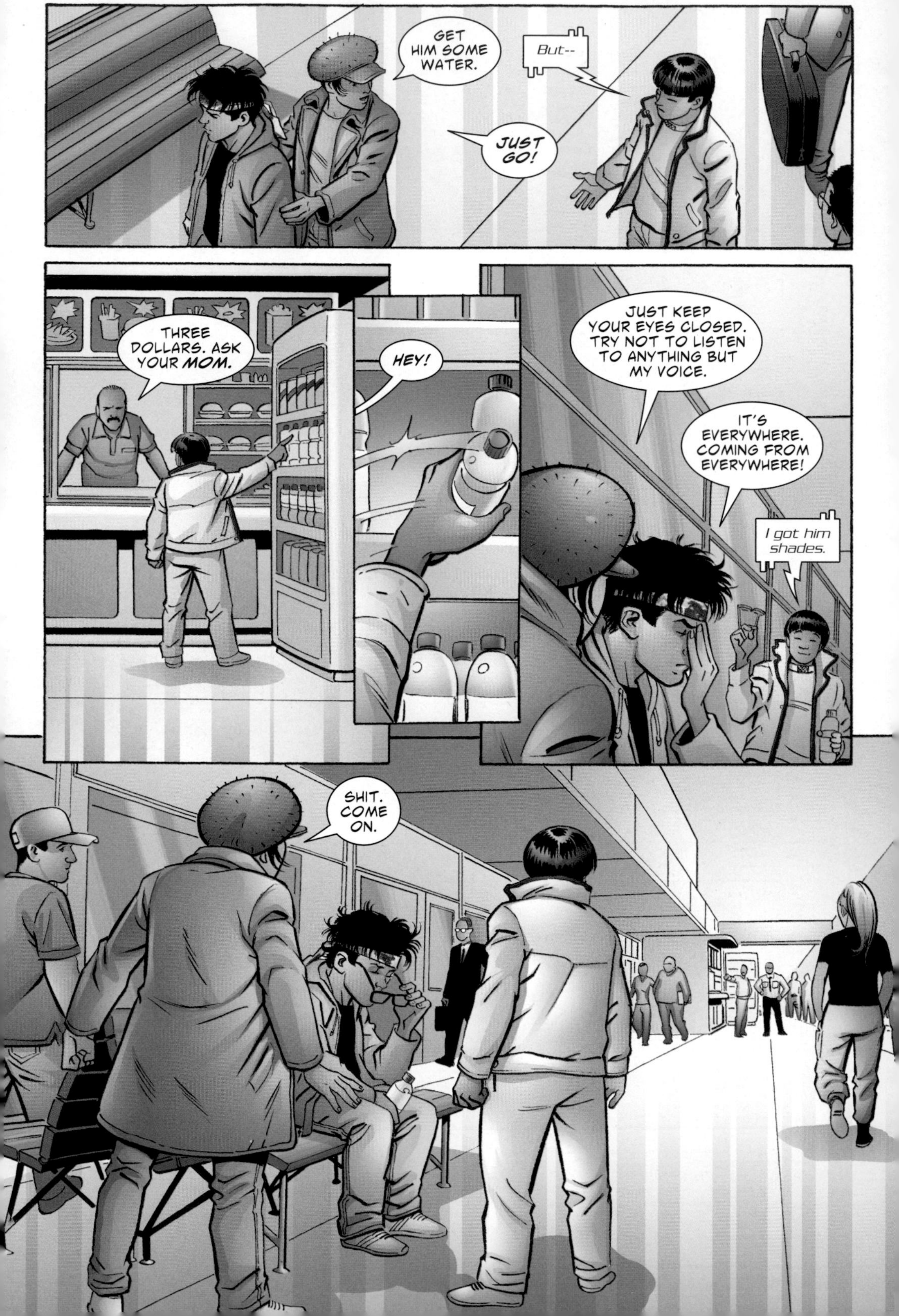
GET HIM SOME WATER.
But--
JUST GO!
THREE DOLLARS. ASK YOUR MOM.
HEY!
JUST KEEP YOUR EYES CLOSED. TRY NOT TO LISTEN TO ANYTHING BUT MY VOICE.
IT'S EVERYWHERE. COMING FROM EVERYWHERE!
I got him shades.
SHIT. COME ON.

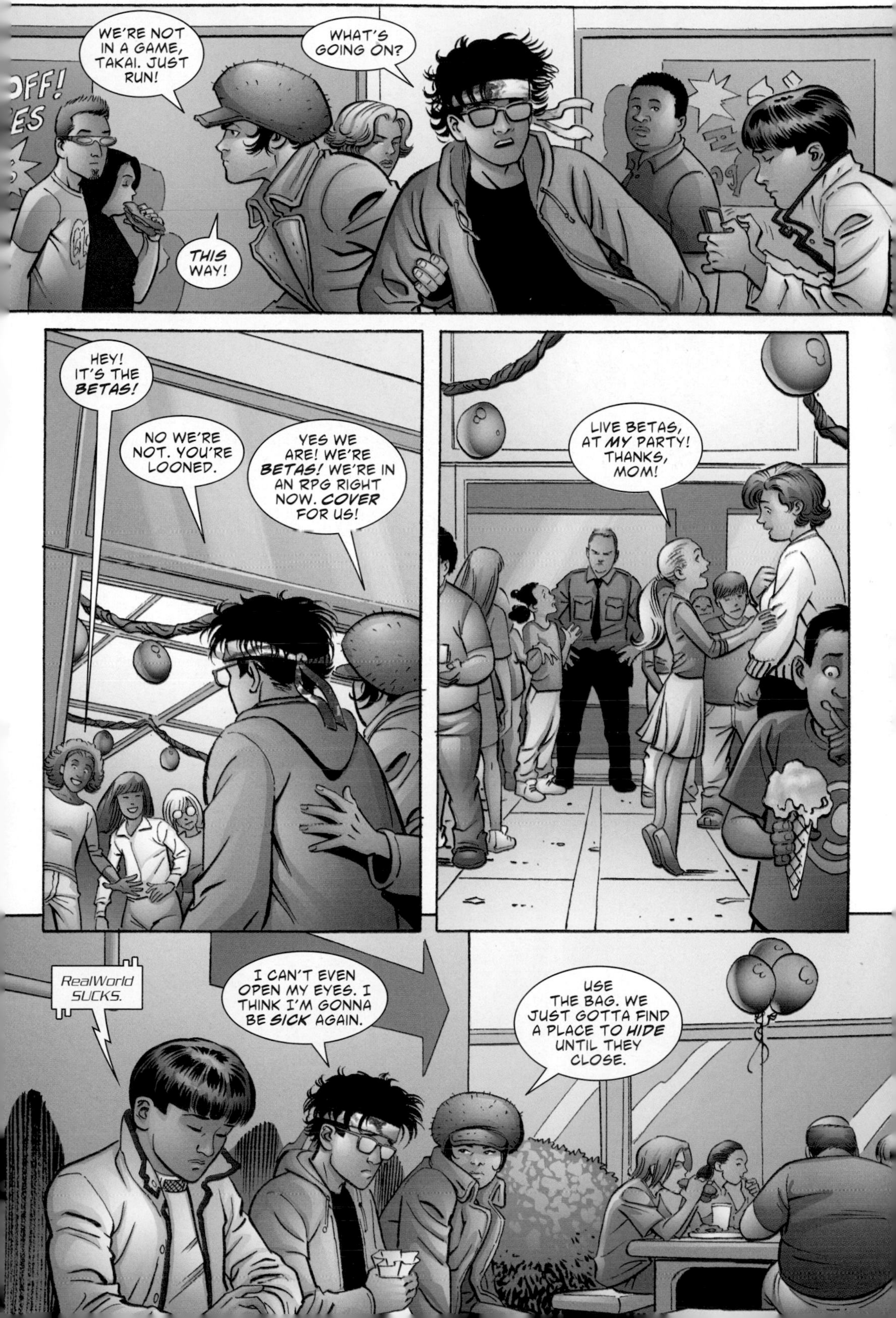
WE'RE NOT IN A GAME, TAKAI. JUST RUN!
WHAT'S GOING ON?
THIS WAY!
HEY! IT'S THE BETAS!
NO WE'RE NOT. YOU'RE LOONED.
YES WE ARE! WE'RE BETAS! WE'RE IN AN RPG RIGHT NOW. COVER FOR US!
LIVE BETAS, AT MY PARTY! THANKS, MOM!
RealWorld SUCKS.
I CAN'T EVEN OPEN MY EYES. I THINK I'M GONNA BE SICK AGAIN.
USE THE BAG. WE JUST GOTTA FIND A PLACE TO HIDE UNTIL THEY CLOSE.

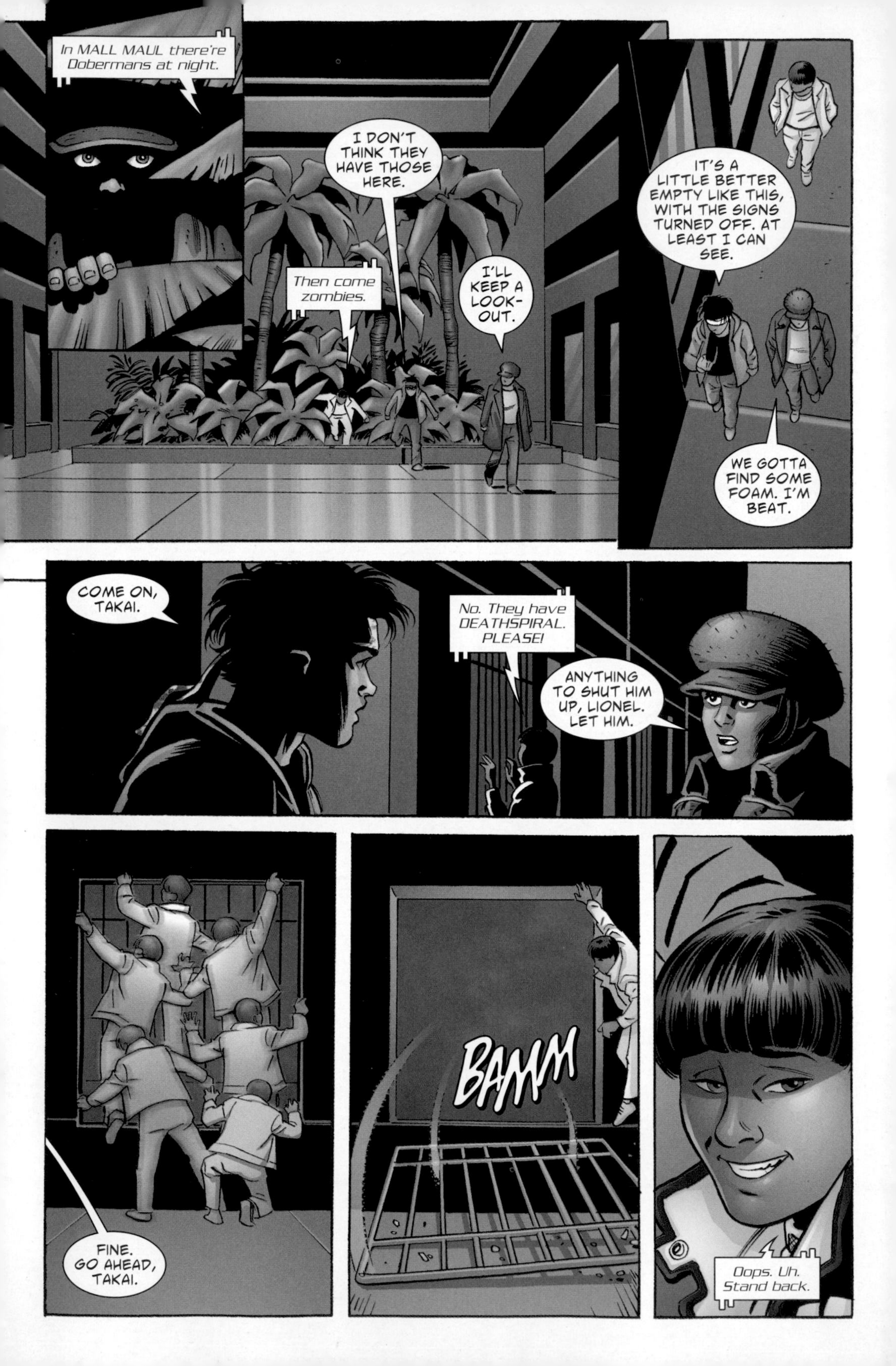

In MALL MAUL there're Dobermans at night.
I DON'T THINK THEY HAVE THOSE HERE.
Then come zombies.
I'LL KEEP A LOOK-OUT.
IT'S A LITTLE BETTER EMPTY LIKE THIS, WITH THE SIGNS TURNED OFF. AT LEAST I CAN SEE.
WE GOTTA FIND SOME FOAM. I'M BEAT.
COME ON, TAKAI.
No. They have DEATHSPIRAL. PLEASE!
ANYTHING TO SHUT HIM UP, LIONEL. LET HIM.
FINE. GO AHEAD, TAKAI.
BAMM
Oops. Uh. Stand back.

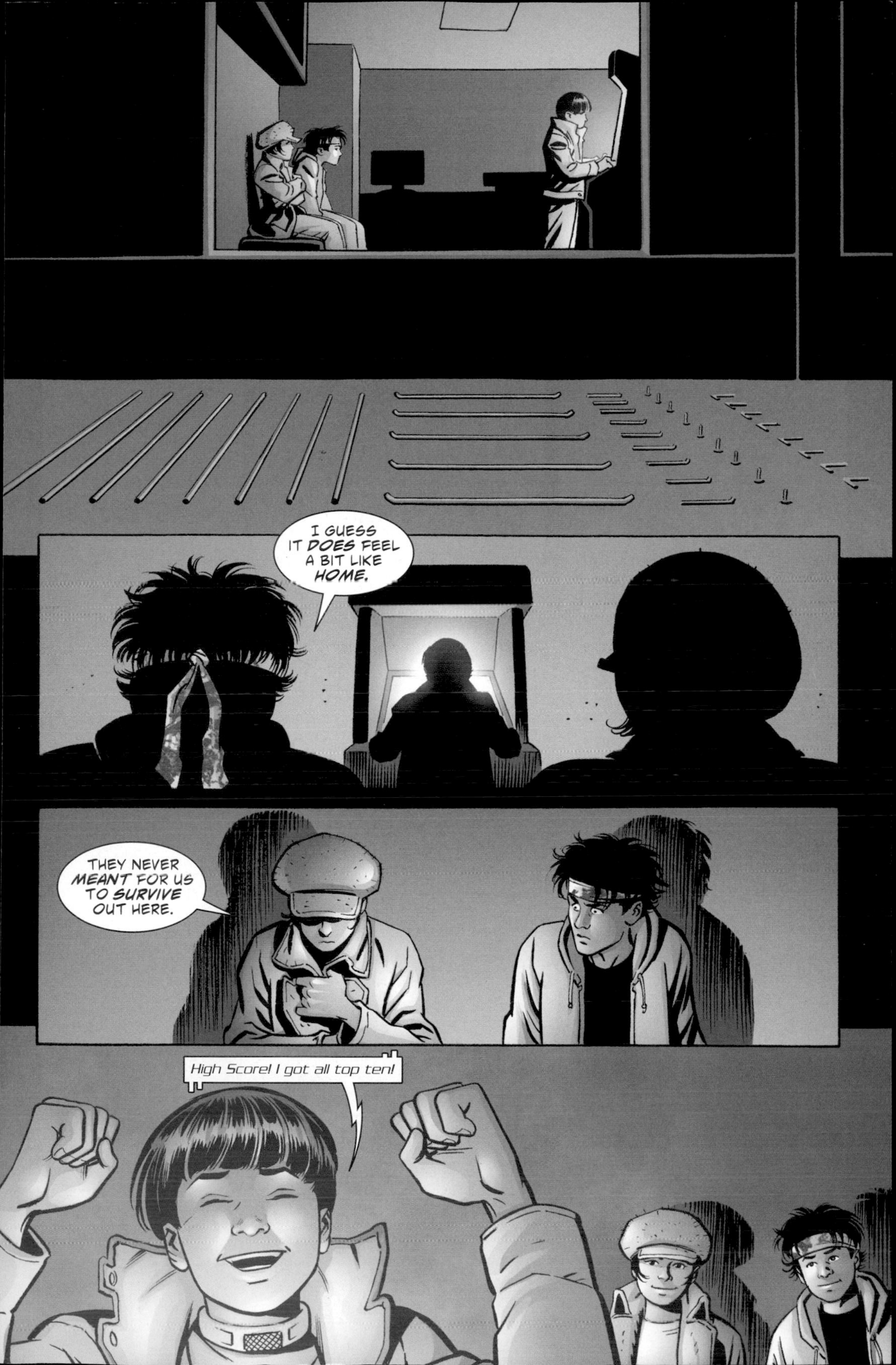
I GUESS IT DOES FEEL A BIT LIKE HOME.
THEY NEVER MEANT FOR US TO SURVIVE OUT HERE.
High Score! I got all top ten!

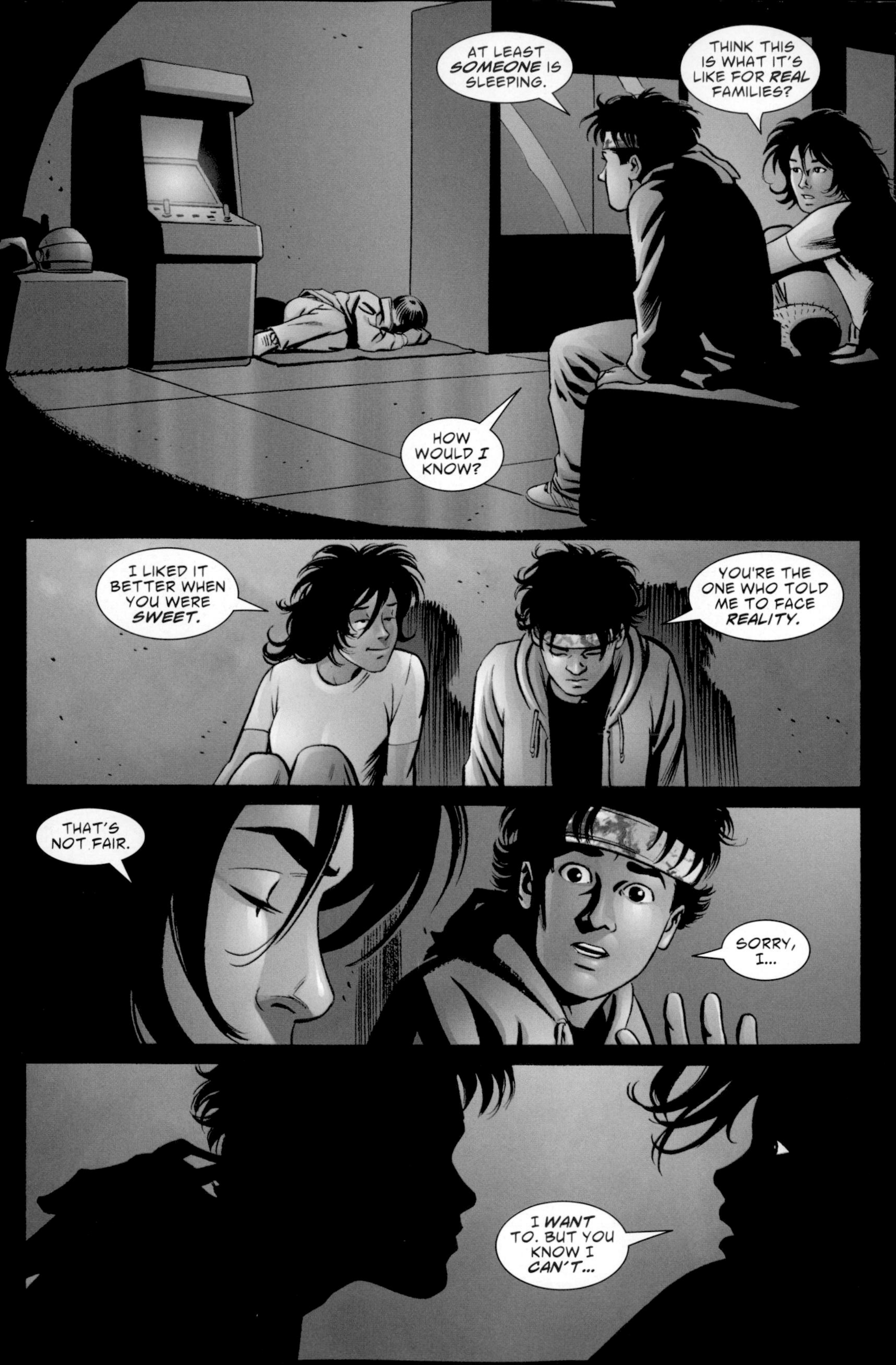
AT LEAST SOMEONE IS SLEEPING.
THINK THIS IS WHAT IT'S LIKE FOR REAL FAMILIES?
HOW WOULD I KNOW?
I LIKED IT BETTER WHEN YOU WERE SWEET.
YOU'RE THE ONE WHO TOLD ME TO FACE REALITY.
THAT'S NOT FAIR.
SORRY, I...
I WANT TO. BUT YOU KNOW I CAN'T...

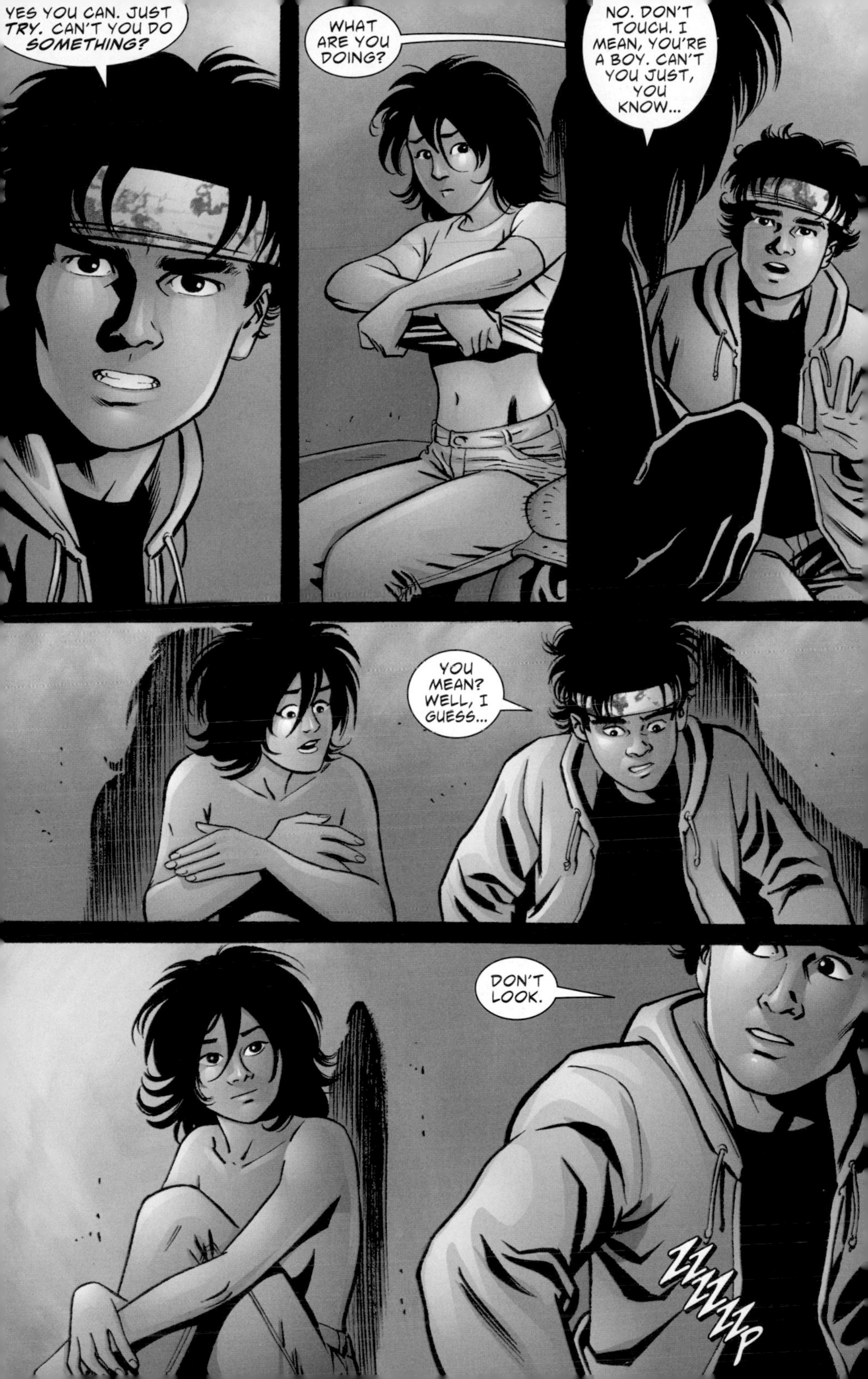
YES YOU CAN. JUST TRY. CAN'T YOU DO SOMETHING?
WHAT ARE YOU DOING?
NO. DON'T TOUCH. I MEAN, YOU'RE A BOY. CAN'T YOU JUST, YOU KNOW...
YOU MEAN? WELL, I GUESS...
DON'T LOOK.
ZZZZZZP

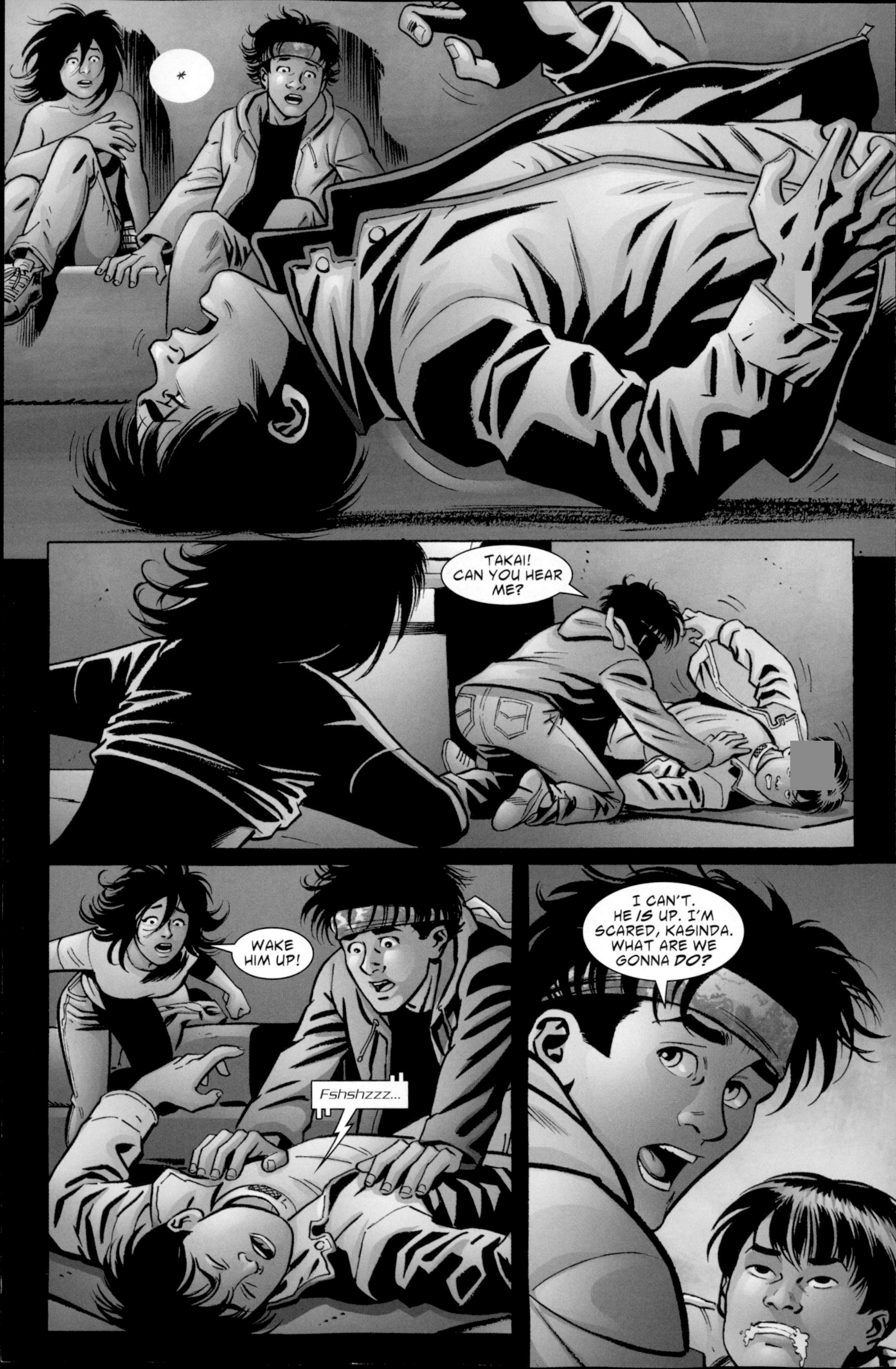
*
TAKAI! CAN YOU HEAR ME?
WAKE HIM UP!
Fshshzzz...
I CAN'T. HE IS UP. I'M SCARED, KASINDA. WHAT ARE WE GONNA DO?

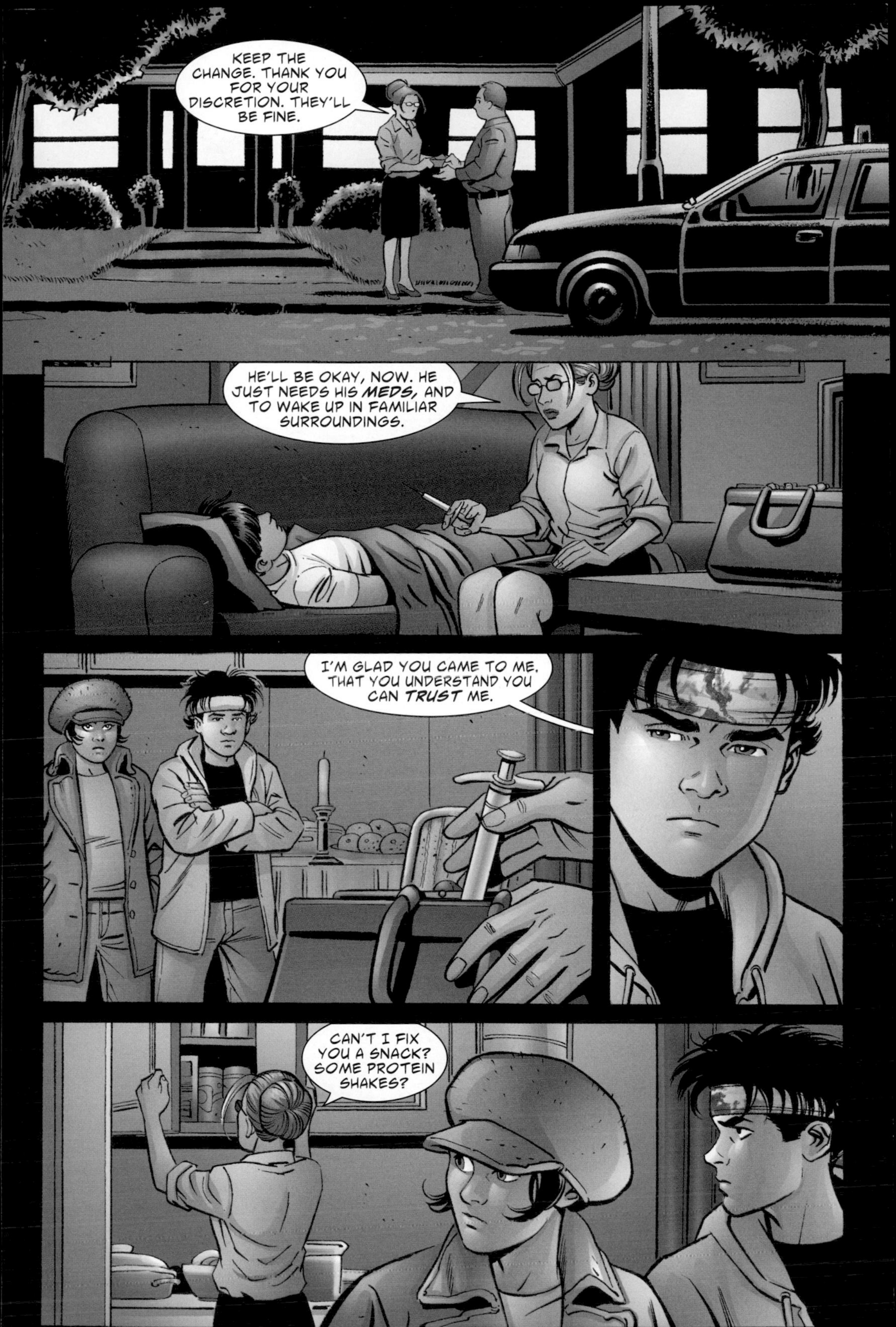
KEEP THE CHANGE. THANK YOU FOR YOUR DISCRETION. THEY'LL BE FINE.
HE'LL BE OKAY, NOW. HE JUST NEEDS HIS *MEDS,* AND TO WAKE UP IN FAMILIAR SURROUNDINGS.
I'M GLAD YOU CAME TO ME. THAT YOU UNDERSTAND YOU CAN *TRUST* ME.
CAN'T I FIX YOU A SNACK? SOME PROTEIN SHAKES?

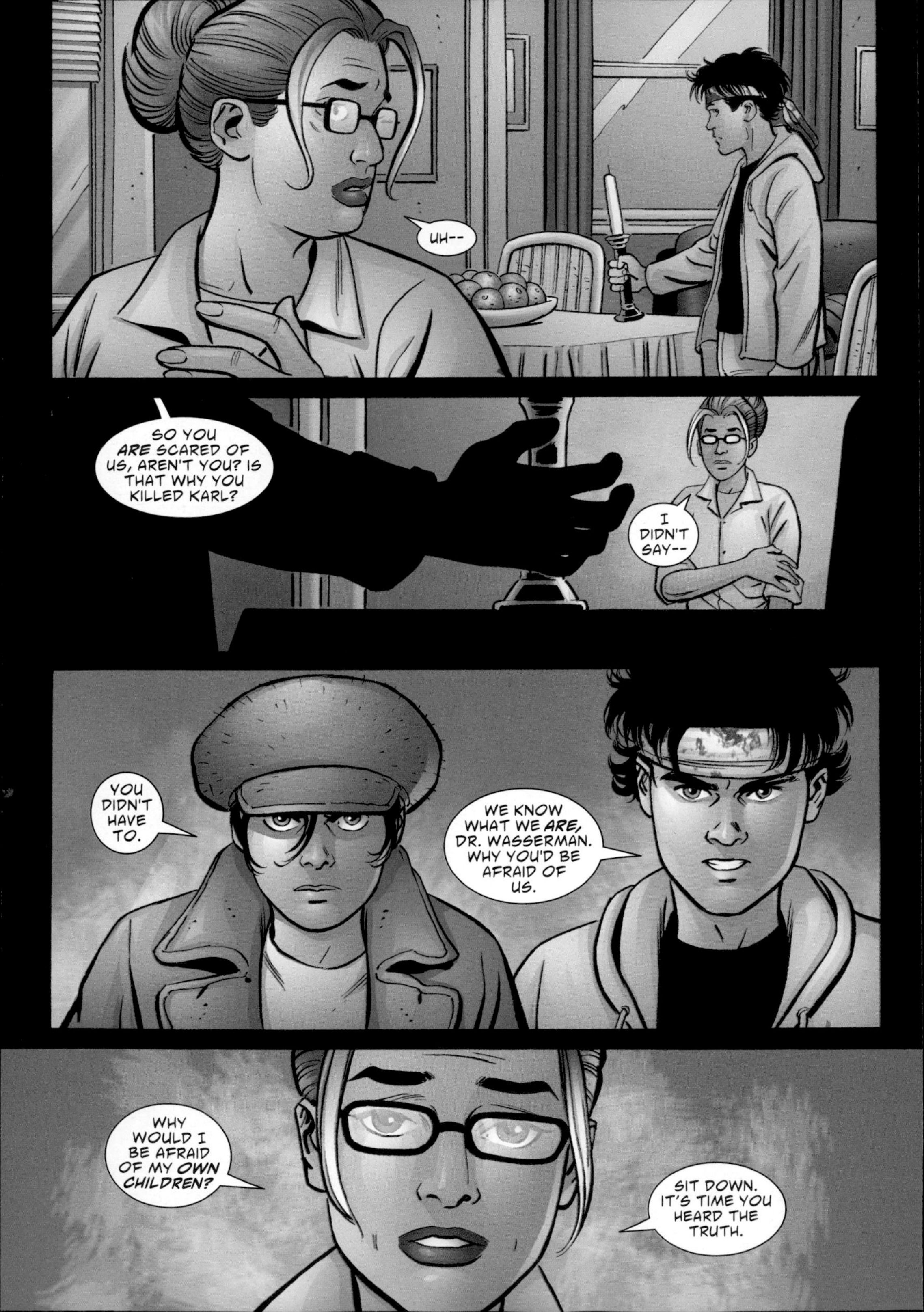
UH--
SO YOU *ARE* SCARED OF US, AREN'T YOU? IS THAT WHY YOU KILLED KARL?
I DIDN'T SAY--
YOU DIDN'T HAVE TO.
WE KNOW WHAT WE *ARE,* DR. WASSERMAN. WHY YOU'D BE AFRAID OF US.
WHY WOULD I BE AFRAID OF MY *OWN CHILDREN?*
SIT DOWN. IT'S TIME YOU HEARD THE TRUTH.

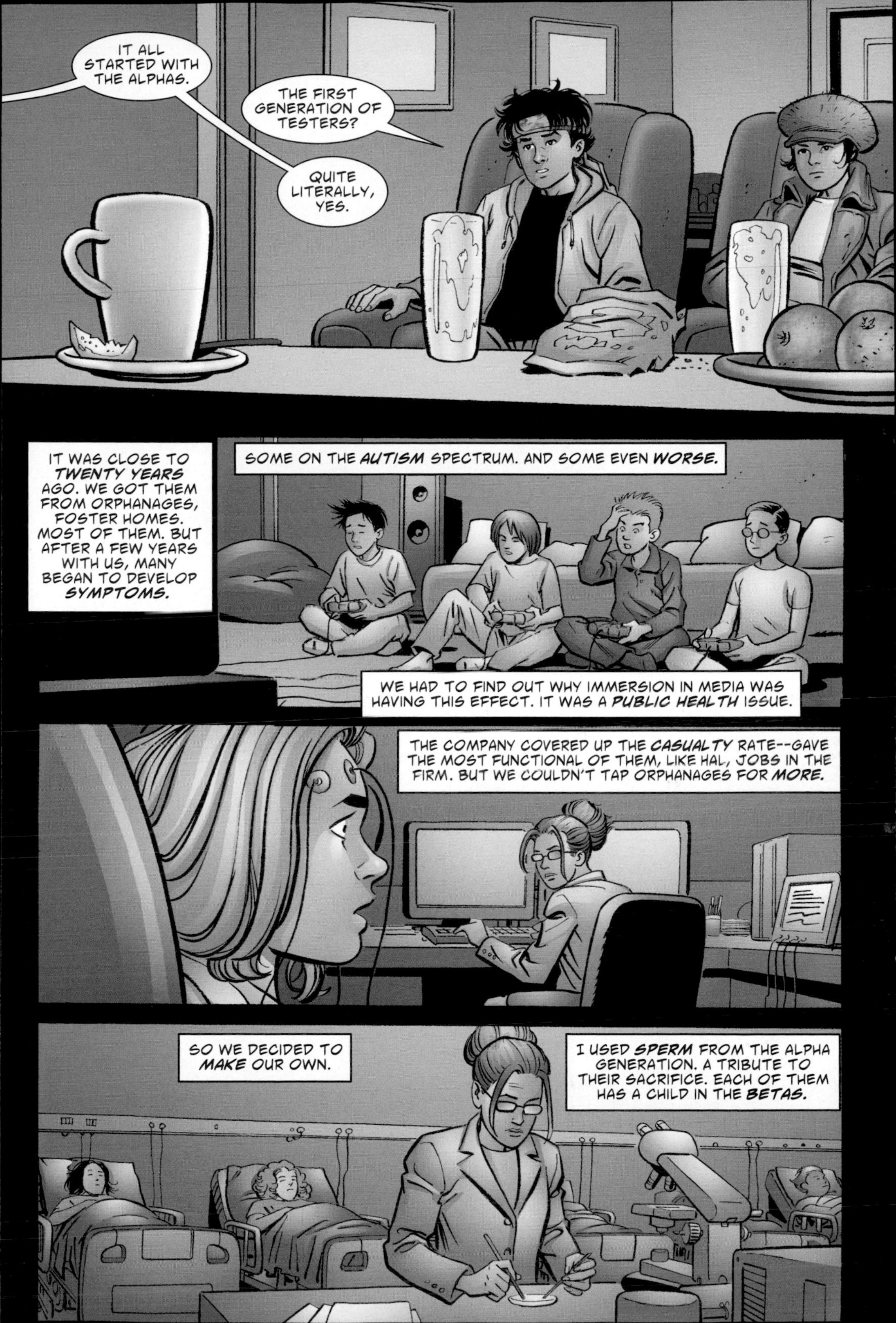
IT ALL STARTED WITH THE ALPHAS.
THE FIRST GENERATION OF TESTERS?
QUITE LITERALLY, YES.
IT WAS CLOSE TO *TWENTY YEARS* AGO. WE GOT THEM FROM ORPHANAGES, FOSTER HOMES. MOST OF THEM. BUT AFTER A FEW YEARS WITH US, MANY BEGAN TO DEVELOP *SYMPTOMS.*
SOME ON THE *AUTISM* SPECTRUM. AND SOME EVEN *WORSE.*
WE HAD TO FIND OUT WHY IMMERSION IN MEDIA WAS HAVING THIS EFFECT. IT WAS A *PUBLIC HEALTH* ISSUE.
THE COMPANY COVERED UP THE *CASUALTY* RATE--GAVE THE MOST FUNCTIONAL OF THEM, LIKE HAL, JOBS IN THE FIRM. BUT WE COULDN'T TAP ORPHANAGES FOR *MORE.*
SO WE DECIDED TO *MAKE* OUR OWN.
I USED *SPERM* FROM THE ALPHA GENERATION. A TRIBUTE TO THEIR SACRIFICE. EACH OF THEM HAS A CHILD IN THE *BETAS.*

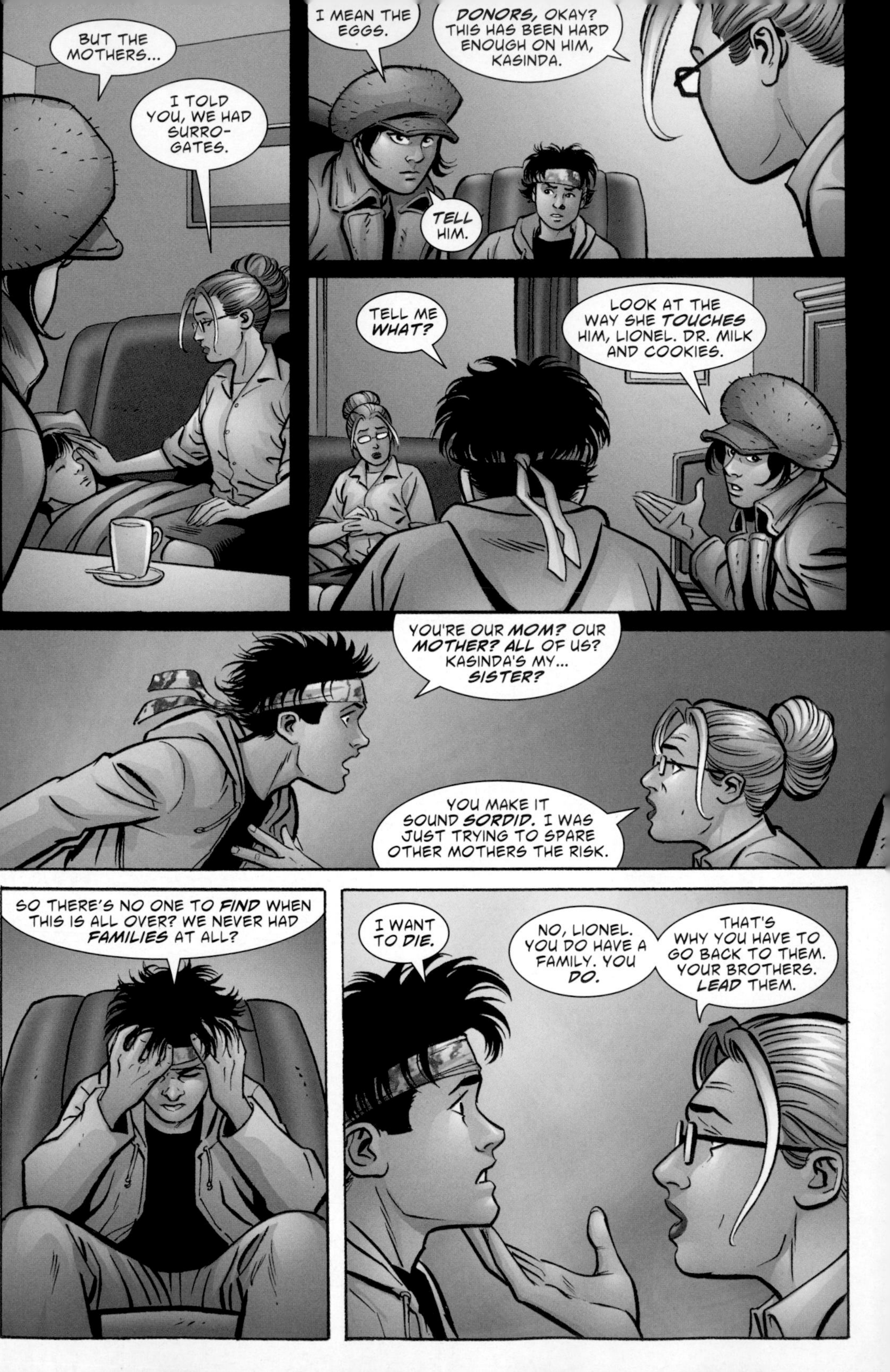
BUT THE MOTHERS...
I TOLD YOU, WE HAD SURRO-GATES.
I MEAN THE EGGS.
TELL HIM.
DONORS, OKAY? THIS HAS BEEN HARD ENOUGH ON HIM, KASINDA.
TELL ME WHAT?
LOOK AT THE WAY SHE TOUCHES HIM, LIONEL. DR. MILK AND COOKIES.
YOU'RE OUR MOM? OUR MOTHER? ALL OF US? KASINDA'S MY... SISTER?
YOU MAKE IT SOUND SORDID. I WAS JUST TRYING TO SPARE OTHER MOTHERS THE RISK.
SO THERE'S NO ONE TO FIND WHEN THIS IS ALL OVER? WE NEVER HAD FAMILIES AT ALL?
I WANT TO DIE.
NO, LIONEL. YOU DO HAVE A FAMILY. YOU DO.
THAT'S WHY YOU HAVE TO GO BACK TO THEM. YOUR BROTHERS. LEAD THEM.

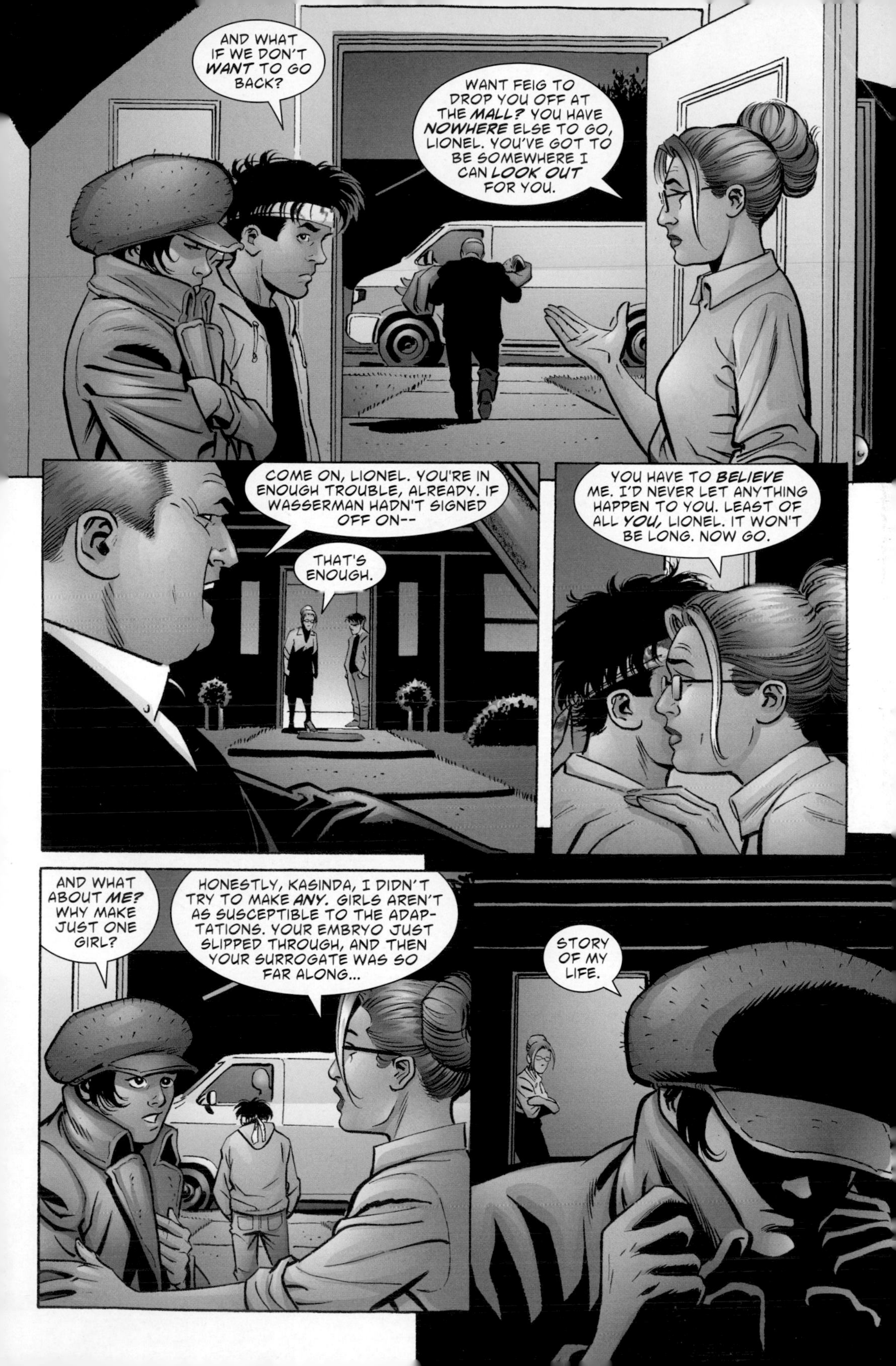

AND WHAT IF WE DON'T *WANT* TO GO BACK?
WANT FEIG TO DROP YOU OFF AT THE *MALL?* YOU HAVE *NOWHERE* ELSE TO GO, LIONEL. YOU'VE GOT TO BE SOMEWHERE I CAN *LOOK OUT* FOR YOU.
COME ON, LIONEL. YOU'RE IN ENOUGH TROUBLE, ALREADY. IF WASSERMAN HADN'T SIGNED OFF ON--
THAT'S ENOUGH.
YOU HAVE TO *BELIEVE* ME. I'D NEVER LET ANYTHING HAPPEN TO YOU. LEAST OF ALL *YOU,* LIONEL. IT WON'T BE LONG. NOW GO.
AND WHAT ABOUT *ME?* WHY MAKE JUST ONE GIRL?
HONESTLY, KASINDA, I DIDN'T TRY TO MAKE *ANY.* GIRLS AREN'T AS SUSCEPTIBLE TO THE ADAPTATIONS. YOUR EMBRYO JUST SLIPPED THROUGH, AND THEN YOUR SURROGATE WAS SO FAR ALONG...
STORY OF MY LIFE.

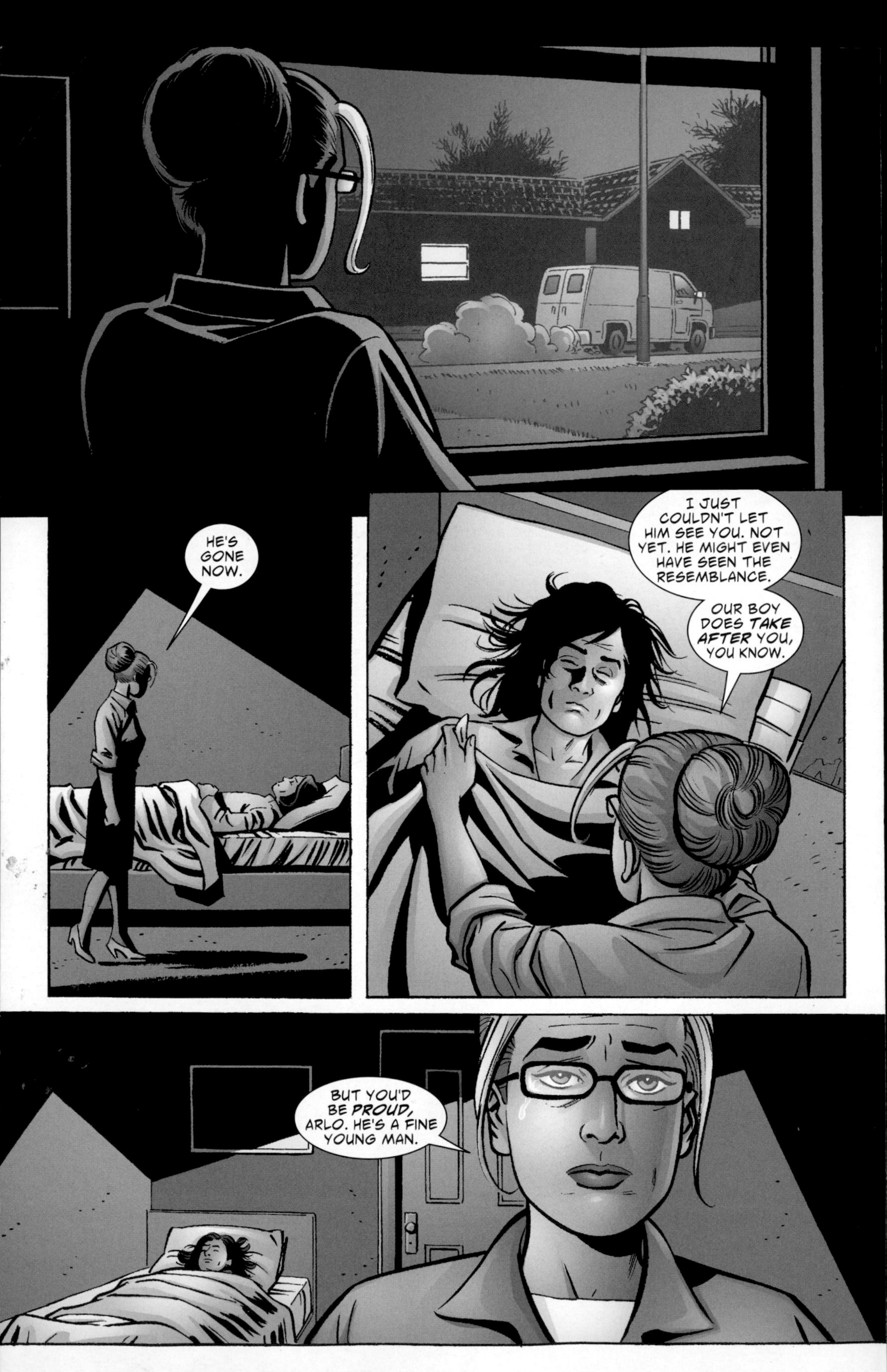
HE'S GONE NOW.
I JUST COULDN'T LET HIM SEE YOU. NOT YET. HE MIGHT EVEN HAVE SEEN THE RESEMBLANCE.
OUR BOY DOES TAKE AFTER YOU, YOU KNOW.
BUT YOU'D BE PROUD, ARLO. HE'S A FINE YOUNG MAN.

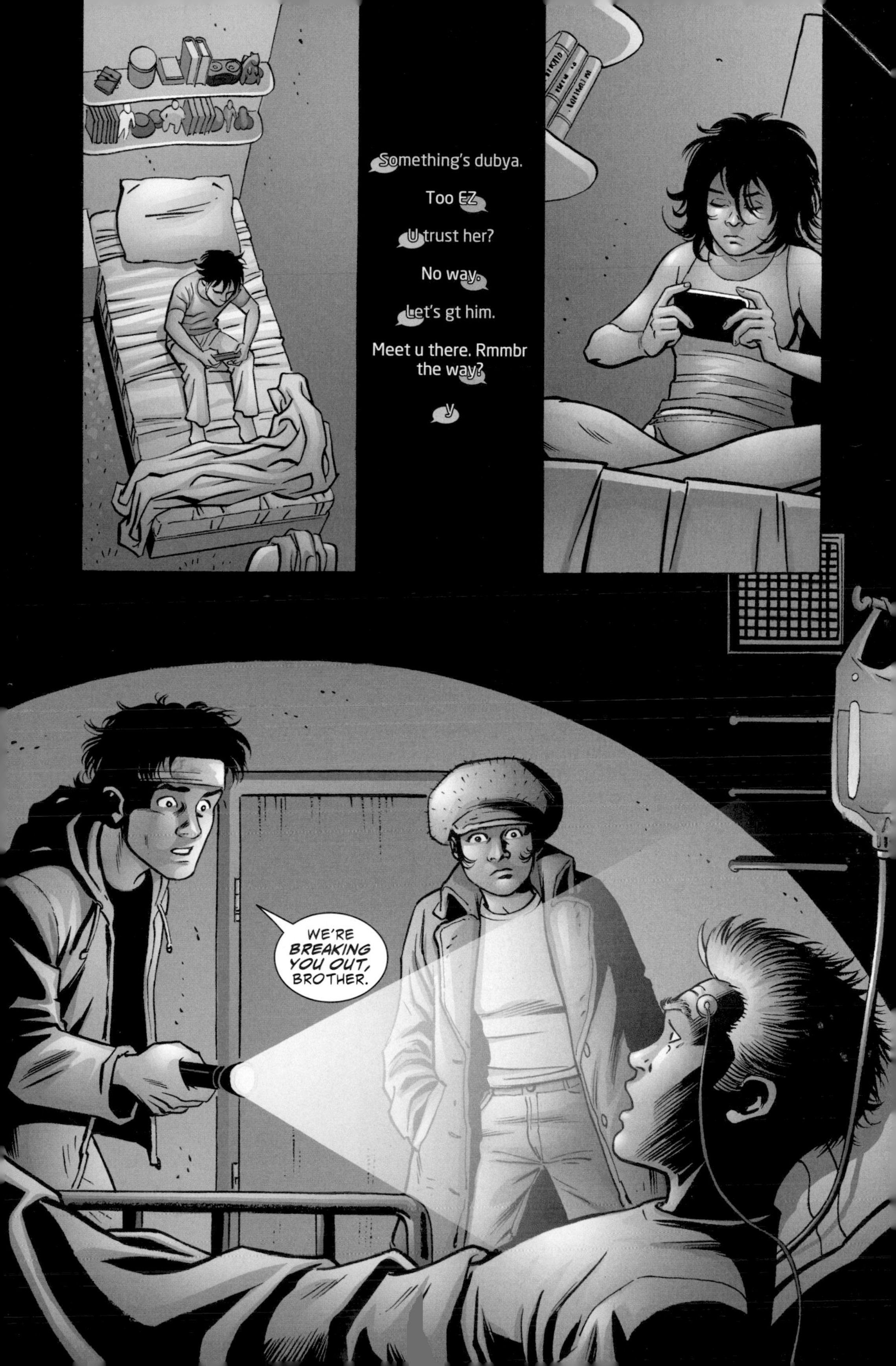
Something's dubya.
Too EZ
U trust her?
No way.
Let's gt him.
Meet u there. Rmmbr the way?
y
WE'RE BREAKING YOU OUT, BROTHER.

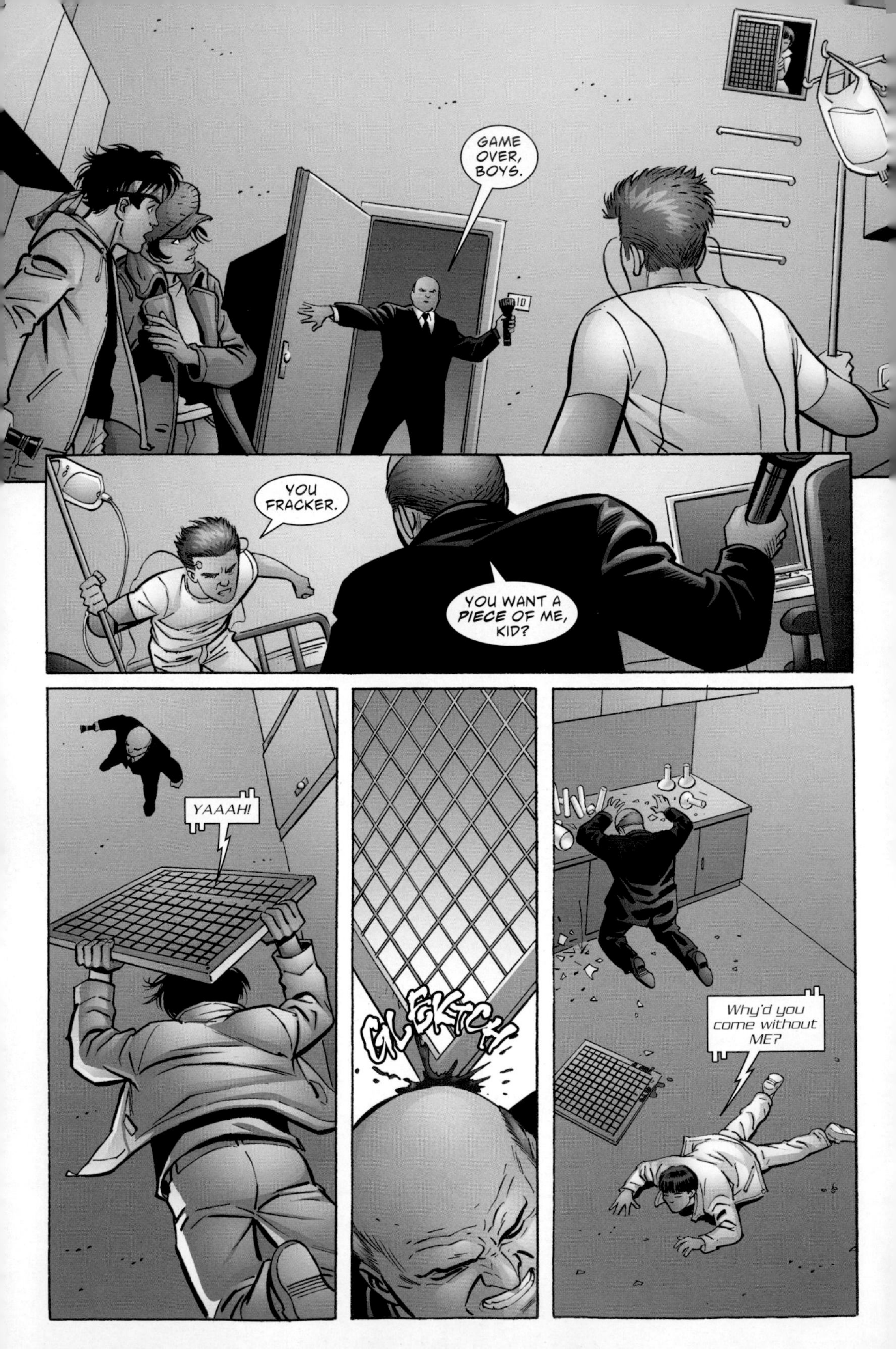
GAME OVER, BOYS.
YOU FRACKER.
YOU WANT A PIECE OF ME, KID?
YAAAH!
GLEKTCH
Why'd you come without ME?

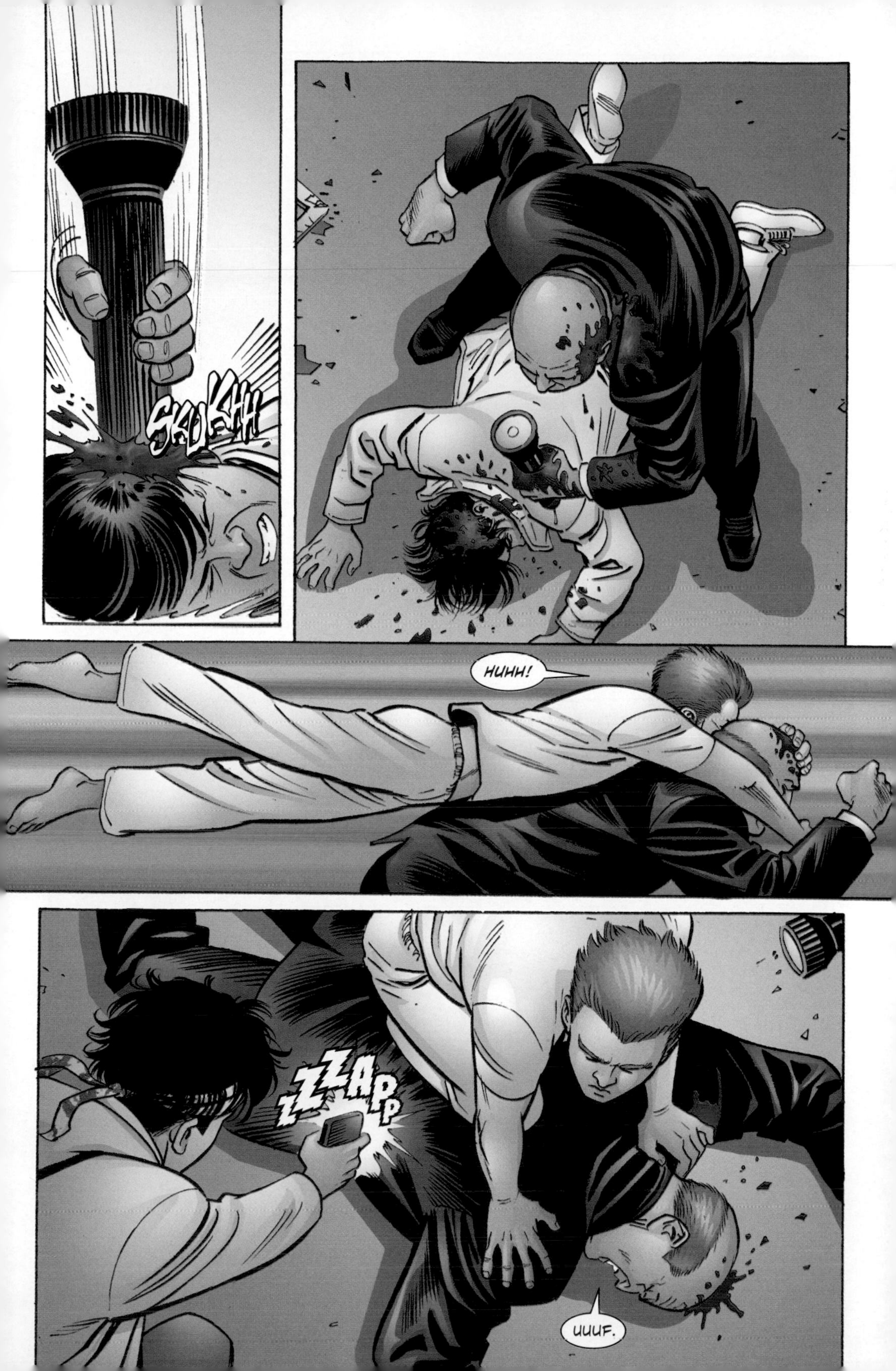
SKLOKHH
HUHH!
ZZZZAPP
UUUF.

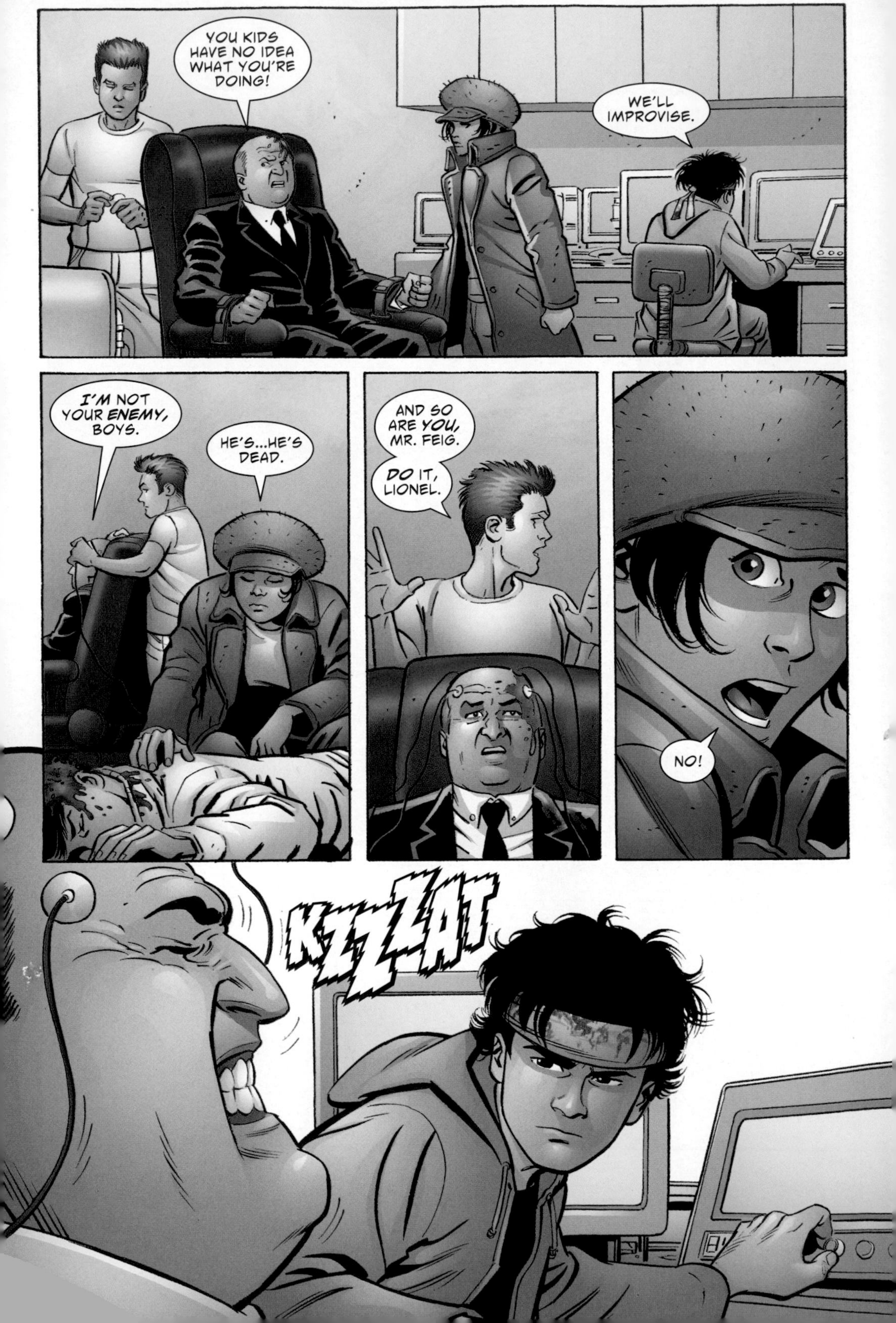
YOU KIDS HAVE NO IDEA WHAT YOU'RE DOING!
WE'LL IMPROVISE.
I'M NOT YOUR ENEMY, BOYS.
HE'S...HE'S DEAD.
AND SO ARE YOU, MR. FEIG.
DO IT, LIONEL.
NO!
KZZZAT

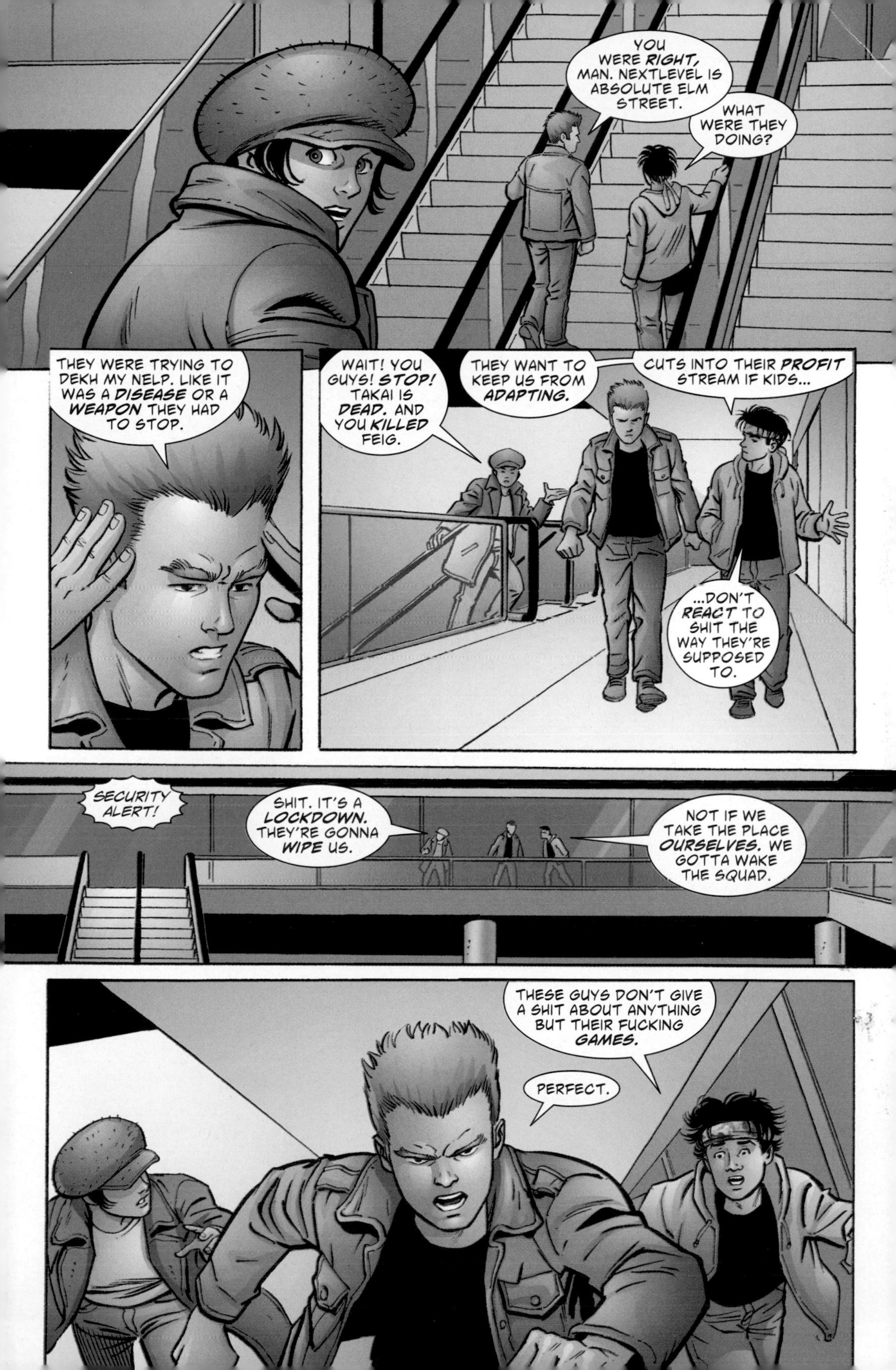
YOU WERE RIGHT, MAN. NEXTLEVEL IS ABSOLUTE ELM STREET.
WHAT WERE THEY DOING?
THEY WERE TRYING TO DEKH MY NELP. LIKE IT WAS A DISEASE OR A WEAPON THEY HAD TO STOP.
WAIT! YOU GUYS! STOP! TAKAI IS DEAD. AND YOU KILLED FEIG.
THEY WANT TO KEEP US FROM ADAPTING.
CUTS INTO THEIR PROFIT STREAM IF KIDS...
...DON'T REACT TO SHIT THE WAY THEY'RE SUPPOSED TO.
SECURITY ALERT!
SHIT. IT'S A LOCKDOWN. THEY'RE GONNA WIPE US.
NOT IF WE TAKE THE PLACE OURSELVES. WE GOTTA WAKE THE SQUAD.
THESE GUYS DON'T GIVE A SHIT ABOUT ANYTHING BUT THEIR FUCKING GAMES.
PERFECT.

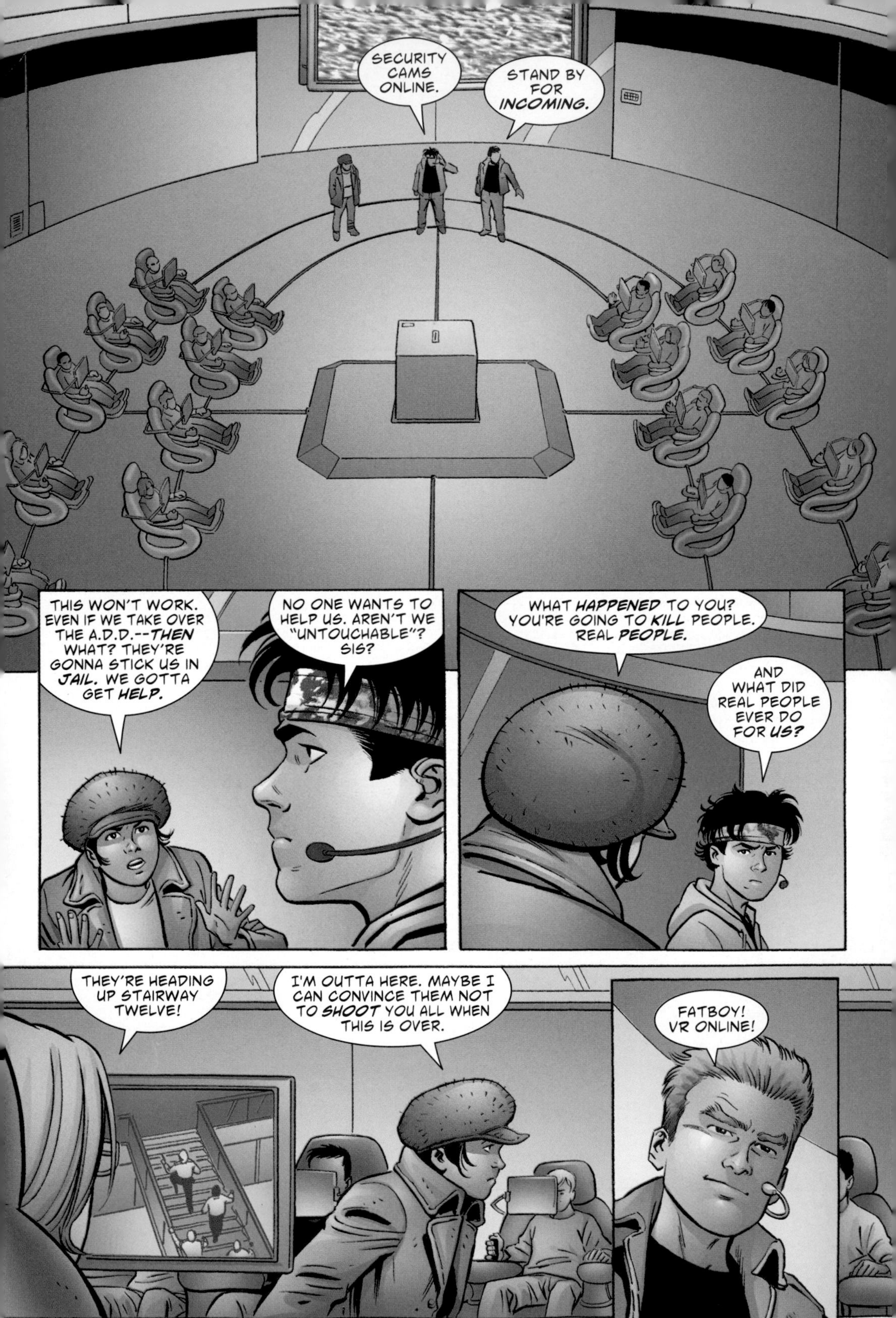

SECURITY CAMS ONLINE.
STAND BY FOR INCOMING.
THIS WON'T WORK. EVEN IF WE TAKE OVER THE A.D.D.--THEN WHAT? THEY'RE GONNA STICK US IN JAIL. WE GOTTA GET HELP.
NO ONE WANTS TO HELP US. AREN'T WE "UNTOUCHABLE"? SIS?
WHAT HAPPENED TO YOU? YOU'RE GOING TO KILL PEOPLE. REAL PEOPLE.
AND WHAT DID REAL PEOPLE EVER DO FOR US?
THEY'RE HEADING UP STAIRWAY TWELVE!
I'M OUTTA HERE. MAYBE I CAN CONVINCE THEM NOT TO SHOOT YOU ALL WHEN THIS IS OVER.
FATBOY! VR ONLINE!

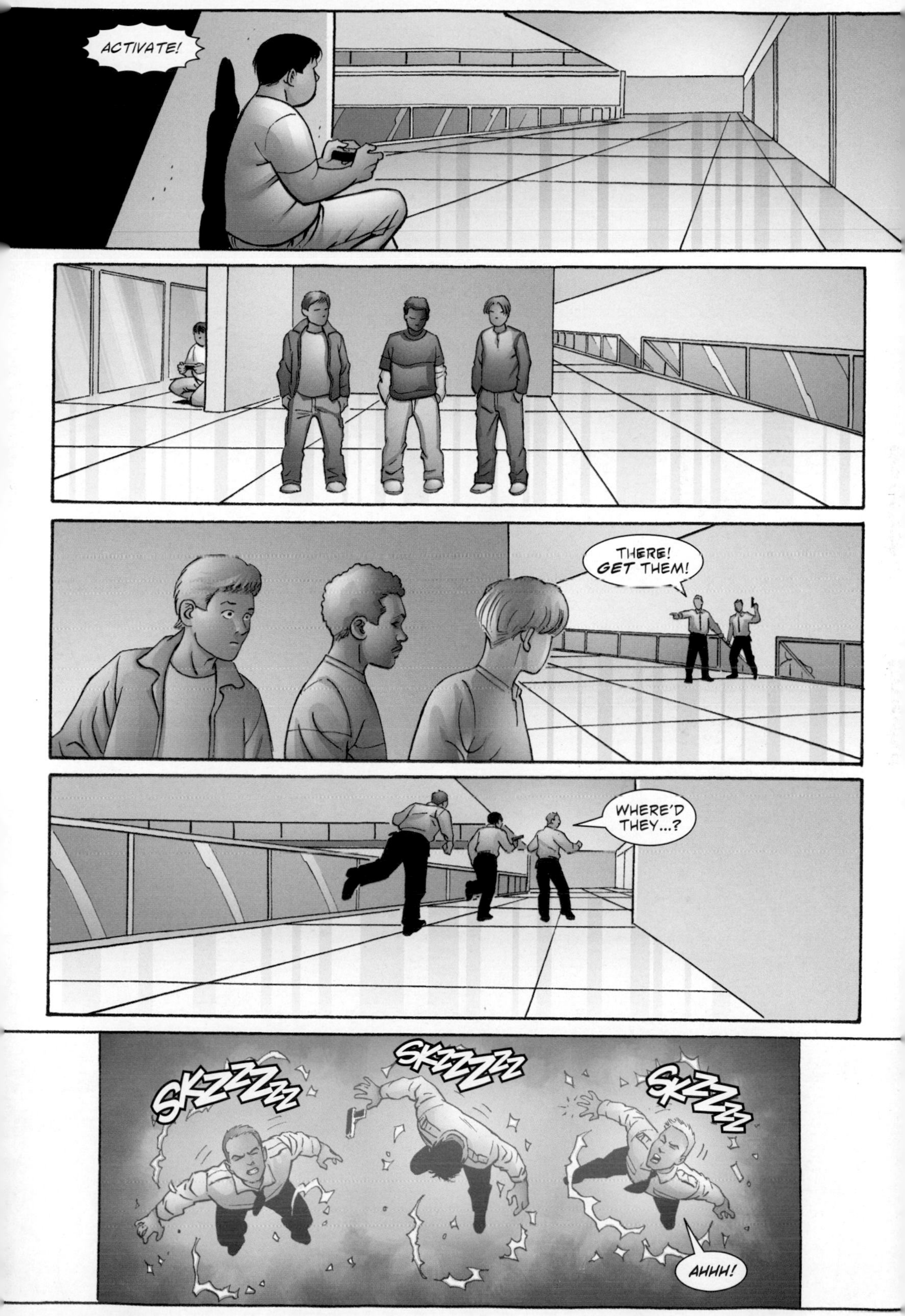
ACTIVATE!
THERE! GET THEM!
WHERE'D THEY...?
SKZZZZZZ
SKZZZZZZ
SKZZZZ
AHHH!

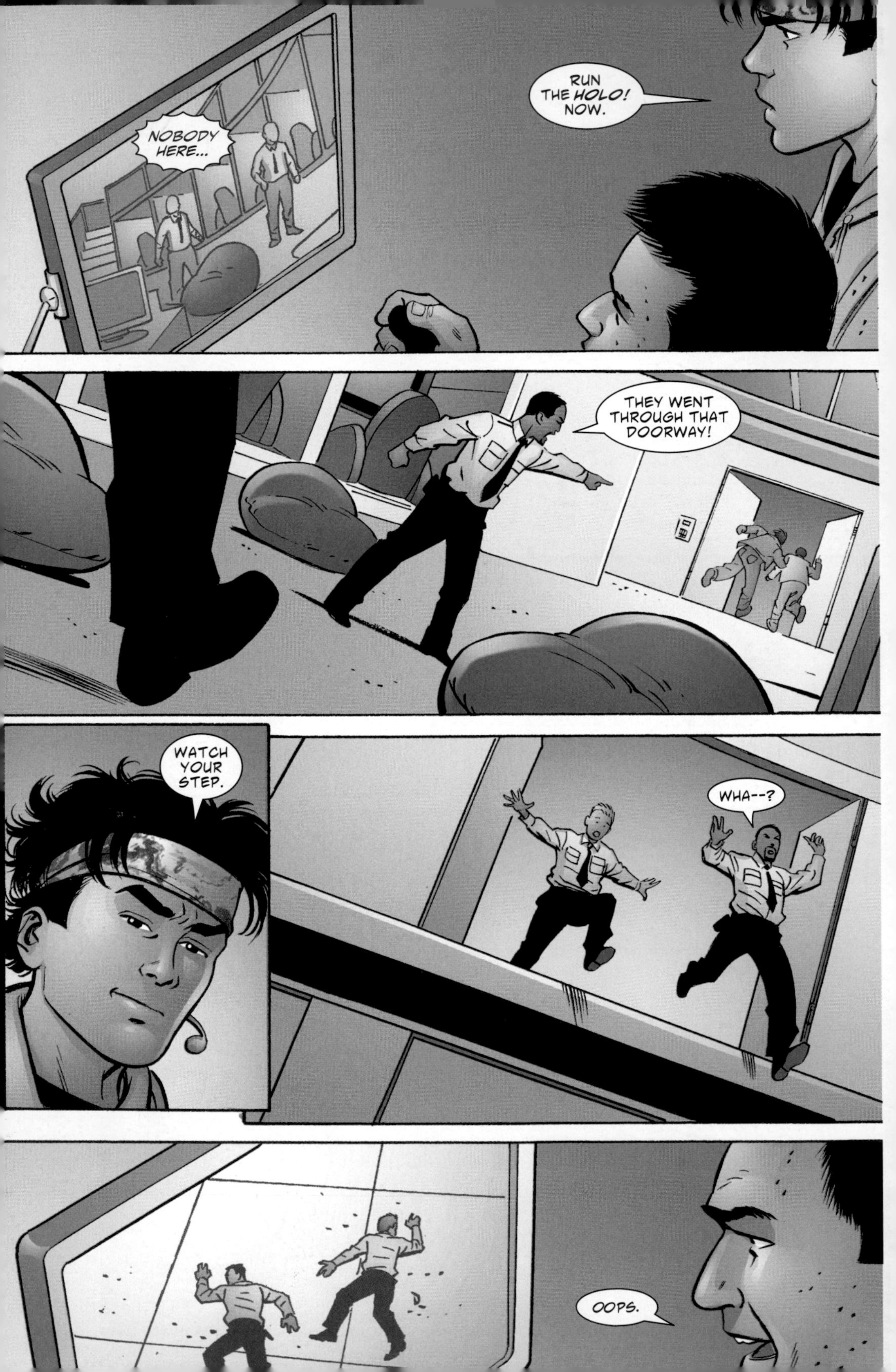
RUN THE HOLO! NOW.
NOBODY HERE...
THEY WENT THROUGH THAT DOORWAY!
WATCH YOUR STEP.
WHA--?
OOPS.

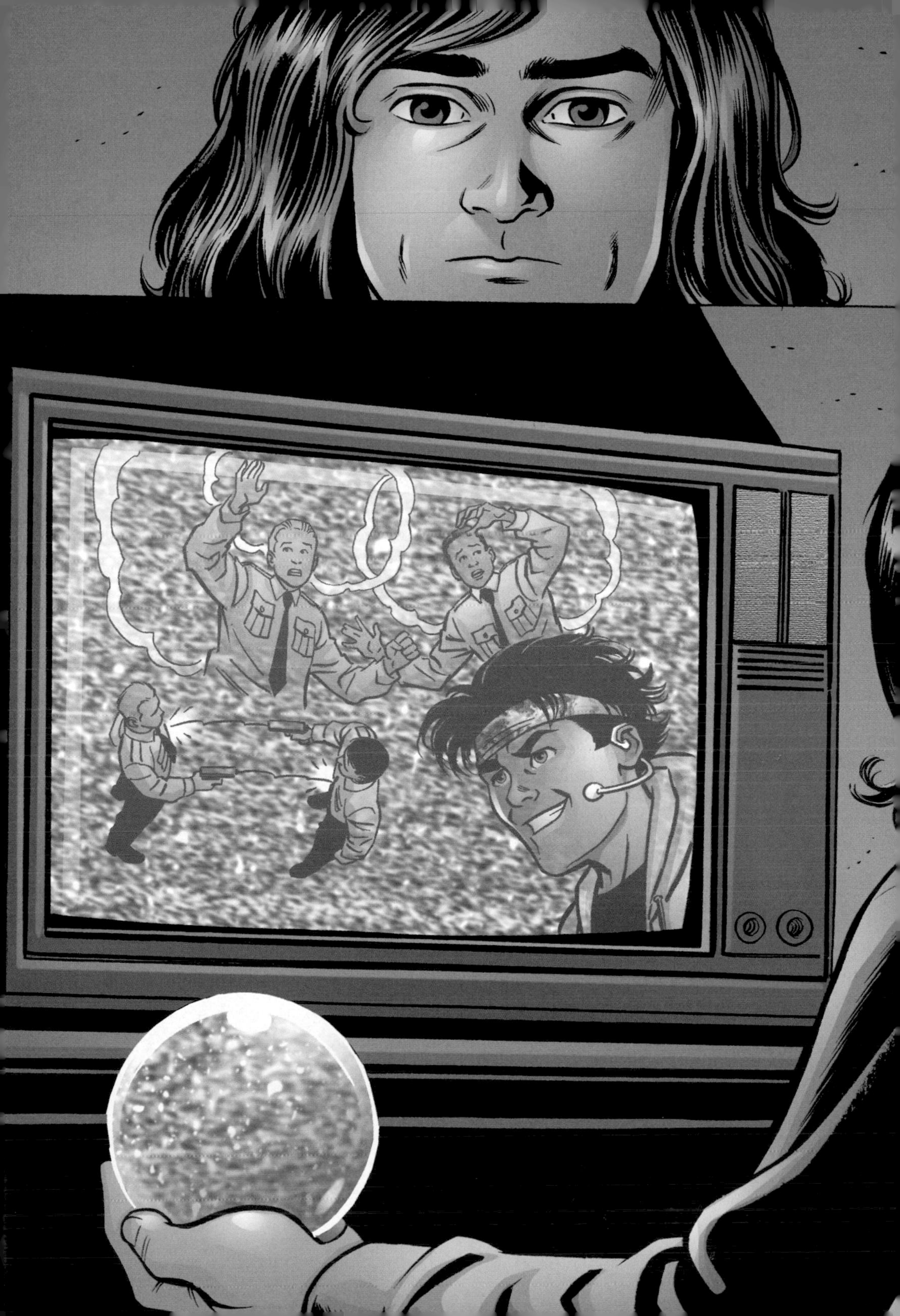

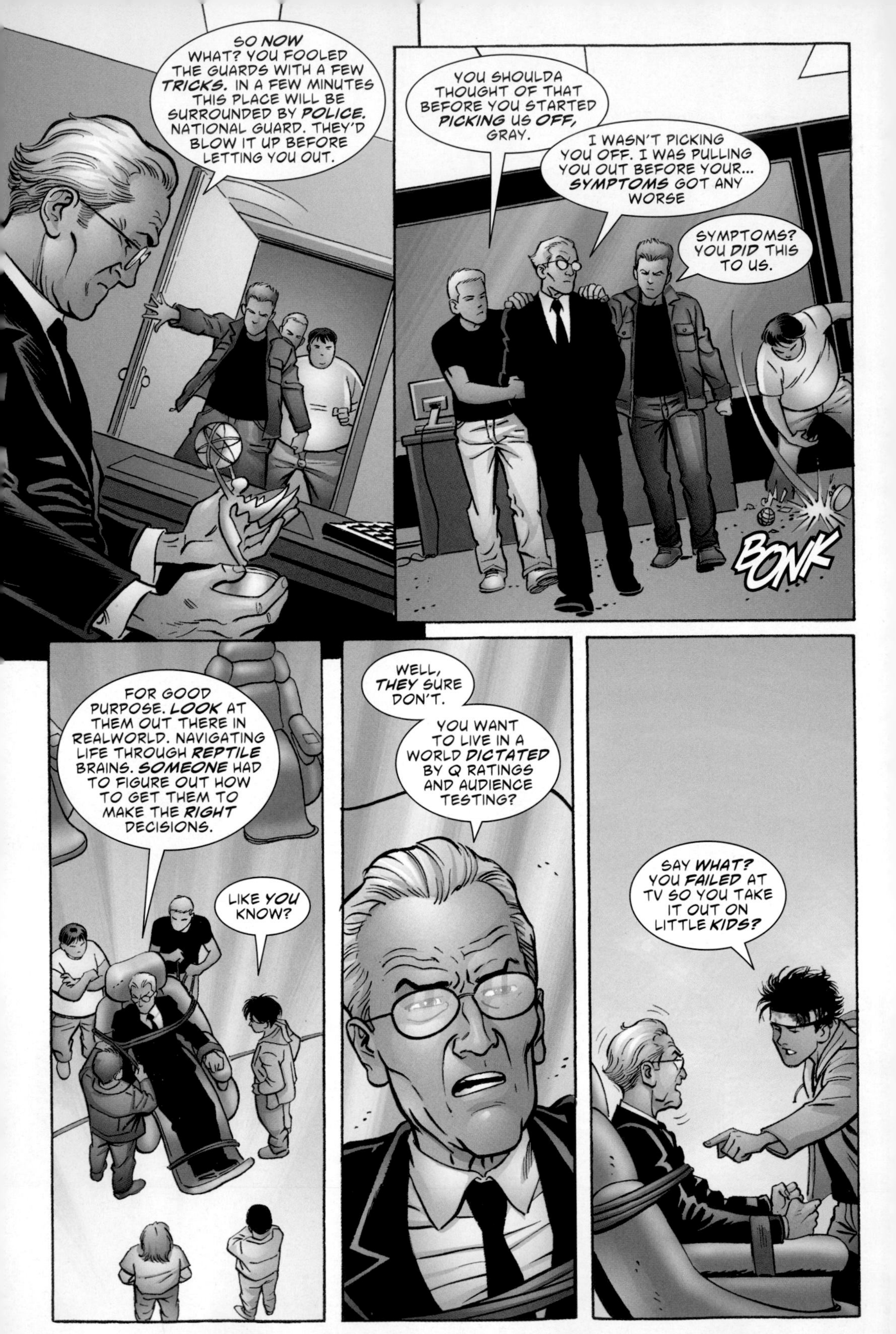
SO NOW WHAT? YOU FOOLED THE GUARDS WITH A FEW TRICKS. IN A FEW MINUTES THIS PLACE WILL BE SURROUNDED BY POLICE. NATIONAL GUARD. THEY'D BLOW IT UP BEFORE LETTING YOU OUT.
YOU SHOULDA THOUGHT OF THAT BEFORE YOU STARTED PICKING US OFF, GRAY.
I WASN'T PICKING YOU OFF. I WAS PULLING YOU OUT BEFORE YOUR... SYMPTOMS GOT ANY WORSE
SYMPTOMS? YOU DID THIS TO US.
BONK
FOR GOOD PURPOSE. LOOK AT THEM OUT THERE IN REALWORLD. NAVIGATING LIFE THROUGH REPTILE BRAINS. SOMEONE HAD TO FIGURE OUT HOW TO GET THEM TO MAKE THE RIGHT DECISIONS.
LIKE YOU KNOW?
WELL, THEY SURE DON'T.
YOU WANT TO LIVE IN A WORLD DICTATED BY Q RATINGS AND AUDIENCE TESTING?
SAY WHAT? YOU FAILED AT TV SO YOU TAKE IT OUT ON LITTLE KIDS?

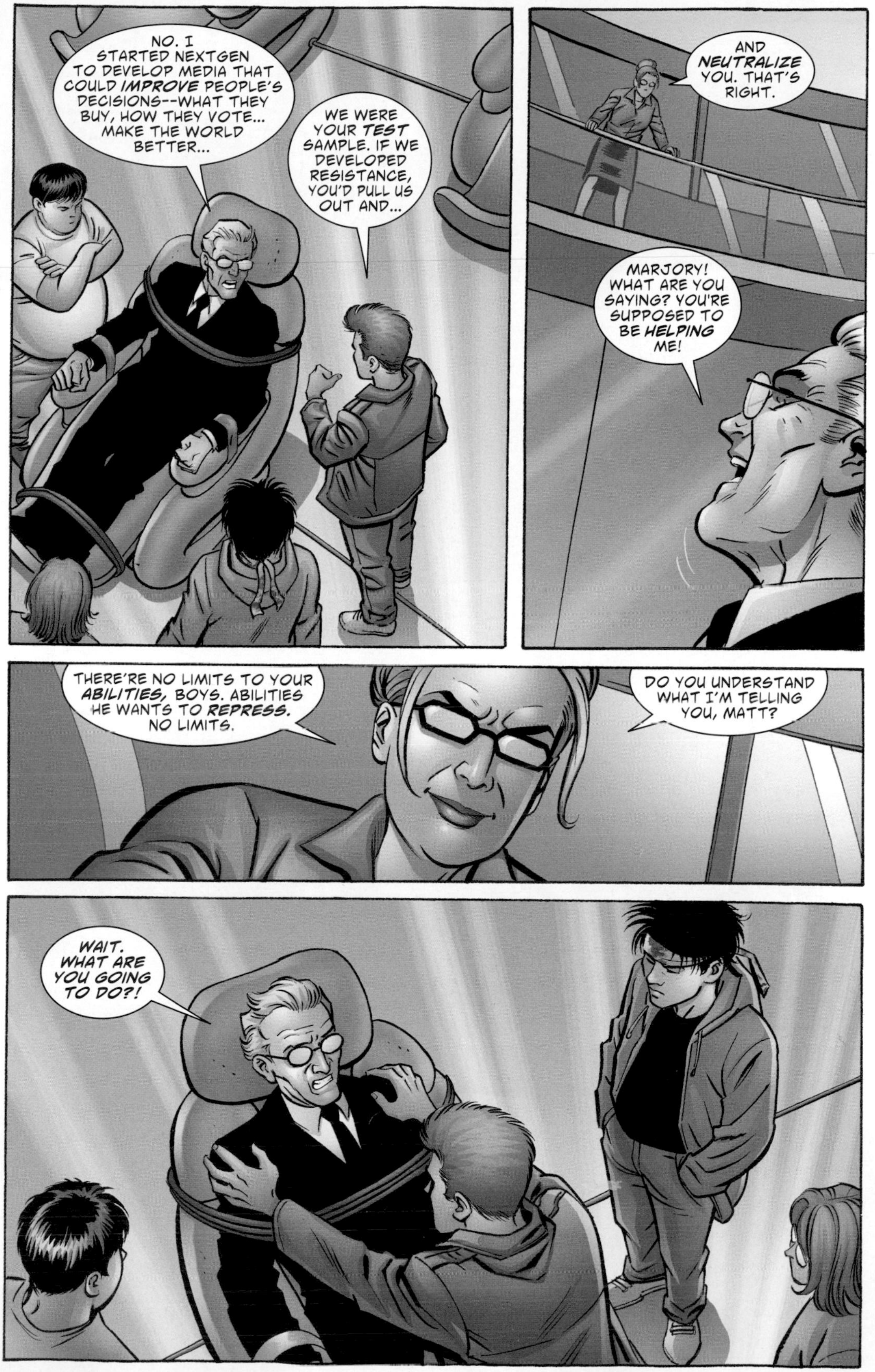
NO. I STARTED NEXTGEN TO DEVELOP MEDIA THAT COULD IMPROVE PEOPLE'S DECISIONS--WHAT THEY BUY, HOW THEY VOTE... MAKE THE WORLD BETTER...
WE WERE YOUR TEST SAMPLE. IF WE DEVELOPED RESISTANCE, YOU'D PULL US OUT AND...
AND NEUTRALIZE YOU. THAT'S RIGHT.
MARJORY! WHAT ARE YOU SAYING? YOU'RE SUPPOSED TO BE HELPING ME!
THERE'RE NO LIMITS TO YOUR ABILITIES, BOYS. ABILITIES HE WANTS TO REPRESS. NO LIMITS.
DO YOU UNDERSTAND WHAT I'M TELLING YOU, MATT?
WAIT. WHAT ARE YOU GOING TO DO?!

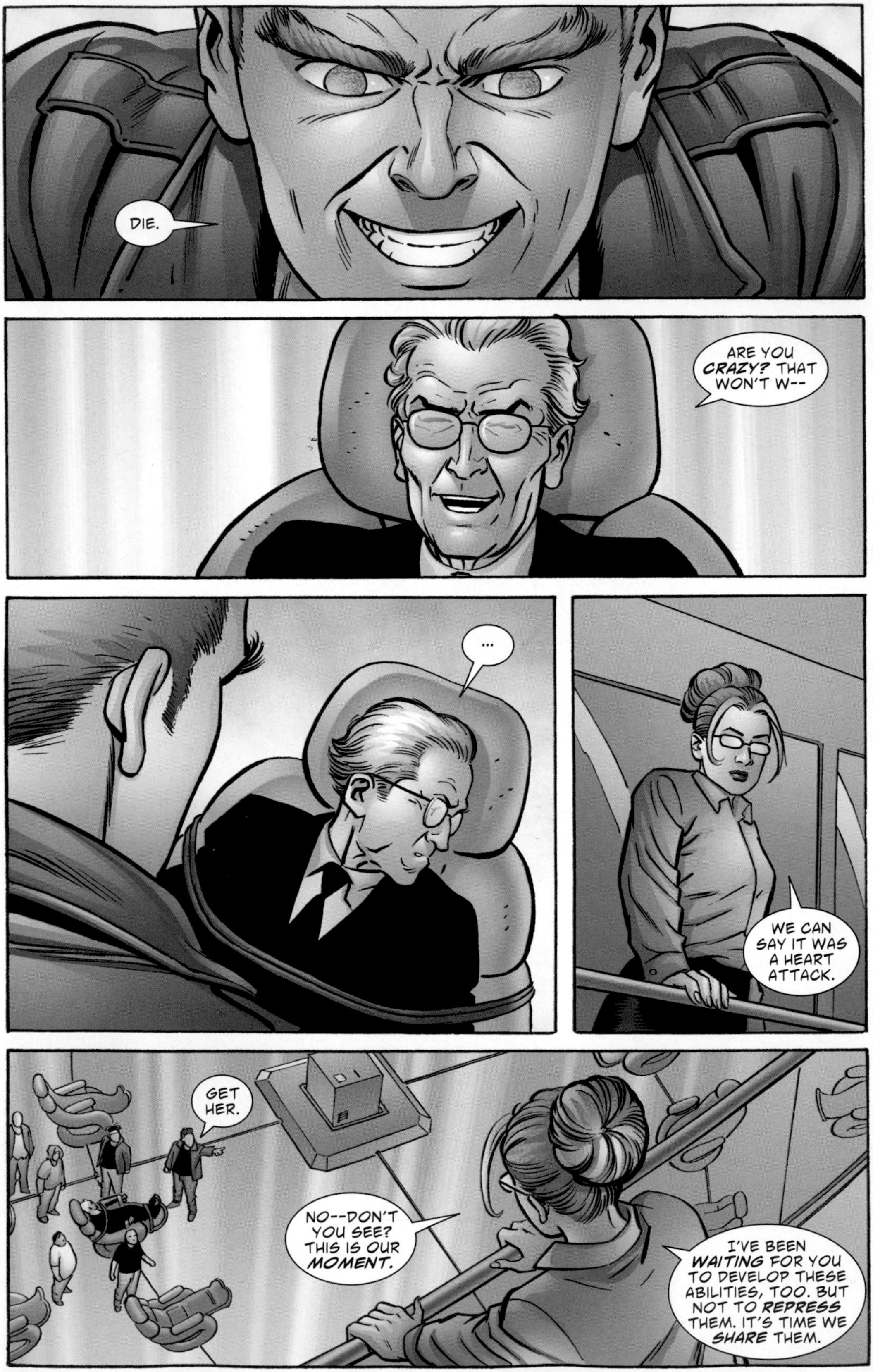
DIE.
ARE YOU CRAZY? THAT WON'T W--
...
WE CAN SAY IT WAS A HEART ATTACK.
GET HER.
NO--DON'T YOU SEE? THIS IS OUR MOMENT.
I'VE BEEN WAITING FOR YOU TO DEVELOP THESE ABILITIES, TOO. BUT NOT TO REPRESS THEM. IT'S TIME WE SHARE THEM.

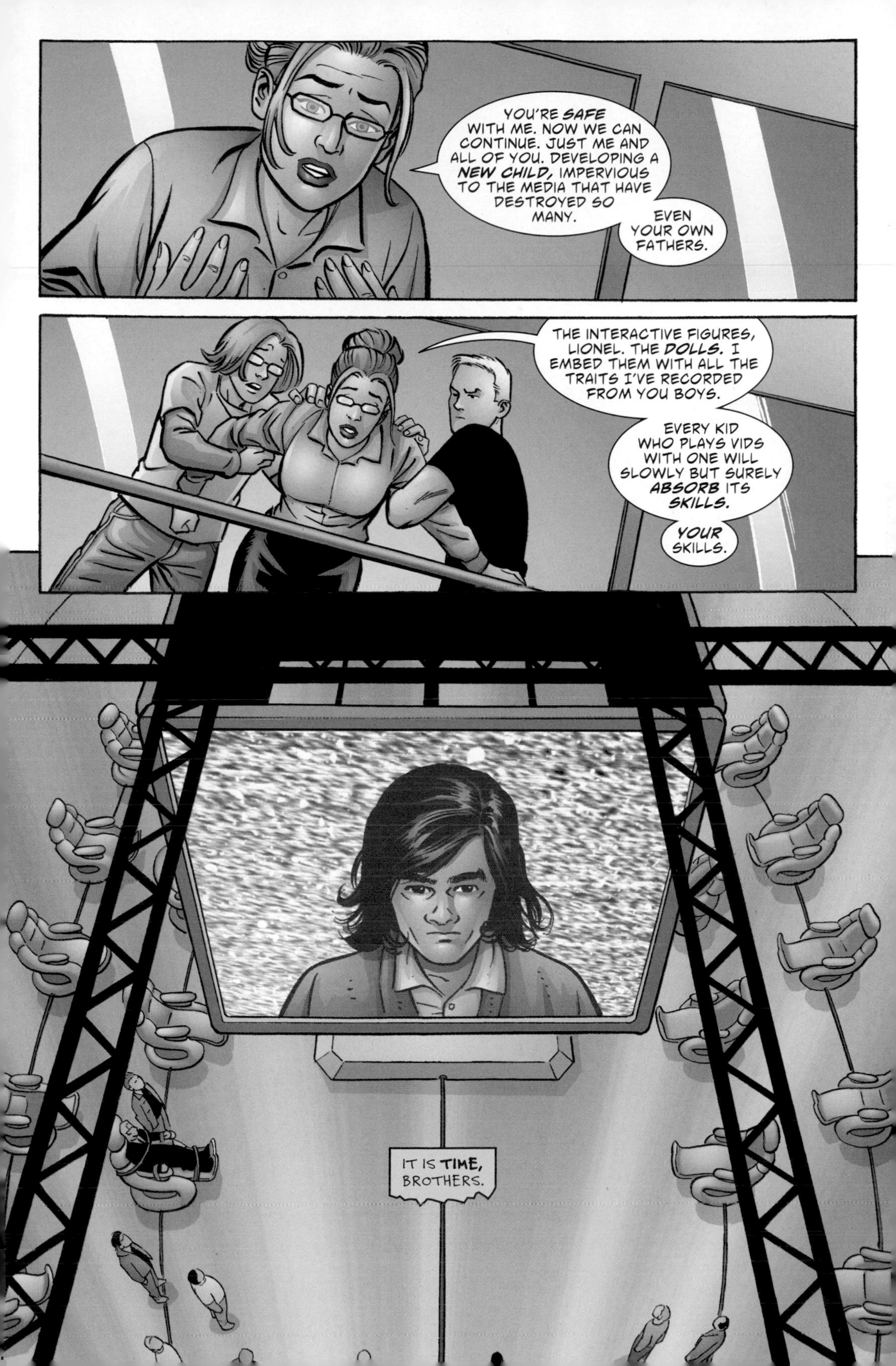
YOU'RE SAFE WITH ME. NOW WE CAN CONTINUE. JUST ME AND ALL OF YOU. DEVELOPING A NEW CHILD, IMPERVIOUS TO THE MEDIA THAT HAVE DESTROYED SO MANY.
EVEN YOUR OWN FATHERS.
THE INTERACTIVE FIGURES, LIONEL. THE DOLLS. I EMBED THEM WITH ALL THE TRAITS I'VE RECORDED FROM YOU BOYS.
EVERY KID WHO PLAYS VIDS WITH ONE WILL SLOWLY BUT SURELY ABSORB ITS SKILLS.
YOUR SKILLS.
IT IS TIME, BROTHERS.

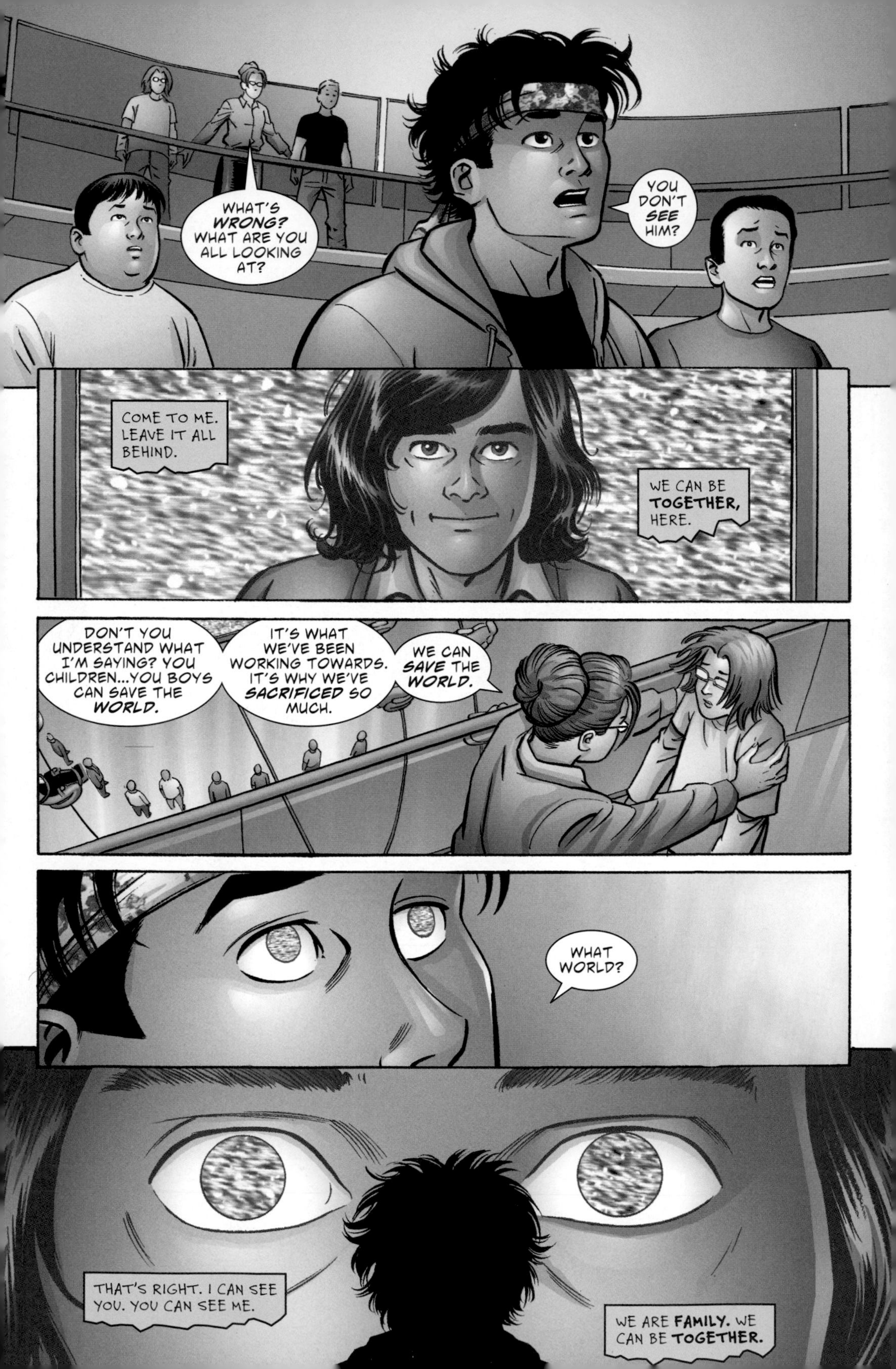
WHAT'S WRONG? WHAT ARE YOU ALL LOOKING AT?
YOU DON'T SEE HIM?
COME TO ME. LEAVE IT ALL BEHIND.
WE CAN BE TOGETHER, HERE.
DON'T YOU UNDERSTAND WHAT I'M SAYING? YOU CHILDREN...YOU BOYS CAN SAVE THE WORLD.
IT'S WHAT WE'VE BEEN WORKING TOWARDS. IT'S WHY WE'VE SACRIFICED SO MUCH.
WE CAN SAVE THE WORLD.
WHAT WORLD?
THAT'S RIGHT. I CAN SEE YOU. YOU CAN SEE ME.
WE ARE FAMILY. WE CAN BE TOGETHER.

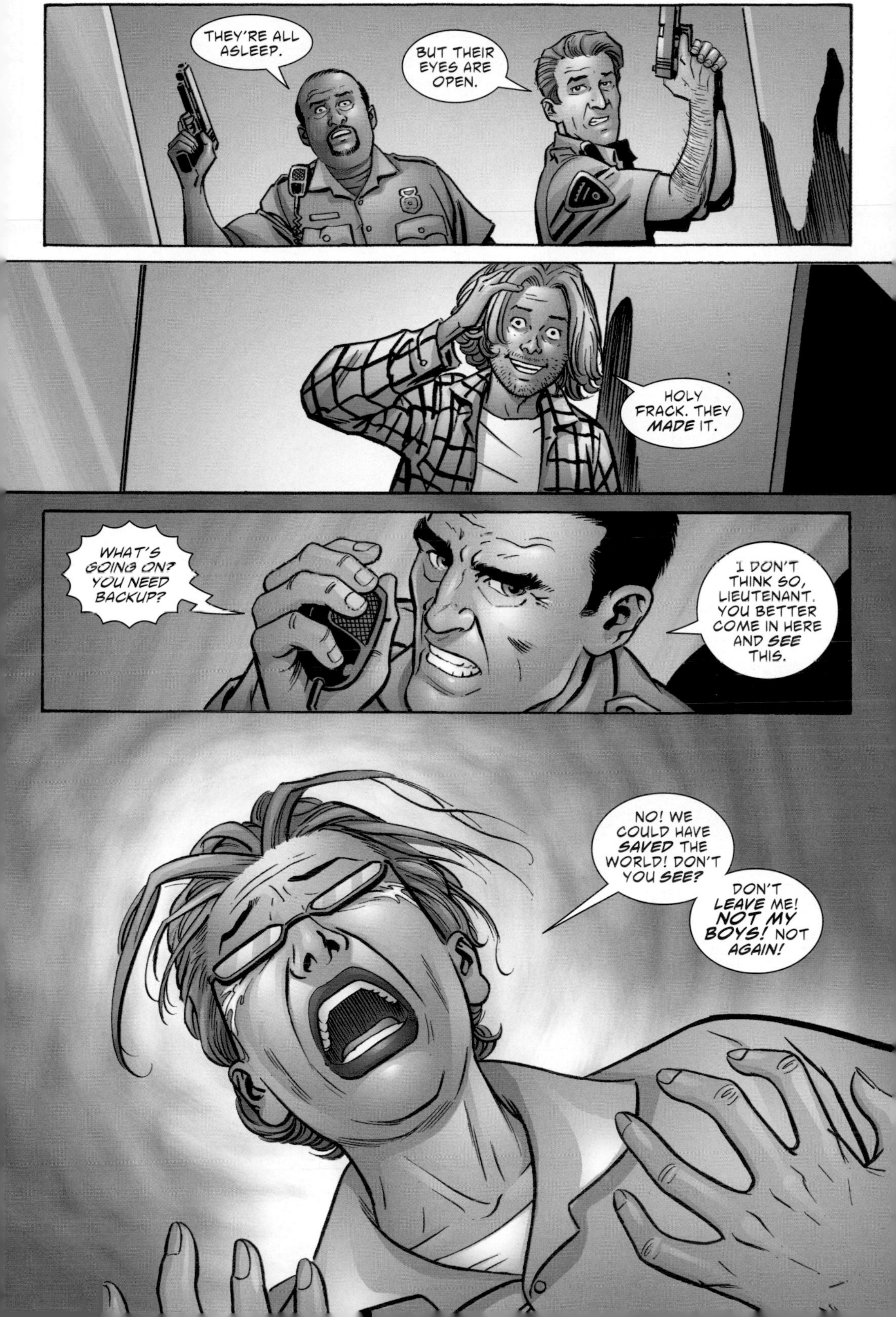
THEY'RE ALL ASLEEP.
BUT THEIR EYES ARE OPEN.
HOLY FRACK. THEY *MADE* IT.
WHAT'S GOING ON? YOU NEED BACKUP?
I DON'T THINK SO, LIEUTENANT. YOU BETTER COME IN HERE AND **SEE** THIS.
NO! WE COULD HAVE ***SAVED*** THE WORLD! DON'T YOU ***SEE?***
DON'T ***LEAVE*** ME! ***NOT MY BOYS!*** NOT ***AGAIN!***

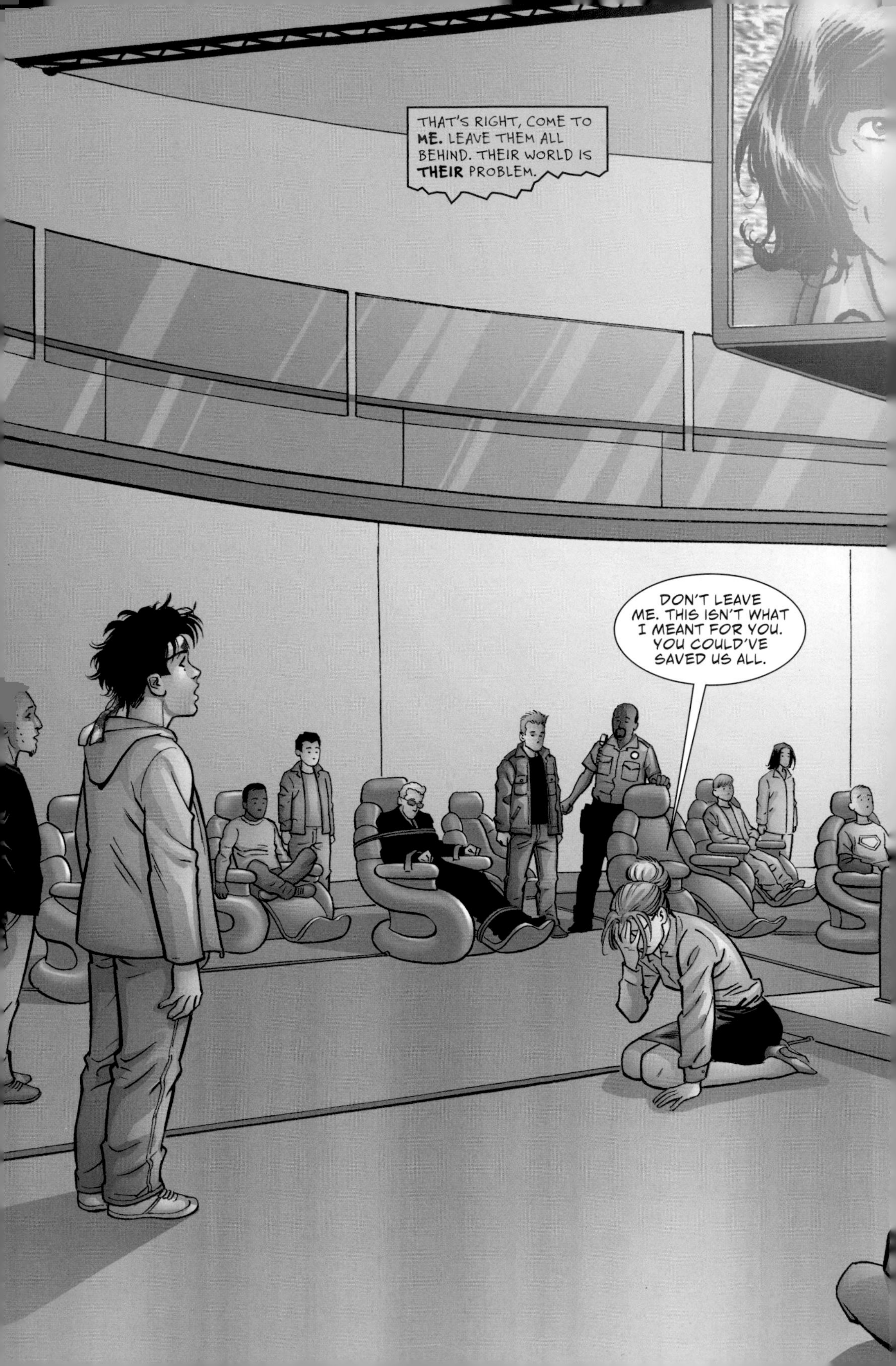
THAT'S RIGHT, COME TO ME. LEAVE THEM ALL BEHIND. THEIR WORLD IS THEIR PROBLEM.
DON'T LEAVE ME. THIS ISN'T WHAT I MEANT FOR YOU. YOU COULD'VE SAVED US ALL.

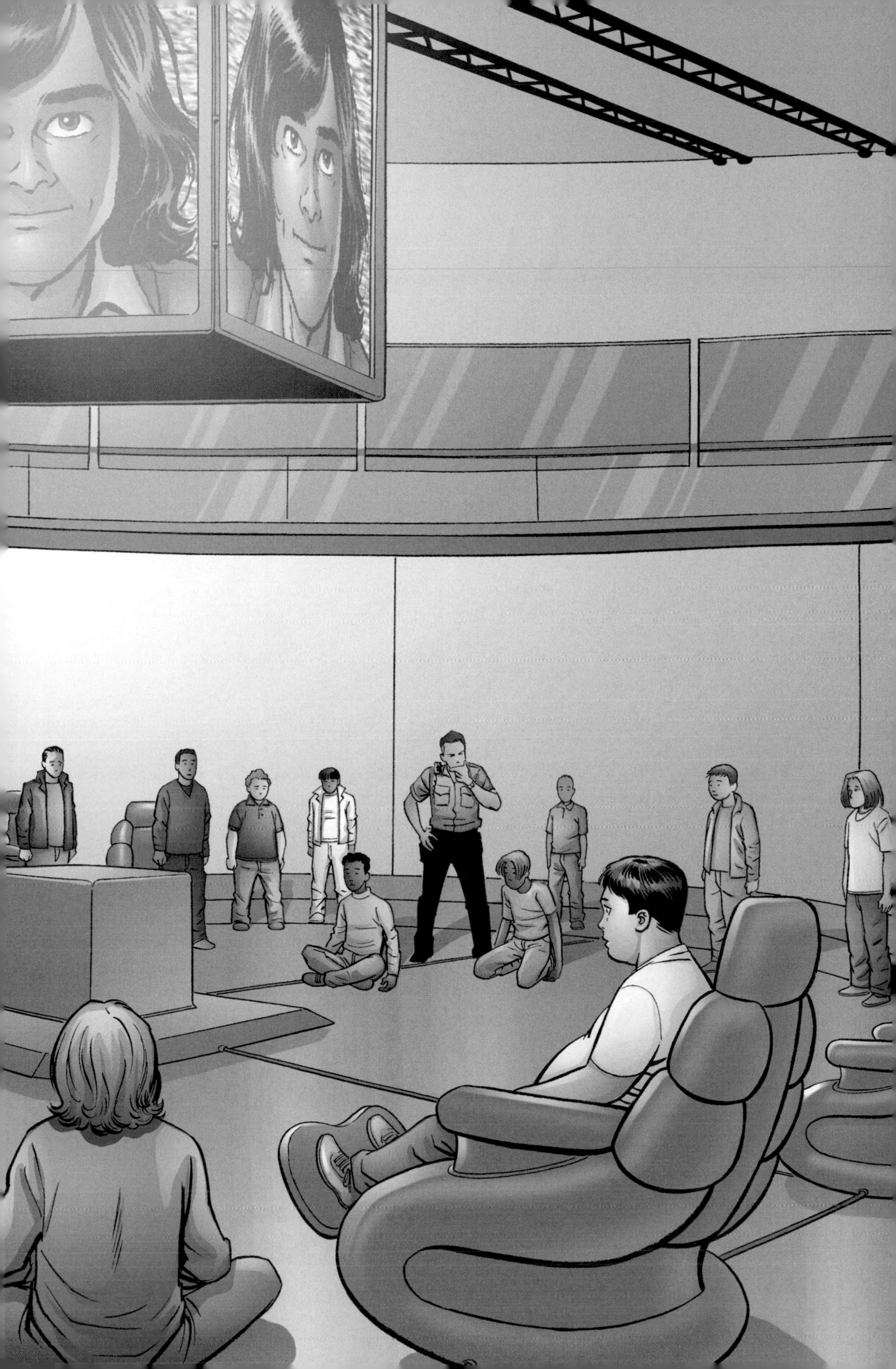

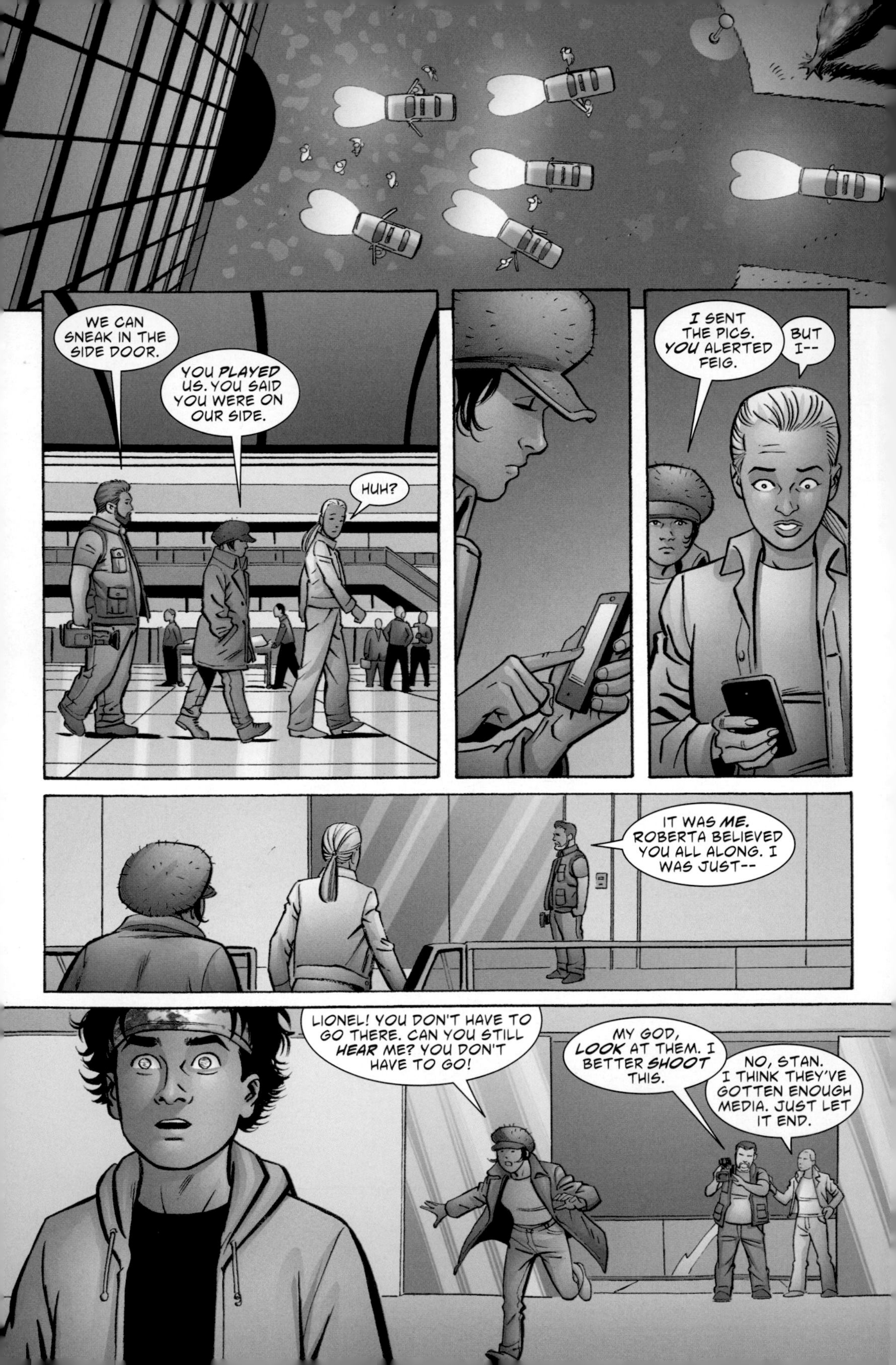
WE CAN SNEAK IN THE SIDE DOOR.
YOU PLAYED US. YOU SAID YOU WERE ON OUR SIDE.
HUH?
I SENT THE PICS. YOU ALERTED FEIG.
BUT I--
IT WAS ME. ROBERTA BELIEVED YOU ALL ALONG. I WAS JUST--
LIONEL! YOU DON'T HAVE TO GO THERE. CAN YOU STILL HEAR ME? YOU DON'T HAVE TO GO!
MY GOD, LOOK AT THEM. I BETTER SHOOT THIS.
NO, STAN. I THINK THEY'VE GOTTEN ENOUGH MEDIA. JUST LET IT END.

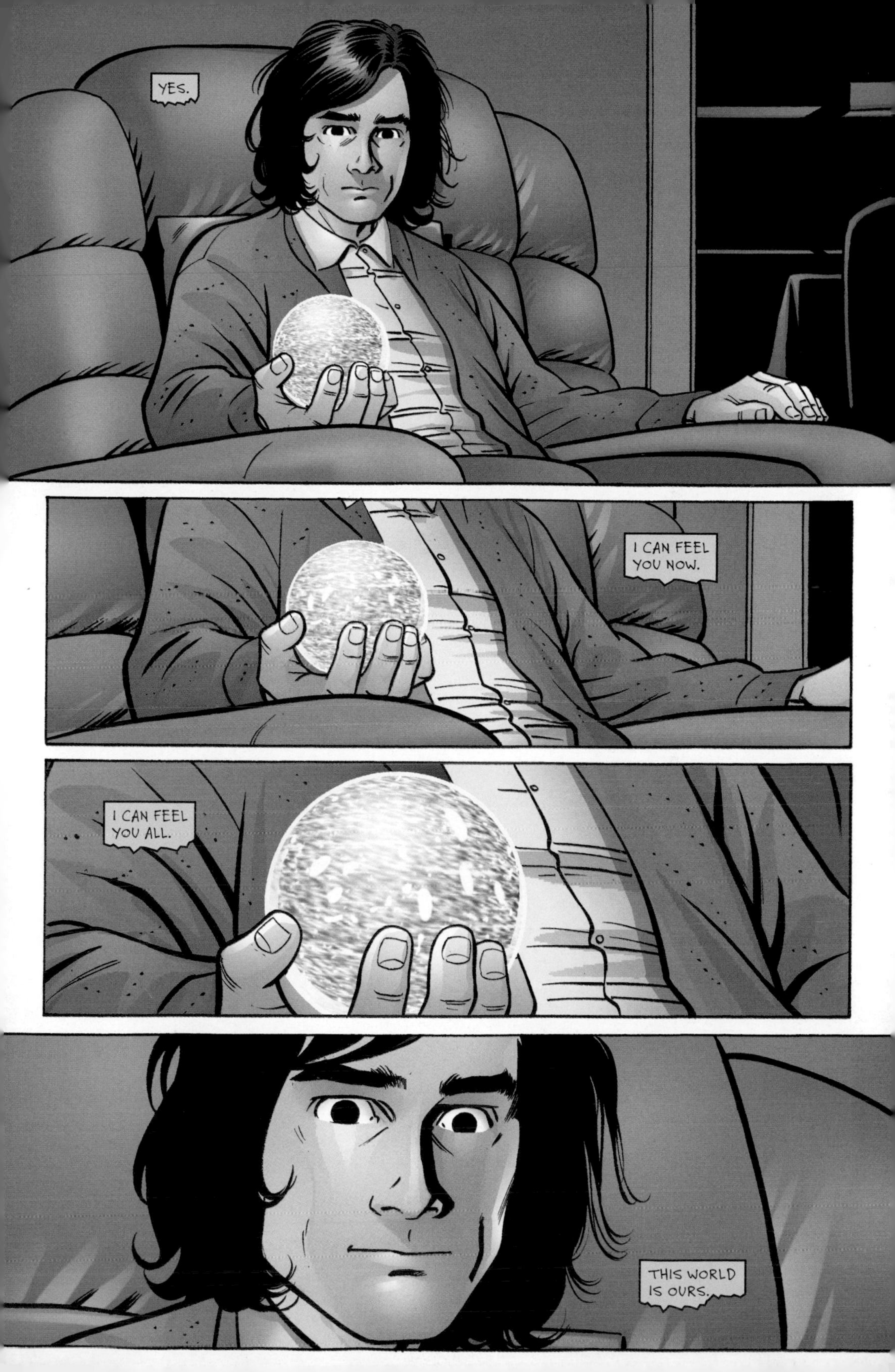
YES.
I CAN FEEL YOU NOW.
I CAN FEEL YOU ALL.
THIS WORLD IS OURS.

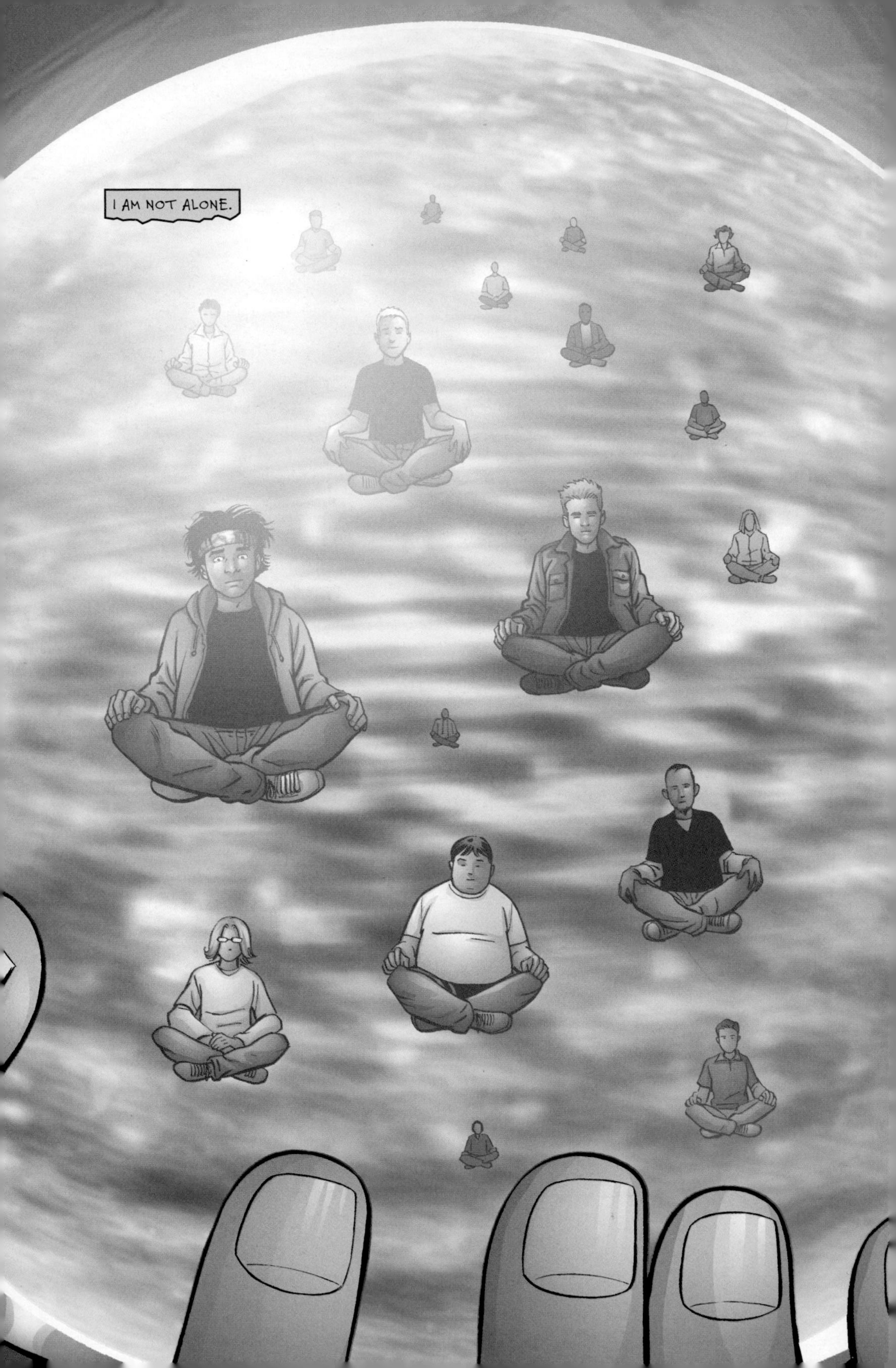
I AM NOT ALONE.

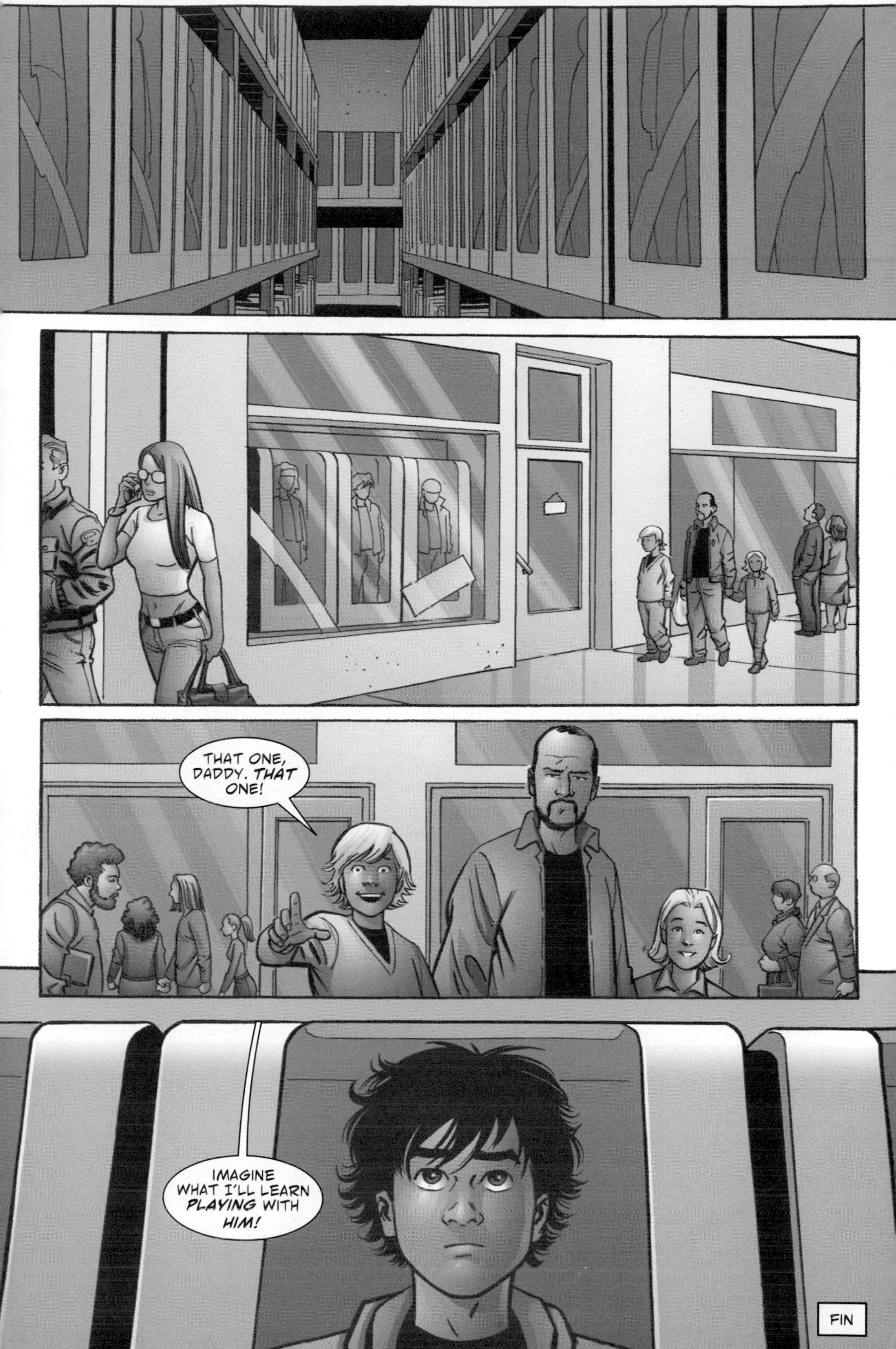
THAT ONE, DADDY. *THAT* ONE!
IMAGINE WHAT I'LL LEARN *PLAYING* WITH *HIM!*
FIN

Douglas Rushkoff, the media theorist and author, has written a dozen books on technology and culture including *Cyberia, Media Virus, Life Inc*, and *Program or Be Programmed*. As a member of the cyberpunk movement and cohort of Timothy Leary and Robert Anton Wilson, he originated the terms "viral media," "screenagers," and "social currency." He has written three award-winning *Frontline* documentaries: *Merchants of Cool, The Persuaders*, and *Digital Nation*, and the comics *ClubZero-G* and *TESTAMENT*.

Goran Sudžuka began working for DC/Vertigo in 1999, co-creating *OUTLAW NATION* with writer Jamie Delano, for which he won the Russ Manning award for Most Promising Newcomer in 2001. He has also worked on the Vertigo flagship series *Y: THE LAST MAN* and *HELLBLAZER*.

Jose Marzan, Jr. has worked in the comics industry for the past twenty years, contributing to such titles as *Y: THE LAST MAN, THE ADVENTURES OF SUPERMAN, THE FLASH, JUSTICE LEAGUE OF AMERICA* and many others. He lives with his wife and son in Florida, where he collects soundtracks and is taking up photography.